*Milton's Poetry of Choice
and Its Romantic Heirs*

Milton's Poetry of Choice and Its Romantic Heirs

LESLIE BRISMAN

Cornell University Press | ITHACA AND LONDON

First published 1973 by Cornell University Press.
Published in the United Kingdom by Cornell University Press Ltd., 2-4 Brook Street, London W1Y 1AA.

International Standard Book Number 0-8014-0666-8
Library of Congress Catalog Card Number 72-13129

Printed in the United States of America by Vail-Ballou Press, Inc.

*Librarians: Library of Congress cataloging information
appears on the last page of the book.*

To Harold Bloom
and Neil Hertz

Contents

Preface

> He was merely "improving the style." But this improvement, which was mainly a process of packing the lines more fully, meant invoking Milton and his sense of the unrelaxing Will; whereas the whole point and delicacy of the first version was to represent a wavering and untrammelled natural growth.
>
> William Empson on Wordsworth, in
> *The Structure of Complex Words*

Coleridge, in the *Biographia Literaria*, defines the secondary imagination as that power which "dissolves, diffuses, dissipates, in order to recreate." While the primary imagination is the "pure agent of all human perception," the secondary is the agent of human creativity, "coexisting with the conscious will."

Why the conscious will? Coleridge would have been happy to put aside all concerns of the will and think rather in terms of Empson's pleasant notion of "untrammelled natural growth." In "Dejection: An Ode" Coleridge deprecates his own plan "by abstruse research to steal / From my own nature all the natural man." Would things not be easier (the poem seems to argue) if one could lay aside considerations of the will and repose in the gentler fiction that imagination has this easy commerce with nature? Empson states the alternatives with almost pastoral simplicity: a romantic poet can choose to represent his process of natural growth, or he can choose to invoke Milton and the "unrelaxing Will." To be fair to Empson one must note that he prefers poetry "to *represent* a wavering and untrammelled natural growth"; the poet wills, or recreates the sense of natural ease. For Coleridge too we must distinguish the exercise of the will from its invocation as another voice. Secondary imagination is found *"coexisting* with the conscious will": though the poet must exercise will, natural desire seems to coexist, to harmonize with creative effort when imagination is operative.

One could call it a failure of will on Coleridge's part that his writing on the subject of the will is lifted—sometimes verbatim—from its German sources. But if we overlook the question of "natural growth" of the idea, we may borrow from Coleridge, or from Coleridge-Schelling, a formulation of what is required to represent the spirit in its wavering and natural state. At moments when secondary imagination is operating, one assumes a kind of Miltonic blindness to the identity of the self as creator and the self being objectively represented in the process of wavering growth. "The spirit (originally the identity of object and subject) must in some sense dissolve this identity, in order to be conscious of it." This dissolution (secondary imagination "dissolves, diffuses, dissipates") is a conscious act ("in order to recreate," to represent spirit), and "self-consciousness therefore is a will."

One may sigh with relief that poetry is not always concerned with self-consciousness, or more particularly that it must recreate such concerns in gentler fictions. But the romantics have a special interest in the representation of self-consciousness, and Coleridge encourages the representation of Milton as the prototype of what he calls the "subjective poet." In this book about Milton, I borrow in my first chapter the romantics' easy distinction between Shakespeare and Milton. Shakespeare's concern, in Coleridge's terms, is rather with the "subjectivity of the *persona,* or dramatic character." For the romantic, Milton stands not only as a model of the conscious will; he is also the object of the will when a poet lays aside the natural man to become a Miltonic bard. Milton himself may be said to take Shakespeare as his "natural," and to reject Shakespeare's sweeter mode for the chaster one he makes his own. (This need not be an accurate assessment of Shakespeare, but it serves Milton as a myth, or consciously willed remaking of the story of his own literary origins; in that remaking lies the poet's freedom.) For Wordsworth, Keats, and Shelley, an original will to assert a more natural self becomes chastened, in confrontation with higher power, into what Wordsworth finds to be a new sense of freedom, "a second will more wise." Blake makes the annihilation of selfhood and the drama of the second will the story of his astonishing *Milton*. And in the *Biographia*'s central chapter about the imagination, Coleridge begins by citing Raphael's address to Adam about the relation of the "one life" to the moral will, and concludes by referring to an essay he intended to prefix to *The Ancient Mariner*. The essay was never written, but that poem itself remains Coleridge's chief account of the primary imagination, a version of the Fall in which no picture of Adamic natural man mitigates the concentration on the will's relationship to imagination.

In *The Burden of the Past and the English Poet*, W. Jackson Bate presents overwhelming evidence that the poets of the eighteenth century felt their literary inheritance to be a burden. In exploring Milton's lightening of the burden of selfhood—for Milton himself as well as for his romantic heirs—perhaps we could reverse the implications of the Fuseli drawing that Bate uses as frontispiece. In contrast to that diminutive figure of the artist, mourning the ruined remnant of a giant foot, we might imaginatively place the figure of the romantic poet putting one foot forward into eternity in defiance of the weeping figures of the past. In Blake's *Milton* the "whole Assembly wept prophetic," but Milton descends to enter Blake's foot. One minute before death in Keats's *Fall of Hyperion,* the poet's "iced foot touch'd / The lowest stair; and, as it touch'd, life seem'd/To pour in at the toes." Keats ascends from the stage where Moneta's voice sounds like a tyranny to the level at which he can make her shed "long-treasured tears." And only Coleridge's natural foot was scalded by Sara's spilt milk; the poet remained behind to enter the Miltonic space of the conversation poems.

The steps in this argument must necessarily be small. One need not itemize a poetic legacy to sense its presence as a burden; but in discussing choice, as Blake declares, and as the study of poetic revision makes clear, we find the poet's art only by examining the "minute particulars." Originally focused more narrowly on Milton, this book has grown wider; to keep it from being still wider, I omit some of those particulars and select from the writings of Milton's heirs the issues that seem most clearly to point back to Milton's achievement. Shelley and Keats are each reviewed in one aspect of their relationship to Milton. Blake requires a separate study, and may seem slighted here. A few pages on *Faust* are included because, having spoken strongly about the burden of Shakespeare, Goethe illustrates as an "outsider" the question of deliberate choice of Milton for precursor. Most attention is necessarily given to Wordsworth, whose revision of himself, like Milton's revision of himself, helps us see Wordsworth's poetry as revision of Milton, and the romantic achievement of both as the poetry of choice.

When Milton's Adam appeals to the "Heavenly Power" for fellowship to share "all rational delight," he is answered mildly: "A nice and subtle happiness I see / Thou to thyself proposest, in the choice / Of thy Associates." Besides the Powers to whose omnific voices this book attempts response, I must name some whose subtleties have been a happiness: Geoffrey Hartman, Charles F. Stone III, Stuart Ende, Barry Weller, Henry Abelove, and Susan Hawk. Their strong inspiration and mild reproof can never be sufficiently heeded.

LESLIE BRISMAN

New Haven, Connecticut

*Milton's Poetry of Choice
and Its Romantic Heirs*

Foreword

"The sibilance of phrases is his
Or partly his. His voice is audible,
As the fore-meaning in music is." Again,

"This man abolishes by being himself
That which is not ourselves."
    Wallace Stevens, "An Ordinary Evening in New Haven"

Milton is everywhere concerned with the act of choosing: the major poems are about temptations; the shorter ones confirm the extent to which poetic composition is the product of continual choice at once ethical and aesthetic.[1] This book explores the way the experience of alternatives is expressed in Miltonic usage and the way poetic influence is expressed in the activity of choice. Milton's choice of biblical material for the major poems may be the most dramatic instance; but the concept of choice is echoed in each option for higher voice over more native strains, and in each romantic's choice of Miltonic voice over the voice he first took to be his own. In Milton the choice is less a matter of whether to allude to Spenser or the classics than a repeated decision for what I call the "Penseroso" over the "Allegro" mode. Not plodding under an imposed burden of the past, Milton and the romantics stand strong and choose a better way.

A poetry about options is committed both to the presentation of the moment of choice as if it were happening now, and to a sense of pattern in time in which past and future are organized around a moment when choices are "present." In Miltonic poetry an image—particularly an ambiguous image, one that suggests a choice of meaning—can stand for larger moments of choice; and language pattern, what happens in syntax and verse effects, can stand for the larger sense of pattern in time. The balance between pattern in time and sense of the moment is so inherently the province of poetry that one is often tempted to respond to that balance by creating or citing analogous poetic moments. When the responding "one" is a romantic poet, Milton's influence takes its most seminal form. But as a common reader of Milton, one can attempt to maintain that balance, aware of how easily it is disturbed when critical discourse weighs on the side of pattern. In outlining the way a poetic moment may be audible in another ("As the fore-meaning in music is"), the pages that follow juxtapose such moments. This "forward" does not pose as an "introduction" to the critical method of the book; it is intended to suggest the rather uncritical way associations occur, and how a poet's second will can revise such association into "criticism" of earlier poetry.

My model for the juxtaposition of moments of indefiniteness is Christopher Ricks, who discusses Milton's "flowing syntax, its terminations no more than hints." Ricks cites an image from *Paradise Lost*, "all things smil'd, / With fragrance and with joy my heart o'erflow'd" (VIII.265–266), and provides what may be the best appreciation of the movement from "things" to "heart" by invoking the lines from Wallace Stevens' "Peter Quince at the Clavier": "So evenings die, in their green going, / A wave, interminably flowing." Ricks goes on to analyze Milton's lines, to clarify the possibilities: what things are smiling with, with what the heart is overflowing.[2] Yet as one reads Milton one does not pause in midline to separate the fragrance from the joy. The lines describe paradise, where all things can smile because of a prelapsarian reciprocity between man and nature; sharper grammar comes only with the Fall, which imposes division between "all things" and "my heart." Stevens is of particular interest here because he too is talking about a paradise, and in a way that makes the linguistic indefiniteness the only means of recapturing paradise. He reworks the story of another biblical garden and recaptures evenings, gardens, Hesperian glory in their "green going." He thus also revises, or reimagines the traditional gardens, and turns what seemed gone into what seems forever "going."

To have things smile, to have the going green, abstracts imagery from the sensory particular in a way that Wordsworth associated especially with Milton. The "going" of the evenings may be compared to the moments in Wordsworth where "the light of sense / Goes out" (*Prelude*, VI.600-601).[3] The resulting darkness lets these lines about poetic power share in a kind of Miltonic blindness. But the grandeur really descends in the going, for the light of sense goes out, "but with a flash that has revealed / The invisible world." The moment of vision captures the temporal ambiguity of a Miltonic moment of choice: the passage looks back, but the poet *now* can say, "I recognize thy glory"; all is seen patterned in time, but the moment seems to be caught right now, in the very enjambment of the clause "the light of sense / Goes out." If a Miltonic image can capture in its ambiguity a choice of meanings, we may say that Wordsworth's equivalent here is the vagueness of the phrase "the light of sense." Is it "sense" signifying reason, rational control of experience, or the sense of sight that is extinguished in this moment when insight takes over? One winces at the thought of "sense" being called a pun, for Wordsworth can no more rest on an easy ambiguity than Stevens can capture the garden except in its "going." Both poets prevent a Miltonic fall by retelling the story, revisiting a moment of choice with the "strength / Of usurpation, when the light of sense / Goes out."

Wordsworth himself associates such awareness of strength with Miltonic obscuring of the sensually particular. In *Descriptive Sketches* he finds a "secret Power" in the ambiguous presence of music, "While o'er the desert, answering every close, / Rich steam of sweetest perfume comes and goes" (1849 ed.; ll. 344–345). If the "going" here is as intangible as the green going in "Peter Quince," the perfume is mysteriously wafted from *Comus;* [4] the moment that mixes odors with Milton's musical term "answering every close" is the moment that mixes sensory apprehension with higher power. Like the dying of evenings and gardens in Stevens, the dying of the light of sense in Wordsworth, is the losing of paradise in Milton—not at one moment, the Fall, but in the rhythmic and grammatical patterns of fall, at moments when the "going" of verse seems to implicate lapse. Beauty is immortal, to use Stevens' phrase, because it is captured in the process of fall so that we sense both the inevitable motion or pattern and the indelible moment or present.

Wordsworth explains sensory abstraction by citing two lines from *Paradise Lost,* "Attended with ten thousand Saints / He onward came, far off his coming shone" (VI.767–768), and pointing to Christ as "lost almost and merged in the splendour of that indefinite abstraction 'His coming.'" [5] The romantic sees the suspension of action become thing: "His coming." As an aesthetic epiphany, this moment becomes a redemption in poetic time that stands for—perhaps replaces—His coming in historical time. The new abstraction from historicity need not be theological revelation; one can wake from dream to find sensually present truth. In "The Eve of St.

Agnes," Keats reaches a moment of "solution sweet" [6] of the
contraries of wakeful time and the dream of stasis: "Into her
dream he melted, as the rose / Blendeth its odor with the
violet." Compare Milton's description of Eve:

> She tempers dulcet creams, nor these to hold
> Wants her fit vessels pure, then strews the ground
> With Rose and Odors from the shrub unfum'd.
>
> [PL, V.347-349] [7]

What is the grammatical status of "Odors"? We read along,
through the word "ground," and expect the nouns that follow "With" to name the things strewn. Stopping to cavil
about the fact that odors cannot be strewn, we see that a sense
impression is being arrested while the sentence simultaneously
moves on.[8]

Smell may be the slightest of the senses, yet what happens
here points to the way the blurring of sense impressions becomes a technique of the poetry of the sublime. Calling the
pines in "Mont Blanc" "children of elder time," Shelley imagines a natural scene in terms of a religious ceremony in
which "The chainless winds still come and ever came / To
drink their odours." Drink odors? There is no question of
echoing Milton here, but there is grandeur aided by a technique elsewhere encountered as a Miltonic inheritance. Keats
makes the connection to Milton a little clearer when he stands
in a Miltonic darkness where he cannot see "what soft incense
hangs upon the boughs" ("Ode to a Nightingale"). He cannot see because this is imaginative space, and the sensory indefiniteness that gives the mind room to play is the indefiniteness that allows incense, rather than more clearly discerned
fruits or flowers, to hang on the boughs. Wordsworth would
find making odors so concrete that they can be hung to be the

very substance of imagination. Turning to Milton, he illustrates how the mind's activity provides the force that keeps the abstract suspended. He cites the image in which Satan like a "Fleet descri'd / Hangs in the Clouds" (*PL*, II.636–643), and comments:

> Here is the full strength of the imagination involved in the word *hangs*, and exerted upon the whole image; First, the fleet, an aggregate of many ships, is represented as one mighty person, whose track, we know and feel, is upon the waters; but, taking advantage of its appearance to the senses, the Poet dares to represent it as *hanging in the clouds*, both for the gratification of the mind in contemplating the image itself, and in reference to the motion and appearance of the sublime objects to which it is compared.[9]

There are a number of passages in Wordsworth's own poetry that capture such poetic power in images of physical suspension. The Winander Boy, for example, heard a voice of nature "in that silence while he hung / Listening" (*Prelude*, V.381–382). Coleridge relates the sense of suspension to the feeling of being interfused with a higher voice when he describes his reaction to *The Prelude* as he sat

> blended in one thought
> (Thought was it? or aspiration? or resolve?)
> Absorbed, yet hanging still upon the sound.
> ["To William Wordsworth"]

As stillness is suggested by *hanging* upon the sound, the moment of arrest becomes one of option. He confronts, at least, the inadequacy of expression, the suspension between the alternate words "thought" and "resolve"; more important, the poet stands between temporal alternatives, between an interfused thought and an inspired resolve, between stasis and motion, inherited tradition and talent to be used.

We must be concerned with the interruption of time and of sensual definiteness at such moments of poetic choice. Furthermore, we must bring concerns about choice to seemingly indifferent moments of arrested time. Simple lines like "Stop here or gently pass," "What men or gods are these?" ask us to linger on the alternatives, as do lines of grander voice:

> Is this the scene
> Where the old Earthquake-daemon taught her young
> Ruin? Were these their toys? or did a sea
> Of fire envelop once this silent snow?
> None can reply—all seems eternal now.   ["Mont Blanc"]

Is this a moment of Miltonic grandeur? Or is Shelley mocking Miltonic voice and using that "or" to contrast with an even more startling alternative, that between such a style and his own? Even if Milton is not noticeably present in such instances, a reading of Milton can make us more conscious of the way the experience of options opens onto perspectives not to be gained simply by adding one suggestion to another. What is Miltonic about moments of choice, whether they are described with or without the word "or," leaps over Augustan alternatives, over the poetry of distinction, to the poetry of what Wordsworth calls "indefinite abstraction." A study that can be said to focus on Milton's "or" cannot be directed toward the couplet poetry that is so often dependent on fine turnings around a verbal or moral option. Pope did not need Milton to write "Or lose her Heart, or Necklace, at a Ball"; but Collins already involved the creative process in posing alternatives, evoking Heaven and Fancy as having "o'erturned th'inspiring bowers, / Or curtained close such scene from every future view" ("Ode on the Poetical Character"). I do not wish to deny the enormous influence of Milton on Pope, but to point out, in passing it by, that it is an influence of a different kind. Pope felt relatively at ease with groves of Eden that "live in description and look green in song"; Wordsworth, weighing the past in the present moment of choice, seems to implicate his whole poetic future in asking of paradisal groves:

> why should they be
> A history only of departed things,
> Or a mere fiction of what never was?
>   [*The Recluse*, ll. 802–804]

We need to cover the ground of choice with less dizzying speed; and it is the prerogative of criticism to revisit the moment of loss that poetry can present in the green going rather than as a history of departed things. I attempt to show also that a prerogative of the romantic poem is to see itself as criticism, looking back at its poetic antecedent as text. Lingering over the moment of loss till infused with its spirit, the new poetic moment becomes Higher Criticism of a higher Word, and the loss of what may have been fiction becomes a real loss. For the poet there are no "mere fictions." As we hear anew echoes of a life that can no longer be called "departed," the moment of choice is translated into the eternal present of poetry. What Wallace Stevens calls the "tragic drone" is still there, but it can "rise liquidly in liquid lingerings, / Like watery words awash." [10]

1. A Better Way*

> You have seen
> Sunshine and rain at once: her smiles and tears
> Were like; a better way: Those happy smilets
> That play'd on her ripe lip seem'd not to know
> What guests were in her eyes, which, parted thence,
> As pearls from diamonds dropp'd.
>
> Shakespeare, *King Lear*

Though "L'Allegro" and "Il Penseroso" are often called companion poems, the extent to which they are successive is an open question. The poems present Milton's most fully drawn alternatives, and the equality of appeal makes the choice a real one. On the other hand, the poems seem to resolve the choice they offer, and even elements of their parallel structure imply progression.

Reading the two poems as a "progress" makes apparent how profoundly intertwined their topic is with their process of creation. The poems are about a choice, and they make that choice as they go along. They create a unity of kind of experience and kind of poetry, building toward that identification, working in time to arrive at the definition of their subject matter that culminates in their endings. In itself each poem is a progress, climbing to a poetic height from which it surveys the ground it has covered and that which lies beyond. "L'Allegro" closes with a vision of immortal verse,

---

* Part of this chapter appeared, in somewhat different form, in the *Journal of English and Germanic Philology*, 77 (1972), 226–240, and is used by permission.

9

> Such as the meeting soul may pierce
> In notes, with many a winding bout
> Of linked sweetness long drawn out,
> With wanton heed, and giddy cunning,
> The melting voice through mazes running.

If the reader's soul meets the music halfway, it recognizes that "melting voice" as the one running through the mazes of the poem. That is the kind of voice we have been hearing, we are hearing at this point in the poem. Music can untwist the chains that tie the soul of harmony only if we emphasize harmony and read "soul" metaphorically. If we read "harmony" metaphorically, and think of the power of music to unchain soul from its bondage to death—read literally or figuratively—we confront what music—or such music—cannot do. For the moment the poetic line suspends its fiction between possibility and impossibility.

Having come this far, the poem then envisions what lies beyond and brings itself to an end by confronting the impossibility of actualizing that vision:

> That *Orpheus'* self may heave his head
> From golden slumber on a bed
> Of heap't *Elysian* flow'rs, and hear
> Such strains as would have won the ear
> Of *Pluto*, to have quite set free
> His half-regain'd *Eurydice*.

The impossible sound is represented by the impossibility of regaining Eurydice, whether one conceives of her soul being bound to death or her story tied to a poetic fiction long since determined. As both fixities turn us away from futurity to what has been, the poem suggests the kind of experience, the kind of poetry that can only be seen as "a better way" when the choice of that way is in the past and no longer recoverable. The greatest delight that the muse of mirth can provide is the evocation of the Orpheus myth; but the poem still longs for strains that "would have won the ear / Of *Pluto*." The dark king could have, would have been won, but can be won no longer. That the old fictions are this alive is half the achievement of "L'Allegro"; that the poem finds the old fictions can be brought back, but not brought forward, is the other part of its achievement, pointing to "Il Penseroso." Seen thus as a matter of poetry, the limitation confronted is a death of the old style, and the present song, "Untwisting all the chains that tie / The hidden soul of harmony," is the last effort of release.

In moving from the first poem to the second a choice is being actualized, and the impossibility of redeeming a choice of the past is transformed into the sense that a choice is being made forever present in the turn from one poem to the other. The Allegro poet ends with a vision of the promised land he can never attain; Eurydice can never be "quite set free," and there are limits to the identity of the musical and experiential achievement, so the poet falls silent at the peak, as if to say, as he does at the end of "In Obitum Praesulis Eliensis," "sed hic tacebo." But the Penseroso poet moves on, at a weightier, more pensive pace, "Till old experience do attain / To something like Prophetic strain." In a sense he will always be moving in that direction, unlike L'Allegro, who stands now at the height of the relationship of song and experience. To this extent the two characters could be said to relate to Milton's own poetic career. In Kierkegaard's terms, "the aesthetical . . . is that in a man whereby he immediately is the man he is; the ethical is that whereby a man becomes what he becomes." [1] The two poems present alternatives, but like

Kierkegaard's "either-or," there is an implicit direction or temporal movement between them from the aesthetic to the ethical, from the world of "L'Allegro" and the kinds of values, the genres of poetry it implies, to the world of "Il Penseroso." The two may be conceived as choices, but choice is actualized when one has moved from the first to the second.

Choosing Either-Or

The act of choice is the essential creative act for Milton; a poem comes into being by excluding certain alternatives in affirming others. "L'Allegro," as well as "Il Penseroso," begins with a selection that defines its nature:

> Hence loathed Melancholy
> Of *Cerberus* and blackest midnight born,
> In *Stygian* Cave forlorn
> 'Mongst horrid shapes, and shrieks, and sights unholy,
> Find out some uncouth cell,
> Where brooding darkness spreads his jealous wings,
> And the night-Raven sings;
> There under *Ebon* shades, and low brow'd Rocks,
> As ragged as thy Locks,
> In dark *Cimmerian* desert ever dwell.

The multiplicity of "horrid shapes, and shrieks, and sights unholy," all the more convincingly packed as a result of the two *and*s, is like the pebbles on the shore that an industrious scholar collects when there are no "spirit and judgment equal or superior " (*PR*, IV.324). The lines of dismissal are temptingly suggestive; indeed, they specify, and thus create objects of poetic contemplation more than do the lines that evoke "the Milkmaid" or "every Shepherd." T. S. Eliot objects, "It is not a particular ploughman, milkmaid, and shepherd that Milton sees." [2] The local habitation and the names which make imaginary beings *be*, are more persuasive in the opening lines than in those more general descriptions.

Perhaps this difference in particularity is just Milton's point. The opening lines of "L'Allegro" suggest the realm of experience that must be purged for the vision to follow, just as poetic vitality will depend on purging the images that may come to the poet's mind with all their particularity and clarity but that do not fit the mood or theme of the passage or work. Creativity for Milton begins with self-denial, and even L'Allegro" begins with "Hence." Its mirthful pleasures are very carefully chosen to direct one on the path to "Il Penseroso," as Cleanth Brooks notes: " 'Public,' convivial mirth, or 'public' melancholy, a funeral in the family—deprive the protagonist of conscious choice and render him chosen rather than choosing. Milton, one feels, is quite as emphatic in his belief that the aesthetic requires a deliberate act of will as was Immanuel Kant in insisting that the ethical involves deliberate choice." [3]

Such choice is actualized in the turn to "Il Penseroso," all the more convincingly because of the choiceness, the delicacy and moderation of mirth that the poem which it implies has just asserted. The "vain deluding joys" castigated by "Il Penseroso" are a rich world whose acknowledgment is a prerequisite for turning to the sage and holy goddess. By first acknowledging the "brood of folly" which "fancies fond with gaudy shapes possess," Milton suggests the multiplicity and vitality of "Those images that yet / Fresh images beget" in Yeats's "Byzantium." * As in Yeats, the superhuman (beyond

* "Byzantium" (copyright 1933 by The Macmillan Company, renewed 1961 by Bertha Georgie Yeats), *The Collected Poems of W. B. Yeats* (New York, 1956), copyright © 1956 by The Macmillan Company; by permission of M. B. Yeats, The Macmillan Company, the Macmillan companies of Basingstoke and London, and the Macmillan Company of Canada Ltd.

the world of "L'Allegro") image or shade that is evoked in the course of "Il Penseroso" depends on the original purging of the other choice, the other way. "Hence vain deluding joys," like "The unpurged images of day recede," and "That is no country for old men," acknowledges a fuller world than the poem ostensibly sets out to argue for. Yeats's process of choice is far less absolute, so that spirit after spirit returns the artistic handiwork to the world of fury and mire. But for Milton the act of creation is more strictly a turning away from the rejected alternatives. It is not enough for images to recede, only to emerge again by the end of the poem; they must be driven "hence." Aestheticism implies a form of asceticism, a denial not because the poet has not had a fuller vision but because the act of creation is an act of choice, a turning, like a religious conversion, from the complexities of experience to the unity and direction of art.

Such is the difference between not seeing that world and seeing it first, not denying its reality but translating it into a higher reality. The dismissal of the world of multiplicities is the first movement toward the higher vision, and the exiting steps are the first steps of the new art form. In Yeats's "Byzantium" "all complexities of fury leave, / Dying into a dance"; in Milton's mask, Comus and his rout dance out the complexities that must be broken off when the Lady, and the simpler moral confrontation, enter the poem. Even in "L'Allegro" itself, as Phyllis MacKenzie writes, the figures "are like dancers in a dance. Each is characterized by stylized movements, executed against a stylized background; and both movement and background are keyed to the rhythm of the central mood." [4] On the one hand, the reality of the dance is the reality of the dancers, and so the "complexities of fury" have to be there to make their graceful bow to the larger world outside; the steps taken to get them off stage are the first steps of the dance. On the other hand, dance requires the strict subordination of each dancer to the mood and design of the whole, so Milton purges the individuated elements which go their own way and realize themselves. Perhaps the best summary of the relationship of the exorcism within the poems to Milton's large aesthetic and moral concerns is the description by Geoffrey Hartman: "The dramatic thing in each poem is the stylistic breach as the speaker turns from anathema to invitation. It is like going from an older world creaking with morality plays and heavy emblems to a brave new world in which man is the master of his mood and his spirit machinery correspondingly fluent. The poems are Milton's notes toward a gentler fiction." [5] The "brave new world" of a new stylistic freedom is an aesthetic miniature of the new world of spiritual freedom opened to man at the end of *Paradise Lost*. Unable to make the kind of renunciation needed in facing temptation, Eve falls from a desire for unlimited experience, and the education of the first parents becomes in part learning to live within the limits newly imposed by God.[6] At least one critic has tried to relate the sytlistic change in the concluding books of Milton's epic to the reintegration into a world of choice, speaking of the "mood of chastened interest." [7]

The drawing of stylistic parallels to a spiritual process is itself a way of distinguishing the two stylistic and spiritual worlds. The unfallen fullness of "L'Allegro" includes "youthful Poets" and their sights, but these are part of an undifferentiated assembly, rather than a higher reality discovered only by analogy. The point becomes less abstract if one considers a passage where, if anywhere, analogies between character and creator could be conceived:

> And the Milkmaid singeth blithe,
> And the Mower whets his scythe,

> And every Shepherd tells his tale
> Under the Hawthorn in the dale.
> Straight mine eye hath caught new pleasures
> Whilst the Landscape round it measures
> Russett Lawns and Fallows Gray.

Here neither the singing of the milkmaid nor the taletelling of the shepherd has any special affinity with the activity of the poet, except that when that tale is told, L'Allegro too must go on to other matters, for his poem is not yet half over. After giving the shepherd his local habitation under the hawthorn, L'Allegro is finished with that image and now looks up, looks elsewhere, for new interests: "Straight mine eye hath caught new pleasures." There is no sense that the period after "dale" marks a still point in a narrowing consciousness, a choice that makes the turn a moment of recognition; it is no confrontation with the limits of self but simply a turn outward, a sally in one more of an infinite number of possible directions. The new pleasures he catches are added to those that have gone before, and the list of landscape objects that follows is held together, like the milkmaid, mower, and shepherd lines, with imagined, if not actual, grammatical *ands*. There is no sense of alternative, as in the turns of "Lycidas" or the turn to "Il Penseroso," no sense of "or," where something is partially negated for something else to follow, where death is subsumed into the poetic process. It is a poem brimming with life, in which there is no death, and therefore no transcendence.

In contrast, the way the poet moves from matter to matter in "Il Penseroso" can suggest the spiritual burden of picking up the narrative of *Paradise Lost* after the Fall. Of the romantic lyric, Hartman writes, "The reflective stopping of the poet, which is like the shock of self-consciousness and may express it in a mild and already distanced form, is a general

feature of Romantic lyricism and related to its penseroso or
'white' melancholy."[8] That the romantic melancholy characterizes Milton's "Penseroso" muse can be seen in the passage
where the poet asks for the company of

> The Cherub Contemplation;
> And the mute Silence hist along,
> 'Less *Philomel* will deign a Song,
> In her sweetest, saddest plight,
> Smoothing the rugged brow of night.

Philomel is introduced with that strange conditional "unless,"
which connects poetic ideas as they are not in "L'Allegro,"
where the *ands* line up one image beside the next, forming a
continuum in which things exist in poetic time as they do
in real space—all there, without the "presence" of one re-
"placing" its predecessor. That is the continuum of mutually
unreproving pleasures; here the continuum is broken with the
word "'less," for unlike shepherds and milkmaids, silence
and the song of Philomel are ordinarily mutually exclusive.
There is silence too in "L'Allegro," but since it is never invoked substantially, it is not negated when the poet turns to
something else: "To hear the Lark begin his flight, / And
singing startle the dull night." "Dull night" is scurried away,
just as the "lively din" in the lines that follow "scatters the
rear of darkness thin." Events and images are joined like
figures in a dance, giving the sense of experience moving
allegro to make room for new experience in unnegating comic
fullness. Watkins notes that "motion Milton identifies with
life itself," and unreproved, unarrested motion makes for the
liveliness of "L'Allegro."[9]

   In contrast to the way singing startles the night in "L'Allegro," night, absence, silence, and death penetrate and are

absorbed into song in "Il Penseroso." The first mode of interruption implies unchecked, free existence in time; the second
implies that strange paradox through which silence is absorbed
into song, absence into presence, to image a kind of inter-
relationship beyond time. Not silence, followed by the song
of Philomel, but silence " 'less" Philomel will sing. (The con-
tracted form of the conjunction helps soften the interruption,
as if respect for the humanized Silence made the bird timid
about dislodging the lady from her present place.) Clock time
turns into the less strict relations of love as the unit measurement of night seems to be glossed over or caressed into continuity. Philomel is found, "In her sweetest, saddest plight, /
Smoothing the rugged brow of night." The image is a favorite one used by Milton to express a gentleness that redeems,
luring time from its swift progress. In *Comus*, for example,
the tempter is himself lured by musical raptures "smoothing
the Raven down / Of darkness till it smiled" (ll. 251–252).
In the mask as in the lyric the present participle "smoothing"
expresses ongoingness, and the timelessness of the motion con-
tributes to, perhaps constitutes, the significance of the gesture's gentleness. Like the angels' caressing care of Lycidas,
the motion is always in progress, never to be consummated.

Our feeling that we have caught the moment is substanti-
ated by the lines that follow: "While Cynthia checks her
Dragon yoke / Gently o'er th' accustom'd Oak." Talking
about something else happening while an action takes place
is fiction's way of giving the moment duration in time. These
lines are modestly self-conscious, saying exactly what they
are doing: what happens "while" Philomel is singing is that
Cynthia checks the movement of time. If song in "L'Allegro"
startles the night, here the night is arrested in song. Poetry
triumphs over the distance that separates one moment from

the next, as it triumphs over the distance that separates the whole song "Il Penseroso" from the song of the bird. Units of space and time dissolve, and Milton speaks directly to Philomel: "Sweet Bird that shunn'st the noise of folly, / Most musical, most melancholy!" All he can voice is her definition, for that makes the nightingale "be." His words are the equivalent in verse of the song of the bird, and the time in which they are spoken is the time which that song arrests.

What happens next is as astonishing as it is inevitable:

> Thee Chantress oft the Woods among,
> I woo to hear thy Even-Song;
> And missing thee, I walk unseen
> On the dry smooth-shaven Green.

The presentness of the song has been a "false surmise," and we are caught in our error, taken aback, and made to confront the absence of what we took to be going on while Milton spoke about the arrest of time and spoke to the bird. Lolling in what seemed an eternal present, we suddenly find that all is lost. The "miss" is a minor confrontation with death, and a shadow of original sin covers the exit of the "guilty" poet, who walks away like his unregarded archetype: "all was lost. Back to the Thicket slunk / The guilty Serpent" (*PL*, IX.784–785).[10] Sympathy extends beyond the awareness shared by poet and reader into the landscape; indeed the poet's ability to evoke the Fall in such remote sounds is an expression of sympathetic vibrancy that itself redeems. Il Penseroso beholds the mistake and loss writ large on the "erroneous" or

> wand'ring Moon,
> Riding near her highest noon,
> Like one that had been led astray
> Through the Heav'n's wide pathless way.

Anticipations of the wandering fallen angels and fallen man
surge up like tears wept for this minor poem's echo of universal fall. In this "almost Shelleyan description," [11] the moon
is like that "wand'ring Fire" which "Misleads th'amaz'd
Night-wanderer from his way" (PL, IX.640). As in the temptation of Eve ("Meanwhile the hour of Noon drew on"), we
see only the vague approach "near her highest noon," for in
the very next line the moon is like one that "had been led
astray," when the timeless temptation is over and all is in the
past tense. The slight shift in image from tempter to tempted
represents the loss of time, and the wandering is, as it were,
postlapsarian.

In Milton's account of the actual Fall, one can point to the
line where Eve plucks and eats; but the "Penseroso" night is
like the night of Eve's dream, where the moment of choice is
itself absent; we see the moment approaching, and then sud-
dently what has been. What is not permitted to be actualized
is the present tense, the moment when choice takes place,
when there really is an either-or and not just a determined set
of events—one and then the next and then the next. If the
sense of loss of the present is an awareness of death, then the
"Penseroso" moon may be said to labor under the burden of
that mystery, "as if her head she bow'd / Stooping through a
fleecy cloud." The delicate pain of absence finds further cor-
relative in the way this passage is related to the absent text,
the parallel passage in "L'Allegro." For unlike the first poem,
complete in its own presence, the second is dependent on the
absence of the first. There is no moon in the "Allegro" daylight, but there are, among other sights, "Mountains on whose
barren breast / The laboring clouds do often rest." The repeated act of resting belongs to "and" poetry, which arrests
sight on a series of objects; "or" poetry images not an accumu-

lation of stops but of "goings," and hence losses. Instead of clouds at rest, Il Penseroso finds the ever distant moon "Stooping through a fleecy cloud." This is not to say that we expect moon and mountains to meet but that we are aware of an "Allegro" pattern not being fulfilled. The stooping moon suggests the void between sequential images that stands for the void between past and future, the failure of one to rest quite on the other. The line that follows the one describing the stooping moon refers not to the resting place of the moon —time does not stop, the present is not to be impaled—but to a new image. There is a period after "Stooping through a fleecy cloud." Then, beginning a different sentence, a thought elsewhere, comes the equivalent of the mountains:

> Oft on a Plat of rising ground,
> I hear the far-off Curfew sound,
> Over some wide-water'd shore,
> Swinging slow with sullen roar.

If colloquialism is appropriate to the relaxation that comes with this turn elsewhere, we can call the change from mountains to plateau a "come-down." Release is not unaccompanied by a sense of loss, and the distance that replaces the "Allegro" ease of sky-earth commerce marks a little death. The far-off sound heard in the gap is the Miltonic ancestor of a romantic line like "Stop here, or gently pass," which stands as epitaph for the experience the poem has brought to life.[12] In tolling for the passing day the curfew tolls too for the present moment that has passed away, for the mute song that is lost as nature retreats into the ongoing "sullen roar" (like the hideous roar" that drowns the song and head of Orpheus). This new, seemingly protracted sound can stand for ongoingness because it has not been checked and held "still." Then an "or" checks that sound too, and the poet looks for some "still removed place," or other images whose introduction by the word "or" suggests the awareness of absence not to be found in "L'Allegro."

The way the moral landscape of alternatives is related to the metaphoric landscape of discontinuous space is perhaps best explained by Arnold Stein. Citing lines describing the efficacy of music, which can chase "Anguish and doubt and fear and sorrow and pain / From mortal or immortal minds" (*PL*, I.558–559), Stein discusses the awareness of loss using a metaphor which it is instructive to place beside the mountain passages of the companion poems. Milton's poetry, he says, "recognizes the tangible and intangible pains, but recognizes too that they can be—not ended but chased; and from mortal *or*—this is the peak, suddenly and quietly mounted, from which all human horizons move magnificently back!—immortal minds." [13] In contrast to the added woes is the perspective that faces the void in nature and apprehends the unfolding vision with awe. One might relate such speculative height to that of Adam's vision in *Paradise Lost*, XI, where man and angel ascend the hill to view historical events laid out in sequence. If "and," as Freud tells us, is the connective of dream, then the sense that those visions are not added one to another, but each approached with misapprehension like a loss, increases the sense that this is no dream but the waking truth. If Adam is to "ascend / In the Visions of God," they must be visions awake to the woes to come. Each sight is like a new awakening, Milton's repeated image for awareness of loss. When Adam dreamed the creation of Eve, he woke to find her "or for ever to deplore / Her loss" (VIII. 479–480); we could hear in that "or" an intimation of the choice to come as well, the choice between loss of Eve and

loss of Eden.[14] In the end Adam is awake both to loss and to
the alternative to loss that corrected vision can apprehend in
Christ.

The language of loss introduced by "Il Penseroso" makes
the turn between the companion poems a kind of irrevocable
fall. In this death of the old style, the awareness of absence
may be compared to the "Lycidas" awareness of "the heavy
change, now thou art gone, / Now thou art gone, and never
must return!" The connectives in the lines that follow these
in "Lycidas" illustrate what has happened between Milton's
companion poems:

> Thee Shepherd, thee the Woods, and desert Caves,
> With wild Thyme and the gadding Vine o'ergrown,
> And all their echoes mourn.
> The Willows and the Hazel Copses green
> Shall now no more be seen,
> Fanning their joyous Leaves to thy soft lays.
> As killing as the Canker to the Rose,
> Or Taint-worm to the weanling Herds that graze,
> Or Frost to Flowers, that their gay wardrobe wear,
> When first the White-thorn blows;
> Such, *Lycidas*, thy loss to Shepherd's ear.

The timeless paradise which has been lost is remembered in
echoes of that universe of unnegating fullness now grown
wild: woods *and* caves *with* thyme *and* vine. Man inherits that
memory of what "Shall now no more be seen," with the
canker *or* worm *or* frost—alternatives whose sameness reminds
us that the real alternative has been lost, bringing "Death into
the World, and all our woe."

What happens in the use of connectives can be taken as an
emblem of the change in the relationship of language and
value. From the standpoint of "L'Allegro," "and" indicates

simply the unfallen full world, and "or" the indifferent turning from one object of interest to another. From the standpoint of "Il Penseroso," "or" acknowledges the experiential
and moral burdens of choice, while the word "and" can signal
a suspect desire to hold on to the fullness in the fallen world.
Kierkegaard says: "The either/or I propose is in a sense
absolute, for it is a question of choosing or not choosing. . . .
In another sense, however, it is only by this choice that ei-
ther/or comes to evidence." [15] One must, to be sure, be careful about throwing on Milton's companion poems the whole
weight of this distinction; to do so might seem like allegorizing
at the expense of the "Allegro" lightness of tone. But on the
other hand one level of meaning of "Il Penseroso" concerns
the turn to language that can bear the weight of such distinction without sacrificing tone. In the mode of language in
which the ethical and aesthetic are one, there are no independent "lighter" works; Milton's corpus appears an ordered
progress in which minor poems prefigure in delicate tone the
major concerns of the epics. The Penseroso, wooing to hear
evensong, missing the chanter of the wood, and walking unseen and solitary, is man contemplating the fact of fall. So
God, wont to hear Adam's evensong of praise, but missing
man, walks unseen and solitary:

> Where art thou *Adam*, wont with joy to meet
> My coming seen far off? I miss thee here,
> Not pleas'd, thus entertain'd with solitude,
> Where obvious duty erewhile appear'd unsought:
> Or come I less conspicuous, or what change
> Absents thee, or what chance detains? Come forth.
> He came, and with him *Eve*, more loath, though first
> To offend, discount'nanc't both, and discompos'd;
> Love was not in thir looks, either to God

Or to each other, but apparent guilt,
And shame, and perturbation, and despair,
Anger, and obstinacy, and hate, and guile.

[*PL*, X.103–114]

The patterns of language are surely not consciously parallel; what they do illustrate is a poetic universe so encompassing that God himself shares the same manner of expression as man, far more than on earth was thought. In the passage from *Paradise Lost* even the connectives are used to reflect the heavy change from the time when options were open, when Adam could choose between the love of God and the love of man, between the open, conspicuous commerce with God and bringing on the world of change and chance. The openness of choice and openness of idiom are lost, and even the language of God ("what chance, what change" is Satan's expression [II.222]) expresses the moral burden of word association. The six *and*s in two lines are a linguistic morass parallel to the moral bog into which man has fallen.[16]

There are no good or bad, fallen or unfallen angels in Milton's companion poems, and it would be a mistake to read them as formal statements of Christian attitudes. But the movement from the first to the second does represent a dedication to a concept of poetry in which each work stands like an angel of a different order serving the same Maker. Their moods or "messages" may be of any weight, but all are in the higher service. The moral burden informs every poetic choice.

Manuscript Choices

The companion poems actualize as poetic product the turn to a chaster mode which is so essentially an element of Milton's poetic process. What we can extrapolate from statements about the nature of creation, and what we can glean from examining manuscript evidence point to the penseroso mode. Beyond allegro fullness of conception, Milton locates creative power in the strength of the selectivity and the care with which the most particular phrase is raised into single service. Any losses in meaning, as choices are made, are sparks on the conscientious forge, evidences of the energy of the more exacting hammer.

Jonathan Richardson reported that Milton "would Dictate many, perhaps 40 Lines as it were in a Breath, and then reduce them to half the Number." [17] We need not be concerned with the historical accuracy of such a remark, but it does dramatize the sense that elimination, saying "not this, not that," was as much a part of Milton's creativity as the original versifying. Revision was a process of deletion of what was not clear or not essential, seldom a matter of enriching suggestivity. Examining the Trinity College, Cambridge, manuscript, Laura Lockwood notes "how seldom he feels it necessary to substitute for words thin in imaginative content those rich in suggestion." [18] The idea of adding a purely embellishing line, one which would "make verbal curiosities the end," was anathema. When lines he had conceived appeared too rich in suggestion, too much in danger of being read as verbal curiosities in themselves, Milton excised with a moral severity that does not condone poetic effect for its own sake. John Diekhoff, whose concern is primarily with the small corrections that improve the quality of the verse, concedes "that the reason for his dissatisfaction was sometimes the extravagance of what he had written." [19]

That a writer should revise with the intent of refining is expected; but that he should have second thoughts about words or passages that are possibly more startling or in themselves more satisfying than those he chooses to retain tells us something of the uniqueness of Milton's poetry of choice. Some of the equivocal corrections from earlier Trinity manuscript readings can illustrate the significance of the motives and achievements of the poet's second will.

C. S. Lewis has perceptively studied the instances in which Milton "subdues . . . in the interests of unity of tone." [20] For example, he quotes the line "and often takes our cattell wth strange pinches," which is present in the Trinity manuscript of *Comus* but omitted in all other texts:

> The first version might have come out of *A Midsummer Night's Dream*. It belongs to the fairy world of real popular superstition; it breathes a rusticity which has not been filtered through Theocritus and Virgil, and a supernatural which is homely—half comic, half feared—rather than romantic. But Milton had gone as near that world as he chooses to go, in the preceding lines; anything more would be out of the convention in which he is writing. He can just venture on the "urchin blasts"; "pinches" oversteps the line drawn by literary decorum. He therefore cancels the verse.

Lewis' account leaves little more to be said—except that for Milton "the convention in which he is writing" clearly has a reality greater than any particular image that fancy could invent. If the passage as it remains is in some way less vital, it is because the laws of literary decorum are for Milton more alive and have a greater right to their being than a petty violation of them. We may prefer the literature which permits "individual beauties" (Lewis' phrase) or moments of immediate apprehension of a world of experience far deeper than the surface coherence of the artistic argument; and indeed Milton will write with an increasing ability to let the vast world repudiated by the chastity of poetry break in with its furies and complexities. But *Comus* is consciously conceived not only as a work to be acted and understood by youths, but as a youthful work, one in which the neophyte poet demonstrates his ability and willingness to uphold the rules of an order above the claims of the fullness of experience.

Revisions in language that suppress expression of the characters' youth are stages of the poet's own initiation. It is as if the writer, giving up the more polymorphous pleasures of characterization for the more austere phrases, rewrites his relationship to nature in a way that spells poetic maturity. For example, the earlier reading has the First Brother envision the encounter with Comus with the childlike enthusiasm and visual realization otherwise reserved for his less philosophical sibling:

> Ile find him out
> and force him to release his new got prey
> or drag him by the curls & cleave his scalpe
> downe to the hips.

"Release his new got prey" is crossed out for the more abstract justice of "restore his purchase back," and between the 1637 edition and 1645, emended to read:

> I'll find him out,
> And force him to restore his purchase back
> Or drag him by the curls to a foul death,
> Curs'd as his life.   [ll. 606–609]

(One can be grateful that those curls did not have to go; perhaps having paid the price of the major excision, Milton could afford not to clip his relation further.) Lewis comments, "There is no question which reading has the more 'punch' in it. Both are full of energy; but the one is physical energy, demonstrable by the actor, the other is moral."

Similar editorial dilution occurs in the brothers' debate

before Thyrsis appears. In the earlier reading the First Brother says:

> I doe not brother
> inferre, as if I thought my sisters state
> secure, wthout all doubt or question, no
> [beshrew me but I would] *
> I could be willing though now i'th darke to trie
> a tough passado wth the shaggiest ruffian
> that lurks by hedge or lane of this dead circuit
> to have her by my side, though I were sure
> she might be free from perill where she is.

First, "beshrew me but I would" is changed to the more decorous, less dramatic "I could be willing." But between the manuscript and the 1637 edition the whole boast is dropped, and "secure wthout all doubt or question, no" becomes "secure beyond all doubt or controversie." Lewis completes his discussion of the passage with the plaintive though good-humored remark, "Not so would Donne or D. H. Lawrence have chosen." While such a judgment may be agreeable, it produces, in the context of a discussion of Miltonic revisions, a sense of incongruity like that Milton must have felt his original verses introduced into the mask. Lewis comments that "the boyish and noble actor, waving his little sword, with his colloquial *i'th' darke* and his picturesque shaggy ruffians and dead circuits, all to be faced in defence of his sister, would to this day be snatched at by any producer anxious to 'brighten up' the dialogue at this point." To wish to brighten up the dialogue, as many a modern adaption of a classic has proven, is to distance—if not to oppose—the text. Either one is committed to the mask, its values and limitations, or one works

* Brackets indicate words crossed out by Milton.

against it by seeking to exploit moments that contrast with its tone. Milton conceived the problem in such either-or terms and so, choosing the mask, deleted the passage. One may agree with Lewis when he bemoans "that dearly bought singleness of quality," provided one recognizes that singleness as the very nature of a poem about chastity, dedicated to a dearly bought singleness of value.

The meticulous avoidance of larger implications in *Comus* seems to contrast with the often startling way *Paradise Lost* implies more than is easily reconciled with the larger purpose of a given context. When the Edenic sun is described as providing "more warmth than *Adam* needs" (*PL*, V.302), or when God counsels taking care "lest unawares we lose / This our high place" (V.731–732), Milton seems to be promiscuously asking for trouble. In contrast to the chaste severity of the mask, the epic raises more issues than it stops to resolve. Yet the proper reading of such passages demands a temperance in choice of meanings which is related to temperance in the poet's choice of words. The persons of the epic are likewise involved in the chastity of choice. For Adam, Eve, and God himself, no less than for the Lady or her brothers in the mask, meaning is everywhere, and moral action, creative action, lies in the act of limitation. Cosmic creation in *Paradise Lost* begins with the retirement of the Father and the passing on of the principle of limitation. The spirit of the Father is carried by the Son, who is enjoined to "bid the Deep / Within appointed bounds be Heav'n and Earth" (*PL*, VII.166–167). He internalizes the principle of denial, which is then externally expressed when he says "No" to the abyss, thus circumscribing the universe. So the poetic son—whose secondary imagination is an echo of the Paternal I AM—comes into his own when he assumes this Urizenic role.[21]

We can compare the work of the first parents in paradise to the labor of revision of the mask. Properly imaging the Creator, Adam and Eve engage in "reformation," the act of re-forming, re-creating, setting new limitations on a garden tending to wild. Adam describes the enjoined task:

> our pleasant labor, to reform
> Yon flow'ry Arbors, yonder Alleys green,
> Our walk at noon, with branches overgrown,
> That mock our scant manuring, and require
> More hands than ours to lop thir wanton growth;
> Those Blossoms also, and those dropping Gums,
> That lie bestrown unsightly and unsmooth,
> Ask riddance, if we mean to tread with ease.
>
> [IV.625–632]

The realm of the mask is one of flowery arbors where the treading is easy. To this end, the speeches are weeded for remarks that suggest more of the corruption of the world than the mask can sustain. The Second Brother, whose childish fear brings him closer to a perception of the actual than the First Brother's philosophic remove, speaks too plainly of this vision when he questions the safety of beauty:

> you may as well spread out the unsun'd heaps
> of miser's treasure by an outlaw's den,
> and tell me it is safe, as bid me [thinke] hope
> danger will winke on opportunity
> and let a single helpless maiden passe
> uninjur'd in this [vast & hideous wild] wide surrounding
>   wast.

The phrase "vast & hideous wild" may provide a more accurate description of the setting in which innocence finds itself in this world than is provided by the limited, protected stage

on which this view of chastity is being presented. But in the
context of the mask the phrase is more inappropriate than
profound. We may agree with the Second Brother that it is
ridiculous to think "danger will wink on opportunity," but
that kind of vision is out of place in the universe of *Comus*,
where nature *is* in accord with moral law and landscape is but
a staged projection of a moral state, an earthly paradise where
a little temperance suffices to defeat all temptation. Milton
therefore changes "think" to "hope," the perception of the
actual to the conception of the ideal. The Elder Brother says:

> where an equal poise of hope and fear
> Does arbitrate th'event, my nature is
> That I incline to hope rather than fear,
> And gladly banish squint suspicion.   [ll. 410–413]

To hope rather than fear is to show faith rather than doubt, to
see with the sight of heaven rather than with the squinting
sight of this world. The Second Brother is, then, not more
experienced but more near-sighted in not hoping that things
will turn out for the best. Milton tones down the line that
most forcefully expressed the actual; "vast and hideous wild"
becomes "wide surrounding waste." [22] He is subduing the
luxury of suggestion, the kind of luxury that Eve, approaching
separation, finds in the garden's "tending to wild" (*PL*, IX.
212). A spectator hearing "wild" might be uncomfortable at
the reminder that the vast world outside this pretty entertainment is all too often hideously out of proportion with the
staged moral order. Perhaps one hearing "wide surrounding
waste" might look at the rather crowded and elaborately deco-
rated stage and smile with the older brother's superior wisdom, knowing that everyone here will pass uninjured. With a
second will more wise, he knows, to twist Wordsworth's

terms, that all shall be saved. The difference in the two readings could stand for the difference in commitment to the
work of art defining its own universe, commitment to sharing
(as do the prelapsarian protoplasts) the labor and value of
creation. Milton revises because, as creator of the world of his
mask, he, if anyone, must be strict in limiting his focus to that
world.

When curiosity is sacrificed for consistency of tone, manuscript change affects not only the individual perspectives but
the total vision of the mask. That the speeches of the Lady,
Comus, both brothers, and Thyrsis are all moderated in the
interests of a more coherent, more limited view points to the
poet himself as ascetic in outlook. Nowhere, not even in the
epilogue, is the suggestion developed that the mask has reservations about the completeness of its perspective. Milton's
commitment to an aesthetic form demands that such reservations be kept in reserve. He does not permit, in metaphysical
fashion, a concept to be surrounded with an aura of second
thoughts about its formulation. For uncertainties about formulation are not "second thoughts" but first thoughts, poetic
intuitions that must be artistically and spiritually converted
from the multiplicity of possibilities to the singleness of
choice.

To rise to "something like prophetic strain" implies a movement beyond vision of what *is* to what might be selected and
thus redeemed. The artistic process of filling in, embellishing,
adding one perspective to another implies, as its end, an art
that holds the mirror up to the complexity and richness of
nature. At its best it can encompass what T. S. Eliot calls "a
thousand small deliberations," and "multiply variety / In a
wilderness of mirrors." Tillyard says that Milton "hated the
unrelated fact generally," [23] and though the process of associa-

tion, the facility of literary imagination could multiply varieties of relations, for Milton this was but the first stage, what preceded the choice that moves from the thousand things perceived to what is singly conceived, from the multiplicity of what was fancied to what is singly imagined. Poets like Blake and Eliot have derided the manner in which the specific is overlooked for the general. But Milton did not need to count fish in order to write the line originally in the tempter's speech: "cramming the seas with spawne innumerable." Such a line, capturing the sense of spawning nature, reflects a mind correspondingly complex, facile with "Those images that yet / Fresh images beget." For Milton the labor of writing is not in proliferating such images but in checking their growth. He has not a mind to say with Yeats, "I sought a theme and sought for it in vain, / I sought it daily for six weeks or so," for the themes are there, cramming, for example, the pages of the commonplace book with the fullness of the seas. Such is the fullness of "L'Allegro," whose promiscuous muse invites company "to live with her, and live with thee, / In unreproved pleasures free." But beyond that vision of inclusion, beyond the mirror, the correspondent universe, the mind exquisitely suited to the natural world, is the selective, higher vision represented in "Il Penseroso," that strain in which experience is carefully sifted into a unity of being.

Choiceness in the Sonnets

The choice by which Milton staunchly abides in mollifying the vision of the characters in *Comus* is not less stringent when he speaks without the mask. The sonnets exemplify this well, since the conventions and impersonality traditionally associated with the form permitted the poet a more inclusive view than that which he might have expressed without the inheritance of the literary form. With Milton the sonnet is deliberately austere.

Sonnet XIV, "On the Religious Memory of Mrs Catharine Thomason," never loses sight of the simplicity of faith appropriate to its occasion. In the Trinity manuscript the poem first began thus:

> When Faith & Love, that parted from thee never,
> Had rip'n'd thy just soul to dwell with God,
> Meekly thou didst resigne this earthly clod
> Of Flesh and Sin which man from heaven doth sever.

The perception of human corruption is inappropriate for the poem. It is to be a comforting and comfortable evocation of heavenly delight, a pastel poem not to be overlaid with a dark impasto of original sin. He therefore changes "clod" to "load," and "flesh & sin" to "death call'd life." Milton does not think in generalities, but having conceived a sharply defined image, goes back and blurs where bluntness is aggressive, personal, and out of taste. In the rewritten line, "Of Death, call'd Life; which us from Life doth sever," wit, what Eliot calls the "alliance of levity and seriousness," replaces "direct sensuous apprehension of thought." [24] Eliot's terms are appropriate here, for ironically they help point to the dissociation of sensibility we can see at work in the manuscript. For Milton that dissociation, far from being a state to be lamented, is an aesthetic and moral injunction. The failure to dissociate the chaste muse from the fury and mire of more immediate images would be a violation of the act of choice, which demands a repudiation along with the dedication to a higher, more single vision. Revising further, Milton excises "journey'd from this dark abode" and concentrates his description of the flight of words and alms on their heavenly destination. They

> Stay'd not behind, nor in the grave were trod;
> But, as Faith pointed with her golden rod,
> Follow'd thee up to joy and bliss for ever.

The poem that results is pure, its harsher harmonies chastened into an absolute statement of that delicate balance which is the sonnet form.

More than the principle of their composition, the notion of *ascesis*, of purification to chaster form is often the very theme of Milton's sonnets. Sonnet XIX, "When I consider how my light is spent . . . ," is perhaps the most familiar example of a text that seems to revise itself, making the prevention of its own murmur both its concern and its formal achievement.[25] We may turn to Sonnet XX, "Lawrence of virtuous father . . . ," for a more extended look at the tone of conscious limitation.

The sonnet invites Lawrence to share an occasion "choice" not only for its quality but its rarity:

> Where shall we sometimes meet and by the fire
> Help waste a sullen day, what may be won
> From the hard Season gaining?

The sense of difficulty in winning that day to waste, the limited attraction forced by the verb "waste," and the reservation of "sometimes meet" argue for a carefully tempered seizing of the day. Dank fields, mired ways, sullen days, frozen earth, and the strong accents of "the hard Season gaining" imply the spareness of any form of pleasure. Appealing to the Attic taste, these reservations make the prospective entertainment as difficult as it is delicate. The painful awareness of the limitations of joys becomes a temperance profoundly spiritual in its quiet overtones of a rejuvenated sense of time:

> Time will run
> On smoother till *Favonius* re-inspire
> The frozen earth, and clothe in fresh attire
> The Lily and Rose, that neither sow'd nor spun.

The tone is that of *consolamini:* and all manner of things shall be well. The enjambment of "run / On smoother" urges pacific equality of accent, and the reinspiration becomes a religious reconciliation to ongoingness.

The only biblical passage combining the lily and the rose is in Song of Songs: "I am the rose of Sharon, and the lily of the valleys. As the lily among thorns, so is my love among the daughters" (2 : 1–2). The passage brings together the spring of renewal and the selectivity that is part of appeal. Milton's sonnet asks, "What neat repast shall feast us, light and choice," and Canticles too relates chosenness to neat repast: "As the apple tree among the trees of the wood, so is my beloved among the sons. I sat down under his shadow with great delight, and his fruit was sweet to my taste. He brought me to the banqueting house, and his banner over me was love." The passage continues with one of the most memorable antecedents of Milton's reinspired frozen earth: "The voice of my beloved! behold, he cometh leaping upon the mountains, skipping upon the hills. . . . My beloved spake, and said unto me, 'Rise up, my love, my fair one, and come away. For, lo, the winter is past, the rain is over and gone; The flowers appear on the earth; the time of the singing of birds is come, and the voice of the turtle is heard in our land.' "

Like the biblical spring, Milton's evocation of pastoral beauty is never far from spiritual service. It is Eliot's rose garden, evoking infinite echoes of the richness of experience only to convert them into the unity of divine service—"the fire and the rose are one." Milton's "hard Season gaining," the winter of the soul's discontent, becomes, like the soul's murmur in Sonnet XIX, a discordant voice turned into harmony, "more bent / To serve therewith my Maker." Spring, the earth newly clothed "in fresh attire," is, like the works and alms of Mrs. Thomason, clad "o'er with purple beams / And azure wings," a vision of the soul at one with God. Rosemond Tuve says, "The soul's home is that place where the conditions of our exile do not obtain." [26] Such are the fields of the lily and rose.

If the resonances of such a vision of rejuvenation seem to extend the sonnet beyond the singleness of devotion, the last phrase of the octet chastens the natural elements of the glorification in rebirth into the purity of worship. It is not that imaginative reality is noticeably confined to theology, but that religious echoes broaden the way of service until it appears as infinite as the secular proliferation it left behind. "The Lily and Rose, that neither sow'd nor spun" evokes its source in Matthew and with it the weight of the New Testament practice of transforming images of nature into metaphors of the godly way: "Consider the lilies of the field, how they grow; they toil not, neither do they spin" (Matt. 6 : 28). With Milton's echo of Matthew the flowers are reborn into emblems of the contemplative life, and the whole octet of Milton's sonnet joins the angelic choir in lines that "also serve who only stand and wait." The invitation to Lawrence to "Help waste a sullen day" becomes, more than a tempered appeal to seize time, a statement of the spirituality of such "waste." "God doth not need / Either man's work or his own gifts" (Sonnet XIX), so time itself and the values that label as "waste" a pause in the world's sick hurry are all blown away by a properly oriented wind, a holy spirit that, like the turtledove heard in the spring, broods over the vast abyss and asserts the godliness of that penseroso pose.

The sestet returns the sonnet to its immediate topic, the dinner invitation, but with reinspired awareness of the unity and godliness of that way. Like "Il Penseroso," it does not dismiss aesthetic pleasures, though they are seen in a different light when they are interposed in the lives of those who stand and wait. The muse of "Il Penseroso" is enjoined to come

> With ev'n step, and musing gait,
> And looks commercing with the skies,
> Thy rapt soul sitting in thine eyes:
> There held in holy passion still,
> Forget thyself to Marble, till
> With a sad Leaden downward cast,
> Thou fix them on the earth as fast.

The religious echoes of the octet of the sonnet are just such "looks commercing with the skies," and the vision of the contemplative life is a vision of that "holy passion still," standing and waiting with all murmurs, all elements of self-expression turned to marble. The death of the self gives rise to the poetry of worship. Once such vision has been approximated, there is no path but down, reintegrating that prophetic strain with living in the prosaic world, fixing the eyes back on earth.

The "Il Penseroso" passage continues:

> And join with thee calm Peace and Quiet,
> Spare Fast, that oft with gods doth diet
> And hears the Muses in a ring.

This descent from lone heights to community—and, specifically, repast—is precisely the movement of the sonnet. Having quietly, in the still small voice of the spring imagery, approached the soul's home, the poem returns to the pedestrian occupation of the soul that serves by bearing the winter yoke and waiting. The "Peace and Quiet" of "Il Penseroso" are the life of the "Lily and Rose, that neither sow'd nor spun," and as the earlier poem continues with "spare fast" and "hears the muses," so the sonnet moves to consider "what neat repast shall feast us" and what "artful voice" shall sing. If the context of both poems is largely secular, both attain to something like prophetic strain within the setting of the natural world. Both evoke aesthetic pleasure, but the drama permitted in "Il Penseroso," like the banqueting of the sonnet, is strictly of "Attic taste." It is a vision of experience, of what it means to live in the natural world, but chastened into the "good part" of knowing that "but one thing is needful" (Luke 10 : 42). After such knowledge the poem returns to the business of Martha, aware that the wasted day is one more service in the life of the patient man.

The line "The Lily and Rose, that neither sow'd nor spun" must evoke not only the verse in Matthew but its context:

Therefore I say unto you, Take no thought for your life what ye shall eat, or what ye shall drink; nor yet for your body, what ye shall put on. Is not the life more than meat, and the body than raiment? Behold the fowls of the air: for they sow not, neither do they reap, nor gather into barns; yet your heavenly Father feedeth them. Are ye not much better than they? Which of you by taking thought can add one cubit unto his stature: And why take ye thought for raiment? Consider the lilies of the field, how they grow; they toil not, neither do they spin: And yet I say unto you, That even Solomon in all his glory was not arrayed like one of these. Wherefore, if God so clothe the grass of the field, which to-day is, and to-morrow is cast into the oven, shall he not much more clothe you, O ye of little faith? Therefore take no thought, saying, "What shall we eat?" or "What shall we drink?" or,

"Wherewithal shall we be clothed?" . . . But seek ye first the
kingdom of God, and his righteousness; and all these things shall
be added unto you. Take therefore no thought for the morrow:
for the morrow shall take thought for the things of itself. Sufficient unto the day is the evil thereof.   [6 : 25–34]

In light of the Gospel the fullness of the natural vision, not
only of the lily and rose line, but of the whole poem is converted to divine service. Matthew's injunction "Take therefore no thought for the morrow" makes the *carpe diem* tone
not something to be overcome but part of the religious *ascesis*
toward *carpe Deum*. It denies involvement with the this-
worldly tomorrow, for which one provides with the security
of Mammon, in order to affirm the eternal morrow and the
providence of God. "No man can serve two masters," Matthew warns, creating the sense of choice that underlies and
redeems the world of experience evoked in Milton's sonnet.
To seize the day is to apprehend the God who "doth not
need / Either man's work or his own gifts." The moment and
eternity are aligned against the worldly workings of time, so
that the invitation to waste a sullen day stands against the
feverish pursuit of goods enjoyed only in time. Heaven, as
Milton says in Sonnet XXI, "disapproves that care, though
wise in show, / That with superfluous burden loads the day." [27]
The lines "Time will run / On smoother till *Favonius* re-
inspire / The frozen earth" thus pose the same opposition as
does the poem "On Time": time runs, but there are those who
stand and wait, flowers in an eternal paradise. "Till" indicates
the temporality, the "directedness" implicit in the concept of
choice, making the invitation of the poem a spiritual call for
the conversion of the involvement in time into a concern with
everlastingness. He who can "interpose" delights ritually en-

acts the ultimate interposition, when a halt will be called to time's race.

The choice posed in Sonnet XX involves a concept of priorities in a double sense, like the "preventing" of murmur in Sonnet XIX. On the one hand, Sonnet XX dramatizes a conversion from a prior state of worldliness to the invited heavenly way. In this sense Milton echoes the kind of transformation Matthew is calling for: "Therefore I say unto you, Take no thought for your life." On the other hand, having established the "priority" of a spiritual path, the poem is concerned in the sestet with what it means to interpose that vision into daily life. This kind of "converting" also takes on added sanction from the model in Matthew: "But seek ye first the kingdom of God, and his righteousness; and all these things shall be added unto you." Establishing the priority of the kingdom of God does not eliminate the need to eat, but eating becomes part of a greater service when acknowledged after the question "Is not the life more than meat?" In light of Matthew's injunction "Take no thought, saying, 'What shall we eat,'" Milton's query "What neat repast shall feast us" becomes a statement of indifference to the particularities of the feast. To be sure, it sounds by itself very much like the kind of concern Matthew is enjoining against, but the vision that preceded has chastened the comestible concern. Once the octet has fulfilled the commandment "Seek ye first the kingdom of God," the rest of the poem fulfills the prophecy that "all these things shall be added to you." "These things" are poetically integrated into the spiritually redeemed natural processes. Earlier lines have already transformed the concern with raiment in the same way. "Wherefore, if God so clothe the grass of the field, which to-day is, and to-morrow is cast into the oven, shall he not much more clothe you," asks Matthew.

Milton writes, "clothe in fresh attire / The Lily and Rose," tempering the poetic involvement in natural beauty not only with the religious overtones of his image but with the awareness of the "hard Season gaining," the limitations in time as in Matthew's phrase "which to-day is, and to-morrow is cast into the oven."

In Matthew, as in Milton, the limitations of the object of the image only add to its attractiveness. Matthew's images from the world of nature are tempered only in the service to which they are put, not in the intensity with which they are couched: "They toil not, neither do they spin: and yet I say unto you, that even Solomon in all his glory was not arrayed like one of these." If the rose and the association of renewal and choice are echoes of the Song of Solomon, Milton is but intensifying that glory in the service of the poem and God. And yet for all its richness the sonnet never loses sight of the sense of limitation, of sacrifice by which natural image is translated into the celestial: "He who of those delights can judge and spare / To interpose them oft, is not unwise." In contrast to the customary praise of Solomon as wisest of men, "not unwise" is praise as moderate as the repast the poem projects. And for all of the sublimation of the secular delights, the word "spare" suggests moderation in just the course for which it recommends that time be spared.[28] Qualification and half-negation seem to be working to disintegrate the very substance of the argument, as if that loss of corporeality were part of the renunciation by which the poem achieves its spiritual vision.

Such extended examination requires, like the sonnet itself, some form of renunciation for the perception of unity. J. A. W. Bennett is undoubtedly right when he points to the mock seriousness of the whole poem,[29] a tone which, permitting connotations of ultimate concern, prevents too high a strain by means of its light, Horatian context. The sonnet, like the repast it images, is "light and choice," but that lightness becomes a measure of the choiceness of the path, the ethereal transfiguration of earthly concerns to concerns about the soul's home. Moreover, the sense in which the poem can be called "witty" is itself more limited, more chaste, than that in which the term applies to the sonnets of Donne or Shakespeare.

What is true of the poetry has its corollary in criticism. Thus R. M. Adams warns against overreading which "corrupts everything and will sacrifice even its own best perceptions for the glare and tinsel of a bit of false wit." [30] One may compare such strictures to Dr. Johnson's quarrel with Shakespeare, that he would have sacrificed the world for a quibble. Johnson's criticism, despite itself, points to a very genuine quality in Shakespeare—that the quibble often reflects a wider range of the world than a sage and serious poet may have chosen to include.

In Shakespeare the witty and the serious combine to create their own world. There is good humor in a line like "Therefore I lie with her and she with me" (Sonnet CXXXVIII), together with a lovely portrayal of an imaginative reality created by utilizing, rather than purging, the world of experience: "And in our faults by lies we flattered be." There is no renunciation, no limitation felt as a prerequisite for the kind of paradise the poem itself creates. Indeed, it is precisely the inclusiveness of Shakespeare, the witty and the serious, playful and painful awareness dancing together, that gives the sense of transmutation "into something rich and strange."

Such a sea change makes the Shakespearean achievement of

a different order from the Miltonic translation to the skies.[31]
The existence of the comparison is part of Milton's poetic, for
the significance of the Miltonic option to climb to another
sphere depends on the measure of earlier greatness. The sea as
symbol of the Shakespearean imagination is crammed "with
spawne innumerable"; it is also a great leveler. In the first
group of Shakespeare sonnets the powerful evocations of the
ravages of time, the claims for the power of poetry, and the
advice to beget an heir all exist on the same plane. That is the
extravagance of some of the couplets:

> Pity the world, or else this glutton be,
> To eat the world's due, by the grave and thee.   [Sonnet I]

> And, all in war with Time for love of you
> As he takes from you, I ingraft you new.   [Sonnet XV]

> Yet do thy worst, old Time: despite thy wrong,
> My love shall in my verse ever live young.   [Sonnet XIX]

The first sonnet sets the tone in the equality of that "or."
Moral injunction and vision of the destructiveness of time are
put side by side, of equal reality, without the Miltonic sense
that the perception of the way things are is but the first step
in the path of a moral progress. Far from turning from time *to*
the young man, Sonnet I unites the addressee and the adver-
sary in the metaphor of the last line: "To eat the world's due."
Combining poetic and generational concerns, the dedication
sets the pattern: "To the only begetter of these ensuing sonnets." In the poems which follow there is no renunciation, no
death that precedes the transcendence. With the freedom of
the "Allegro" bird, the poet's mind changes state "Like to the
lark at break of day arising / From sullen earth, sings hymns

at heaven's gate" (Sonnet XXIX). There is no ladder to be scaled, no experience from which one must turn aside. (Indeed, the neglect of one aspect of experience is a subject of the sonnets.) Speaker, subject, image, the ostensible addressee, and all aspects of the natural world exist on a level. Sonnet III concludes: "But if thou live rememb'red not to be, / Die single, and thine image dies with thee." Artistic and experiential realities are in easy commerce with each other; the image is of equal importance, if not identical with the thing itself.

Is Tom o' Bedlam the "thing itself," a man, or symbol of man? A cursory glance at the tragedies finds unrenouncing inclusiveness there too and helps explain why so much of Shakespeare belongs to the "L'Allegro" world. Shakespeare's is the kind of "immortal verse" of which "L'Allegro" sings, not the penseroso verse created by an "immortal mind that hath forsook / Her mansion in this fleshly nook." He needs no such forsaking. When the Clown in *Antony and Cleopatra* calls the queen a "dish for the gods," we do not move from the earthy idiom to the "immortal longings" of this noble act; [32] without denial, the play remains grounded in sensuous reality at the same time that it finds out new heaven, new earth. (The whole play is perhaps more about its allegro ambivalence, its insistence on having it both ways, than about the significance of the alternatives themselves.) On a different journey toward the union of sensual and spiritual reality, King Lear looks at Poor Tom: "Unaccommodated man is no more but such a poor, bare, forked animal as thou art" (III.iv). Literature loses a clear sense of identity as mirror and laps the soul into a confrontation with the "thing itself." At the end of *Lear* mythic and natural meanings are inseparable in Kent's "journey," and Albany's fiat, "fall and cease," refers as much to the end of the play as the end of the world. Kent asks, "Is this the promis'd end?" Edgar queries, "Or image of that horror?" (V.iii. 265–266). As the two questions seem to measure each other's self-consciousness, there is no temporality and no choice to be made in that "or." Compare the infinitely more limited, more chaste ending of the Miltonic piece in which Shakespearean echoes, if anywhere, are to be found: [33] "Or if Virtue feeble were / Heaven itself would stoop to her" (*Comus*, ll. 1022–23). In contrast with the drama of living in time and patiently enduring that temptation which is implicit in Milton's "or," Shakespeare's is almost replaceable with "id est." It is the promised end—that is, the image of that horror. The whole scene cries out "id est," "This is so," more *so*, closer to "the thing itself" than will be imaged outside the play or seen by the young, those who with the audience, go on to ordinary experience. Such apprehension is beyond logical sequence, beyond any sense that the final vision has been achieved by purgation of any imaginative element brought to that consummation. There is no alternative in that "or," because the voice is authoritative—things here imaged are *so*.

Shakespearean language takes a stand for its own transcendence, as it were, by straddling the "or," by weighing substantially on either foot like an Antony bestriding the ocean. The delights of Shakespearean language are dolphin-like, too; "they show'd his back above / The element they lived in." The apology for such metaphor is that if one must generalize about Shakespearean and Miltonic vision, the distinction must recognize a difference in relation of language to reality, and the distinction must be one that can cope with the discordant overtones of an idea of imaginative progress. From the perspective of Miltonic language, imagination must now follow a better way, while Shakespearean language can be said to have taken a broader, more inclusive way. Milton gives us Hesperian fables, "if true, here only"; Cleopatra says:

> nature wants stuff
> To vie strange forms with fancy; yet, to imagine
> An Antony, were nature's piece 'gainst fancy
> Condemning shadows quite.   [V.ii]

This is to have it both ways, to insist on a transcendent picture of Antony and to insist that his reality transcends that which could be pictured.

Here is another passage that insists in the manner of the romances on apprehending the realm of grace as the furthest addition to, not negation of, unaccommodated nature:

> You have seen
> Sunshine and rain at once: her smiles and tears
> Were like; a better way: Those happy smilets
> That play'd on her ripe lip seem'd not to know
> What guests were in her eyes, which, parted thence,
> As pearls from diamonds dropp'd.
>
> [*King Lear*, IV.iii.19–24]

Robert Heilman properly notes how language is being wrought to unusual complexity, and that fact is surely related to the difficulty editors have had with both grammar and significance.[34] In Milton there must never be any doubt about which is the "better way." Here, the question whether the phrase belongs to the simile that precedes or to the one that follows is a quibble that stands for the straddling of the "or," the supreme equivocation that the scene is about. A firsthand rendition of the scene or an unadorned narrative of it is out of the question, and the difficulty of metaphoric language is appropriately confronted in trying to describe Cordelia, who from the beginning has been associated with the inadequacy of verbal expression. Cordelia represents a higher unity of feeling and seeming where patience and sorrow, pathos and goodness exist as simultaneous alternatives.

The Gentleman is having trouble because contrary impulses must be expressed without introducing negation. Blake says, "There is a place where Contrarieties are equally True. / This place is called Beulah." In the mundane world, as in the world of metaphor, "The Negation must be destroyed to redeem the Contraries." [35] We could say that just as there is, in Blake, a higher Eden where contraries are not equally true —they exist rather in intellectual warfare for superior truth— so Milton will present an Eden to Shakespeare's Beulah. Within Shakespeare, however, this Beulah moment approaches the highest harmony. Call the contraries sunshine and rain. The combination represents an arrest in time of what is ordinarily experienced consecutively rather than simultaneously, though the speaker is clearly picking out the most naturalistic, the most familiar analogy to help explain an emotional state. But the familiar and naturalistic are not enough; if one compares the unnegating simultaneity of sunshine and rain, still the smiles and tears were a *better* union than natural metaphor could express. Beyond simple paradox, a second comparison must be introduced, and the linguistic arrest of time between the two already implies the association of arrest with choice and an apprehension of a higher order. For one stands between the metaphors, as one stands on the "or" that separates "promis'd end" from "image," to achieve a greater height than could be expressed simply as "image."

Language is at this moment at its most self-conscious extreme and can only escape by acknowledging "seeming" and introducing an image of unself-consciousness: the smiles seem "not to know" the tears. In a false surmise of independent metaphorical existence, the smiles become innocent of the tears and their grief, and negation is thus transmuted into a higher innocence. Since smiles "really" cannot know tears, the greater fiction carries the greater truth. The reworking of the description of smiles and tears then produces a double metaphor, combining the temporal image of "guests" and "parting" with the atemporal jewelry analogy. Linguistic alternatives thus bring the passage to a kind of incarnation: metaphoric simultaneity represents the arrest of negating, progressive time in a moment of grace. "A better way," in the sense of "a better way of putting things," is a miniature of a better way of ordering time from the simple natural metaphor to the one where only fictional ignorance—"seem'd not to know"—can express the complexities of emotion in a contrary world. In Miltonic terms it is as if language were pointing to an allegro fullness (sunshine and rain), a turn from the inadequacy of that expression, and then to "a better way," a penseroso "parting thence" and a redemption in time.

Reading this kind of transcendence into the Shakespearean moment of linguistic self-confrontation may seem less out of place when one considers that Cordelia, if anyone, is a symbol of a grace that redeems from the general curse. In Milton, "a better way" is always in some sense an echo of the better way offered to history through Christ. Even as removed a salvation as that which the Attendant Spirit offers in *Comus*, "another way" after the rod has been lost, carries such overtones.[36] Grace gets implicated in the very language of fictional alternatives and turns a striding of the word "or" into an either-or confrontation.

If evidence were needed that Milton felt the force of the Shakespearean way, it is openly found in the poem "On Shake-

speare." The terms of that praise not only establish Milton's
sense of what has been done before him, but point to the
direction his own career will take: "Thou in our wonder and
astonishment / Hast built thyself a livelong Monument." As
great as that monument may be, it rests on an earthly sensibility
of how wide a range of experience it encompasses. Shakespeare's "easy numbers flow" in all directions, unlike Milton's
attempt to stem the tide of imaginative suggestion and by slow
endeavoring art to ascend "higher than the sphery chime."
Shakespeare's domain is defined as horizontal, as wide as the
sea it straddles, shoring all on its encompassing level. In
"L'Allegro" it takes in the whole countryside, where "sweetest *Shakespeare*, fancy's child, / Warble[s] his native Woodnotes wild." Fancy is that capacity of infinite extension in
which image and experience are on the same plane, and a play
can create "new Heaven, new earth," where the "promis'd
end" is actualized in its image.[37] Shakespearean tragedy belongs to the world of "L'Allegro" as much as does comedy.

For Shakespeare, image begets image, and the new meaning
fulfills rather than usurps the life of the old. But for Milton
an image or simile fades before it assumes its proper place in a
greater order. Sabrina, for example, can be seen as an image of
cleansing virtue, but it is "far closer to the main line of Milton's intent to let the water-virtue connection quietly disappear the minute it ceases to help our understanding of the
images and begins to make demands on its own account."[38]
Each meaning is assumed into the work, its family of meanings,
when one sees its death, the limit of its vitality. And Milton
contrasts such self-denial with the profligacy of Shakespeare's
muse: "thou our fancy of itself bereaving / Dost make us
Marble with too much conceiving."[39] The immensity of the
"brood" overflows the Shakespearean moment and infringes

on our ground, trampling "our fancy." Shakespeare "violates"
us in the way Comus threatens the Lady:

> if I but wave this wand,
> Your nerves are all chain'd up in Alabaster,
> And you a statue.

Shakespeare does "make us Marble"; he fulfills that of which
Comus remains but a feeble literary ghost, recalling, as
G. Wilson Knight notes, Prospero and his rod. But the powers
of that rod are lost or renounced between Shakespeare and
Milton. Comus does not make the Lady marble, but only
momentarily motionless. Prospero is dead, and there will be
no more resurrected Hermiones; the brothers lose Comus' rod,
and the loss, as Knight says, "reflects a wider poetic loss," [40]
the renunciation of the full Shakespearean power in order to
serve a higher power. Hence Milton apprehends the Shakespearean imagination in terms that imply the rejection of it.
The qualified praise of "too much conceiving" is the first step
toward the chastity of choice.

Knowing that the fancy is bereaved of itself in too much
conceiving, Milton renounces the poetry of infinite suggestiveness to bring that fancy to a new life. It is a chastening
"either-or," and Milton moves from the multiplicity of the
eithers to the singleness of that *or*, the vertical *ascesis* to penseroso "Service high and Anthems clear." Like the lady in
Sonnet IX, Milton shuns the "broad way and the green" and
labors "up the Hill of Heav'nly Truth," the better, the chosen
path. Shakespeare stands behind him; *King Lear* ends with a
caveat to all future writers and readers: "we that are young /
Shall never see so much, nor live so long." As if responding to
that cry, Milton does not try to see so much, to encompass

such a panorama of emotive experience within the single artistic perspective. In a certain sense Eliot was right when he pointed out that "Milton may be said never to have seen anything," [41] for it is not in the perception of any thing of this world that ultimate reality lies. When the self will be bereaved anew, its loss will dissolve the "Penseroso" poet "into ecstasies / And bring all Heav'n before [his] eyes."

There are two kinds of monuments of unaging intellect. Dissolving bounds between image and nature, author and audience, Shakespeare built a "livelong Monument" that does "make us Marble." For Milton these dissolutions must be limited, and the identity of the soul itself preserved for its higher sphere. Looking back at the limit of dissolution, Milton chooses a penseroso muse who retains her integrity by not uncovering all:

> Come, but keep thy wonted state,
> With ev'n step, and musing gait,
> And looks commercing with the skies,
> Thy rapt soul sitting in thine eyes:
> There held in holy passion still,
> Forget thyself to Marble. . . .

Unlike Shakespearean power, which makes *us* marble, this perceptual metamorphosis of the muse maintains the wonted state between art and audience. The revelation of Miltonic power must be strictly limited, just as the "saintly visage" of the muse, itself too bright, must appear veiled. Finally, since poetry cannot capture but can only momentarily approximate prophetic strain, the muse's eyes retain their soulful looks only

> . . . till
> With a sad Leaden downward cast,
> Thou fix them on the earth as fast.

Sadness accompanies the knowledge that unearthly vision must be lost for the sake of continuity on the earth, just as panoramic vision of the earth must be narrowed for the sake of prophetic sight. Accepting blindness for insight, Milton chooses a better way.

2. A Moment's Space*

> She knows all their notes,
> That gentle Maid! and oft, a moment's space,
> What time the moon was lost behind a cloud,
> Hath heard a pause of silence; till the moon
> Emerging, hath awakened earth and sky
> With one sensation, and those wakeful birds
> Have all burst forth in choral minstrelsy,
> As if some sudden gale had swept at once
> A hundred airy harps!
>
> Coleridge, "The Nightingale"

A choice is necessarily belied when it is written about. The writing comes after the choice has been made, and writer and reader, knowing the outcome, must suspend disbelief to pretend that there was a choice. If something has already happened in a certain way, it cannot be said that another way is a possibility. Only an act of imagination, a conscious falsification of the facts as they are now known, a determination to examine the "not" as if it were of equal reality with what was, can represent choice. To capture alternatives is to make what is not *be*.

In this light the question whether "L'Allegro" and "Il Penseroso" represent equal courses or mark a progression from the first to the second is a measure of the achievement of these poems. The worldfullness of "L'Allegro" must be presented with an appeal comparable to that of "Il Penseroso" to re-create the experience of facing aesthetic and moral options. The problem is a miniature of that posed in *Paradise Lost*, where the poet must not only justify the way things have

* Part of this chapter appeared, in somewhat different form, in *The Yearbook of English Studies*, 1 (1971), 78–81, published by the Modern Humanities Research Association, and is used by permission.

gone, but present the case as if the way they have not were for the moment still an option. In a sense Adam's options are the poet's writ large, and the subject matter of Milton's epic is its own poetic process; to recreate the sense of alternatives, to recapture choice, is to recapture the past, and to recapture is to redeem it.

History is against the poet, who must put off his knowledge of what has been. Against the awareness of the weight of human events that separate us from the Fall, the poet works to recreate the feeling of the presentness of the past and the suspension of what has in fact already occurred. Bergson says, "When we have to do with a feeling, it has no precise result except its having been felt; and, to estimate this result adequately, it would be necessary to have gone through all the phases of the feeling itself and to have taken up the same duration." [1] Any literary representation of states of feeling is a falsification of those states; to know completely the feeling of alternatives, the conditions of an action, is to be actually performing it. The poet necessarily summarizes and fictionalizes, but attempts to take the reader through the experience of alternatives.

He works against both the feeling that things must happen a certain way and the knowledge that they have already occurred: "The determinist . . . takes refuge in the past or the future. Sometimes he transfers himself in thought to some earlier period and asserts the necessary determination, from this very moment, of the act to come; sometimes, assuming in advance that the act is already performed, he claims that it could not have taken place in any other way." [2] In *Paradise Lost* the first "sometimes" can look like God's foreknowledge, the second like the reader's knowledge of history. To a lesser

extent the problems are the same in the early poems we have
looked at. In the sonnets plan is posed against process; the
sense of a speaker working out doubts, murmurs, and reservations occurs within the confines of predetermined form. In
Comus our knowledge of mask conventions, the circumstances
of this particular one, the overriding presence of Thyrsis, and
the constant limitations of language of which the manuscript
changes are an index all work to eliminate the threat and the
possibility of alternatives occurring in any but the expected
manner. To all the arguments about the progression from
"L'Allegro" to "Il Penseroso" one must add the physical fact
that one poem "follows" the other. Though one editor has
even tried to actualize their nature as alternatives by printing
them on facing pages, the fact remains that one still reads
successively, in time, one choice after another. *Paradise
Regained* is the consummate expression of such temporality,
for alternatives are presented as temptation and answer. Even
interpreted as most ambiguously divine, Jesus, we know, is not
to be tempted—which leaves only Satan to divest himself of
knowledge for the sake of the illusion of freedom.

How is the nature of alternatives to be expressed when
language itself imposes temporal pattern? " 'L'Allegro' or 'Il
Penseroso' " is not the same as " 'Il Penseroso' or 'L'Allegro.' "
As emblems of ethical attitudes, literary history, and Milton's
own development, the terms separated by "or" represent progression as well as alternative. The problem is one Milton will
carry into every simile and periodic sentence of his epic.
Bergson says, "We set our states of consciousness side by side
in such a way as to perceive their simultaneity, no longer in
one another, but alongside one another; in a word, we project
time into space, we express duration in terms of extensity, and

succession thus takes the form of a continuous line or chain." [3] If this is true of our representation of states of consciousness generally, it is especially applicable to *Paradise Lost*, in which time is constantly being turned into space, from the fall of the angels, "Nine times the Space that measures Day and Night" (I.50), to Michael's projection of history on a plain. The difficulty is that spatial representation of time, "linear" representation, obscures the sense of presentness on which alternatives, if they are not to be merely successive states, depend. Seeing things in succession, projected on a "time-line," "does not show the deed in the doing but the deed already done." It "does not signify the time which is passing but the time which is past," and which once past, strikes us as "determined." [4] Northrop Frye says, "The straight line, where there is no real present and everything is annihilated in the past as we are drawn into an unknown future, is the fallen conception of time." [5] To represent choice, the poet must give the illusion of time not fallen but falling, turning from unfallen to fallen state. He must recapture the sense of *durée*, of the presentness of the moment of choice.

The Moment of Arrest

"Lycidas" is especially suited to a study of the way Milton apprehends the arrest of time, because it is about such arrest: Lycidas is "dead ere his prime." It is a poem about the cutting off of human life, the cutting off of human time. But from the very beginning it is not only Edward King whose time is cut short; in what is itself a poetic identification cut short Milton shares the arrest. At least one critic is surprised: "To pass from the fate of one's friend to one's own fate is normal in pastoral elegy—we think of Shelley, Tennyson, and Arnold. But in *Lycidas* the move is made with what seems inexcusably indecent haste. By the twentieth line Milton is engrossed in himself." [6] The shock of recognition of the poet's self-absorption is one way the reader shares the poem's sense of abortive arrest. Even before the startling turn to the speaker's own death, the opening of the poem sees subject, poet, reader, and scene under the blight of premature death. The berries are plucked while yet harsh and crude, the leaves shattered before the cycle of the seasons would make them die a natural death. There is an extraordinary identification of the writing of the poem with the arrest of life. One can associate poets with laurels as one associates pastoral, convention, and art generally with artifice, that which is not "natural," but Milton insists further that the writing of this poem, the attaining of this crown, is a killing, a self-conscious and "untimely" termination of growth and decay in time.

"Lycidas" thus begins with an aesthetic theory: art fixates ideas and emotions previously in flux; every poem is a death. Natural death, like subjection to the forces of the "mellowing year," the "season due," seems kind in comparison to the suddenness and violence with which the prime is anticipated in art. The poem itself is not permitted to reach a prime for these larger significances to emerge, but begins with them, conceived as it were in original sin—the central fact of premature death encompassing King, Milton, reader, and poem. Rosemond Tuve arrests further circumlocution: "*unripeness*—the flaw is in our entire condition." [7]

The little we know of the composition of "Lycidas" from the corrections in the Trinity manuscript confirms our conception of the way the poetic process is intertwined with the subject of premature arrest. We may take as a model the lines Milton first wrote: "I come to pluck your berries harsh and crude / before the mellowing year." The sentence as such dies

a natural death at the end of its brief span, but Milton, instead
of letting it rest, forces his "fingers rude" between the berries
and the natural year and marginally adds: "and with forc't
fingers rude / Shatter your leaves before the mellowing year."
He is here, as everywhere in the poem, shattering the placid
pastoral surface to insert himself, disturbing the simplicity of
a succession of thoughts and images all of a kind in order to
surprise us with something more profound, a new dimension
from which to view in perspective the path we thought we
were following.

The poet's relationship to the poem he is writing undergoes
continual change. "Deliberation," Bergson says, "really consists in a dynamic progress in which the self and its motives,
like real living beings, are in a constant state of becoming." [8]
The literalist point that a poem is not a "living self" is less
significant than the distinction in genre, for deliberation is not
exactly what "Lycidas" is made of, nor do we ever meet anything like a living poetic whole that seems to "grow," to move
forward out of its internal momentum. There are, rather,
shattered fragments that have to be recharged from without
after each grinds its way to a halt. "It should be read," as
Northrop Frye says about *Paradise Lost*, "as a discontinuous
series of crises." [9] The continuum in which thoughts modify
themselves is the core of the sensation of living in time: "Pure
duration is the form which the succession of our conscious
states assumes when our ego lets itself *live*, when it refrains
from separating its present state from its former states." [10]
Reading "Lycidas," however, involves a repeated separation
from the state of consciousness evoked by previous lines. The
poem begins by addressing the laurels and myrtle, and grows
increasingly involuted, only to break out in line 15 with an
address to the Muses. Nor is it only a matter of the changes in

address and the fresh impetus with successive verse paragraphs; the poem is constantly turning back upon itself in self-consciousness epitomized by the hypothetical poet:

> So may some gentle Muse
> With lucky words favor my destin'd Urn,
> And as he passes turn,
> And bid fair peace be to my sable shroud.

The going-out of self, the universalization of the problem of death leads back to a confrontation with his own death.

In contrast to the deliberation that Bergson holds to be the essential awareness of living in time, self-consciousness involves a break with *durée*, a gap through which the self becomes separated and comes to an awareness of its mirrored image. The "uncouth swain" pauses over Lycidas; but Lycidas' condition is one to which all mankind is subject, so the "uncouth swain" takes the place of Lycidas, while the hypothesized "gentle Muse" takes the place of the "uncouth swain." In a recognition of involvement, the awareness that swain and Lycidas are both subject to death leads to hypothesizing a "gentle Muse," generating an image of the experience of recognition. In contrast to "deliberation," to "cognition," *re*cognition involves a return, facing of an alternate self. The moment of turning, when motion in one direction is arrested and motion in the opposite direction is about to begin, is the still point at which the present is captured and alternatives are real.

It is important that the moment of recognition is the awareness of one's own death, for the connection underlies the story of the tree of knowledge and of death and sin which stem from it. Eating the fruit cuts off the moment when choice was real, and cuts man out of the ongoing present that was paradise, the eternal life he was to enjoy there. In this sense the knowledge of one's own end is the recognition of original sin; it is recaptured when the poet, proceeding along the line that his task is to weep for Lycidas, stops short, stops the sense of linear time, in the recognition of his own death. The Hebrew word for repentance is *tishuvah* ("answer" or "return"), and it is such a return which the gentle Muse accomplishes, such an answer which the poet returns to the question of why Lycidas died. Having gone along weeping for the shepherd, he is taken aback by sin, coming to self-awareness in the recognition that that is not the way. The sense of the present moment comes into being when one realizes that the path one is on is not right, and one must go back in order to go forward, must apprehend past as present in order to proceed to future. Kierkegaard says, "One discovers that there is something which must be done over again, something which must be revoked." [11] The violation of time is the achievement of self-awareness. It is T. S. Eliot's still point, and as he says in *Burnt Norton*, "to be conscious is not to be in time."

Part of the achievement of Milton's lines is the way the poet makes the reader participate in the recognition of the uncouth swain. Reading "So may some gentle Muse," one is prepared for an analogy in which the hypothetical term is interesting for a comparison but in some sense less real. The reader, too, is taken aback, for the lines drive home the awareness of death, penetrating out of what now seems to have been pastoral fiction into immutable truth. This is the strange beauty of a poem in which the repeated attempts at constructing a lovely fiction "fall, gall themselves, and gash gold-vermilion" (like Hopkins' windhover) into more splendid truth. What happens to "some gentle Muse" happens to the similes for death a few lines later:

As killing as the Canker to the Rose,
Or Taint-worm to the weanling Herds that graze,
Or Frost to Flowers, that their gay wardrobe wear,
When first the White-thorn blows;
Such, *Lycidas*, thy loss to Shepherd's ear.

Not until the last line is the reader struck by the fact that these statements of lethal agency have not exactly been pictures of landscape mourning in pathetic fallacy nor lesser analogies "to compare great things with small." The word "such" explains the word "as"; in this poem about death all facts of death are equally "such," equally so. They are the same thing, and far from being pretty conceits or belittling analogies, assert the overwhelming universality of that of which Lycidas' death is emblem and instance. With this one must go back and reinterpret "Who would not sing for *Lycidas?* he knew / Himself to sing, and build the lofty rhyme." All sing for Lycidas, for that is the song of everyone's own death. Lycidas himself knew how to sing, and he knew how to sing of himself, as Milton is doing in this poem and as every poet does when the fiction of song turns to the awareness of "knew / Himself."

If one objects that such moments of self-consciousness seem less well defined than they might be, it is important to realize how essential to their experience that tenuousness is. If the moment is "extended," it takes dimension in time, with parts of varying degrees of pastness, and is no longer an apprehension of the present. The still point, given duration, becomes not a moment of awareness but part of the poetic line. Self-consciousness if protected becomes a confrontation with the void, or, since there are no words directly describing the activity of the mind, the attempt to elaborate it loses it and becomes talk about something else. One could compare, as does Geoffrey Hartman, the repeated moments of "Lycidas" with the attempt in romantic poetry to take a longer look, a firmer grasp, only to note the moment retreating to the point where it began, back into landscape or some person or event external to the self.[12] Milton sometimes extends the moment if his purposes are other than the startling confrontations of "Lycidas." In the Nativity Ode, for example, time is politely halted for an extended look at the moment of Incarnation, with the poet coming like one of the magi to take his turn at admiring the Christ child. The arrest of time, far from being a personal confrontation, is a public pronouncement: "This is the Month, and this the happy morn" identifies the original with every subsequent Christmas. One could say of stanza IV that the cry "O run, prevent them with thy humble ode" addresses the muse; but it is, of course, a self-address, and startling in the way it leaps, in poetic parallel to the act of faith it represents, to deny all the intervening years between Christ and Milton. The lines which follow draw that self-confrontation into the meeting with Christ, self-awareness into religious awareness:

> O run, prevent them with thy humble ode
> And lay it lowly at his blessed feet;
> Have thou the honor first, thy Lord to greet,
> And join thy voice unto the Angel Choir,
> From out his secret Altar touched with hallow'd fire.

Milton is not looking at Milton but at God, and the voice, instead of being startled at hearing its own echo, joins the shepherds and the angel choir. The moment of isolation has become sixteen centuries of Christian community.

Such transformations are an integral part of the way Milton

presents the Christian conception of history, where the moment can be protracted because all time is simultaneously present to the mind of God. Incarnation, the intersection of the eternal and the temporal, is a moment that really "extends" over the subsequent course of Christian history, offering for all time an alternative that redeems time because it is constantly there. The turn Incarnation gives to human events, unlike that of the hypothetical muse of "Lycidas," is not an instantaneous apprehension but a conversion in time. Thus, for example, in the poem "On Time" the meditation on eternity picks up and accompanies to its consummation the poetry which seemed to have ground to a halt in the first half of the poem. Elsewhere Milton uses verbal turns—not still points but dynamic sweeps of sentence and historical structure—to apprehend the pattern of eternity working itself out in time. Bergson writes, "If curves are more graceful than broken lines, the reason is that, while a curved line changes its direction at every moment, every new direction is indicated in the preceding one." [13] When the direction of history is in God's hands, each new direction is foretold, and religious grace is like physical movement in time. In *Paradise Lost* this extended or "curved" turn has much to do with sentence structure, especially with repetition. It is worth exploring the way the rhetorical device of repetition is used, for it can indicate the relationship of the poetics of choice to the pattern of history.

Excursus: Repetition

If one thinks of a sentence line spatially, repetition is a way of defining the encompassed ground. A closely knit repetition seems to deny space and impel a collapse of terms, a fall.

When the bower in Eden is described as "with flow'rets deck't and fragrant smells; but *Eve* / Undeckt" (*PL*, V.379–

380), we may scurry for the clothing of righteousness; but we hear lurking in the pun the undoing to come. Bentley objected to the passage: "And does not *With flourets deck'd, but* Eve *undeck'd*, so closely cohere, as not to be parted?" [14] The "coherence" of the phrase leaves no room for objection; Eve is undecked "save with herself," and the mind that would separate nakedness from being one's own best ornament is the mind that would intrude into paradise, like Satan. Bentley asks, "Why come *fragrant Smells* between? *Eve* did not use Ointments and Perfumes, as *Homer's* Goddesses did." Here Bentley's spatial term, fragment smells coming "between," is appropriate to the violation of space that one can discuss more generally as a function of ambiguity. [15] We recognize in the rich fragrance of the simile that is there introduced, the parallels of judgment, mistake, war, death, and history that can be drawn with the Judgment of Paris; we know the consequences of appetite "rais'd by the smell / So savory of that Fruit" (IX.740–741) that will ultimately come between Eve and bower, clothed mankind and naked paradise.

If one conceives of intrusion or disruption between repeated words as satanic, then undisturbed repetition can be a way of expressing accord with the heavenly scheme. Raphael exclaims:

> O *Adam*, one Almighty is, from whom
> All things proceed, and up to him return,
> If not deprav'd from good.   [V.469–471]

Though depraved from good, Satan acknowledges that God "deserv'd no such return / From me" (IV.42–43). Perfect return, the *regressus* of the soul to its source, is distinguished from the divergent path of the soul which swerves and continues to fall. The first is reserved for man; the second is the eternal bane of the fallen angels. (They want nothing better than one stroke to determine, "and not need repeat" [VI.318], perhaps even more than they want the determination in their favor.) In the largest sense verbal repetition is related to the godly return; Michael addresses Adam so:

> But longer in this Paradise to dwell
> Permits not; to remove thee I am come,
> And send thee from the Garden forth to till
> The ground whence thou wast tak'n, fitter Soil.
>
> [XI.259–262]

We have already heard God's law forbid "longer in that Paradise to dwell (XI.48), as we have heard Michael bidden to "send him from the Garden forth to Till / The Ground whence he was taken, fitter soil" (XI.97–98). The return of these phrases from Michael's lips comes as an expression of perfect obedience, the enactment in time of what, in arrested time, can be seen as pattern.

Within a given unit of verse, repetition is a way of arresting verbal time and capturing in the verse itself the actuality of choice. The reader comes across a word or phrase, goes on, confronts the same expression, and realizes that he must have turned in the interim if he is back on the same ground. Yet since he is still there, he is still innocent, having, as it were seen but not actually followed an alternate course. Repetition can thus capture the conditions of choice, the moment when one senses fallenness but has not actually fallen. God tells Raphael to talk with Adam:

> such discourse bring on,
> As may advise him of his happy state,
> Happiness in his power left free to will,
> Left to his own free Will, his Will though free,
> Yet mutable.   [V.233–237]

While thus stating the conditions of freedom, the recrossed verbal ground focuses on what may be lost between the word and its repetition. The relation between repetition and fall here is like the relation of repetition to creation I discuss below, and is one way verbal pattern connects Milton to the romantics' concept of creation as fall; I point this out to emphasize the connection of creativity to morality, a linkage Wordsworth develops from the stern voice that speaks such admonition.

Raphael carries out the same dramatic choice as God's words imply when Raphael presents Adam with the return of Abdiel as a model of temptation conquered, choice successfully made. Abdiel is congratulated by God, who tells him:

> the easier conquest now
> Remains thee, aided by this host of friends,
> Back on thy foes more glorious to return
> Than scorn'd thou didst depart, and to subdue
> By force, who reason for thir Law refuse,
> Right reason for thir Law.   [VI.37–42]

The easier conquest, the second return, contrasts with the mischoice captured verbally in the repetition of the last two lines. It is always remarkable how Milton gets spatial and metaphysical meanings to be one for God. Here the angels of Satan's party, who as yet have not physically fallen out of heaven, are presented, not as already fallen but in the very act, right now refusing the rule of right reason, as if Adam and reader have time arrested for them and face choice while they watch the angels fall.

If repetition is associated with choice, we may expect that the moment of turn will not always be apprehended innocently.

There are many minor instances in *Paradise Lost* like the one when Eve addresses Adam after the night of her troubled dream:

> I this Night,
> Such night till this I never pass'd, have dream'd,
> If dream'd, not as I oft am wont, of thee,
> Works of day past, or morrow's next design,
> But of offense and trouble, which my mind
> Knew never till this irksome night.   [V.30–35]

The two *dream'd*s and the three *night*s contrast with the innocent passing of time represented by the choice there used to be of "Works of day past, or morrow's next design." Eve is accustomed to a notion of time in which the present moment, the "or" of choice, does not arrest the easy passage from past to future, a passage in which one moves indifferently without weighing on the moment. Instead she has been confronted with an arrest that prefigures, as she will come to learn, her arrested attention by the tree at the noon hour.

The association of repetition with arrested presentness comes to the surface when Milton speaks *in propria persona* about his own time:

> Standing on Earth, not rapt above the Pole,
> More safe I sing with mortal voice, unchang'd
> To hoarse or mute, though fall'n on evil days,
> On evil days though fall'n, and evil tongues.   [VII.23–26]

"Evil days" refers not only to the Stuart Restoration but to all time between fall and redemption in which Milton and man in general are caught. The whole invocation is an arrest of narrative time in which the poet, who has been "up led by thee," pauses to request "like safety" in the return to earthly time and space, thus distinguishing his journey, not only from that of Bellerophon, whom he mentions here, but from a classic model of the artist's journey in Book I:

> from Morn
> To Noon he fell, from Noon to dewy Eve,
> A Summer's day. [I.742-744]

Repetition seems to pause over the action as if to make room for the distinction between fall as moral choice and as physical consequence. We hear a parody of the relationship of Creator to creation, on the model of word and enactment in the Genesis account.[16]

Both the summer's day and the noon hour recur as emblems of suspect stasis, suggesting that repetition focuses on the moment of danger of fall. Valéry talks about language as just such difficult "passage":

Each and every word that enables us to leap so rapidly across the chasm of thought, and to follow the promptings of an idea that constructs its own expression, appears to me like one of those light planks which one throws across a ditch or a mountain crevasse and which will bear a man crossing it rapidly. But he must pass without weighing on it, without stopping—above all, he must not take it into his head to dance on the slender plank to test its resistance! . . . Otherwise the fragile bridge tips or breaks immediately, and all is hurled into the depths. Consult your own experience; and you will find that we understand each other, and ourselves, only thanks to our *rapid passage over words*.[17]

Comus' and Satan's desire is to dance on the slender plank and arrest continuity; but clearly the attempt is not necessarily fallen, for weighing on words is one of the marks of God's own speech. He declares, for example, that man "upheld by me" will stand on even ground, will walk a re-enforced bridge "by me upheld" (III.178–180); the repeated words physically seem to support, to stand under man going over the ground of choice. Though Adam and Eve fall at the initial crossing, God will

> clear thir senses dark,
> What may suffice, and soft'n stony hearts
> To pray, repent, and bring obedience due.
> To Prayer, repentance and obedience due,
> Though but endeavor'd with sincere intent,
> Mine ear shall not be slow.   [III.188–193]

It may be "vain attempt" to try to distinguish by structural rules between the rhetorical device used by God and the precarious balance that points to the Fall, or between the renewed, recrossed ground opened to man "upheld by me . . . by me upheld" and the difficult ground crossed by Satan, who "with difficulty and labor hard / Mov'd on, with difficulty and labor hee" (II.1021–22). The undercut satanic ground looks like the underscored divine one, for both emphasize the crossing and the implied choice. Yet occasionally the word pattern itself can point to the difference in moral burden.

Satanic repetition is often directionless, pointing to the sense of being lost in treading in its own footsteps. Thus Satan talks to Eve:

> Of Death denounc't, whatever thing Death be,
> Deterr'd not from achieving what might lead
> To happier life, knowledge of Good and Evil;
> Of good, how just? of evil, if what is evil
> Be real, why not known, since easier shunn'd?
> God therefore cannot hurt ye, and be just;
> Not just, not God; not fear'd then, nor obey'd:
> Your fear itself of Death removes the fear.   [IX.695–702]

This is language "in wandering mazes lost," and repetition marks, not a single turning point, but a repeated recoiling back upon itself. Milton imitates it when describing Satan as serpent:

> He sought them both, but wish'd his hap might find
> *Eve* separate, he wish'd, but not with hope
> Of what so seldom chanc'd, when to his wish,
> Beyond his hope, *Eve* separate he spies,
> Veil'd in a Cloud of Fragrance, where she stood,
> Half spi'd.　[IX.421–426]

The words "wish'd," "hap," "hope," "spies," "spi'd" form a maze that suggests lack of a moral as well as of a temporal direction. In contrast, the repetitions in God's speech about prayer and repentance instance an ordered universe.[18] The relationship of the line "To pray, repent, and bring obedience due" to the line "To Prayer, repentance and obedience due" is the harmonious relationship of man to God. The first presents man offering three things; the second, God responding to them.

Still more closely tied to God's order of time are the repetition and turn in the lines "He with his whole posterity must die, / Die hee or Justice must" (III.209–210). Technically the alternative offered by Christ comes next, introduced by the word "unless." But it is prepared for in the repetition, which readjusts the terms of history. The return of the word "die" creates a still point where history seems both to end and to continue along the alternate route, catching the turn of events in the turn of the line. The "or" can imply distinction between the rule of law by which "hee"—man—must die, and the rule of mercy, by which justice must die. Together these verse effects anticipate the redemptive possibility offered in the "unless," thus creating an interposed space in which we apprehend alternatives as simultaneously present. If the effects seem too small, if too much seems to depend on what happens between the lines, we may say that the dimensions involved reflect the relationship of the moment of divine choice to the expanse of human history. But the best exposition of the point is Milton's own in another poem.

"Upon the Circumcision" points to the way the moment of godly presence is integrated into historical futurity. The poem approaches a still point, in verbal miniature of Incarnation, at the end of the first part of its inverted two-sonnet structure. The second half begins, "O more exceeding love or law more just? / Just law indeed, but more exceeding love!" The word "but" comes like the word "unless" in the previous example to break insignificant alternates into new possibility. The first line poses two alternatives in perfect stasis; the second restates them in a way that moves along, that integrates the alternatives into history, making the Incarnation the point on which history hinges, with Mosaic law before and "exceeding love" after.[19] Taken together, the two lines represent the coming of Christ. The first presents love as an alternative to law, as something which would arrest the workings of justice; the second apprehends justice as the working out of love in time, and proclaims with Jesus, "Think not that I am come to destroy the law, or the prophets: I am not come to destroy but to fulfil" (Matt. 5 : 17). It is an integration back into time like the delicate one of the Nativity Ode, where "wisest fate says no"—not yet. Mercy must come through time, not violating but fulfilling that which has been foretold.

The rest of "Upon the Circumcision" is about the way love and justice, time and the moment, are mutually inclusive. On the side of justice and the operation of love in time the poem says, we "were lost in death" (past); now, at the circumcision, Christ "seals obedience first with wounding smart" (present); at the Crucifixion, huge pangs "will pierce more near his heart" (future). Such is God's order in time. But on the other hand, the central lines are simultaneously an extraordinary assertion of the way all events in Christian history are taken out of time:

> And that great Cov'nant which we still transgress
> Entirely satisfi'd,
> And the full wrath beside
> Of vengeful Justice bore for our excess.

That "rigid satisfaction," as it is defined in *Paradise Lost,* is "death for death" (III.213), the fulfilling of justice in time that is love, and does not occur until the Crucifixion. The remarkable phrase "which we still transgress" violates the poem's time to make all subsequent history as present to Christ as Christ is to us "still."

What "Upon the Circumcision" illustrates in so dense a manner is the way the moment of poetic arrest, integrated into succeeding lines, can represent the moment of temporal arrest integrated into succeeding time. In a lesser poet so theologically and paradoxically convoluted an argument would tend to obscure the simple tone. But a phrase like "which we still transgress" manages to relate poet and reader more directly to the time and topic than one would have imagined possible without violating the formal terms in which the poem is conceived. The choiceness of the verse is the way it points to something that is not there, something that has been given up or made past in the process of choice. There is something refreshing in the phrase "which we still transgress," as there is in the opening words of "Lycidas," "Yet once more." The one phrase could be didactic, the other tired, but both succeed in

suggesting the freshness of the new periods of time they discover. For a moment the sense of loss over time that has lapsed
is transformed into awe at a heavenly vision which we apprehend in the closing.

The relationship of such a depiction of time to the concept
of choice is most substantially expressed in the longest of the
repetitions in Milton's poetry. At the close of *Paradise Lost*,
Book X, Adam turns to Eve and says:

> What better can we do, than to the place
> Repairing where he judg'd us, prostrate fall
> Before him reverent, and there confess
> Humbly our faults, and pardon beg, with tears
> Watering the ground, and with our sighs the Air
> Frequenting, sent from hearts contrite, in sign
> Of sorrow unfeign'd, and humiliation meek.

The lines depict Adam in the "Prayer, repentance and obedience due" which God's own repetition foretold. So Milton
enacts that reconciliation, repairing the breach between the
narrator's and God's knowledge and the characters' involvement in the events:

> So spake our Father penitent, nor *Eve*
> Felt less remorse: they forthwith to the place
> Repairing where he judg'd them prostrate fell
> Before him reverent, and both confess'd
> Humbly thir faults, and pardon begg'd, with tears
> Watering the ground, and with thir sighs the Air
> Frequenting, sent from hearts contrite, in sign
> Of sorrow unfeign'd, and humiliation meek.

The phrases that Adam and the poet share bring the two together, and the loss that is the Fall is repaid with the feeling
that time itself has been lost or transcended.

Verbal repetition thus illustrates the relationship of the

poetic depiction of choice to the arrest of the present and the relationship of choice to the sense of absence or loss as one passes between alternatives. If the moment of choice, the moment of loss, cannot be apprehended without belying its momentariness, repetition points to going over the duration before and after the moment as fiction's means of talking about the moment. To an extraordinary extent, repetition itself moves us with the consolation of ongoing time. When the line "For Lycidas is dead, dead ere his prime" seems to stop short and center on the fact of death, the next line, "Young Lycidas, and hath not left his peer," [20] consoles with its continuity: "Young Lycidas" is still there. The return of "young Lycidas" does not simply contrast with a full stop on "dead," for the earlier line itself anticipates and establishes the rhythm of ongoing time by stopping with "dead" and picking up, after the caesura, with the same word. Going over the fact of loss is poetry's way of redeeming it. Though never as facile as such explanations, the poem can move us most with the direct acknowledgment of the difference between poetic continuity and experiential discontinuity: "But O the heavy change, now thou art gone, / Now thou art gone, and never must return." The return of the verse contrasts with and acknowledges the irrevocable disparity from human experience in time, from the hard fact that there is no return. In this sense the structure of the statement of loss makes it express consolation in the same way as does a statement of consolation. Compare the line "Weep no more, woeful Shepherds weep no more." The first "weep no more" stops and questions the rightness of iambic pentameter motion; the second, reconciled with it reconciles stasis with motion, and death with the timeless pattern that ends in resurrection. It is the supreme repetition.

The Moment of Arrest—Continued

The question "why must man go unready?" Rosemond Tuve points out, "dwells in the cadences and inhabits the frail and lovely figures." [21] "Lycidas" is a poem which prevents its own murmur, posing the question in a way that arrests and answers it. "Sorrow begins by being nothing more than a facing towards the past, an impoverishment of our sensations and ideas, as if each of them were now contained entirely in the little which it gives out, as if the future were in some way stopped up." [22] Though "Lycidas" begins with the condition of sorrow, the grief Johnson expected, it reconciles its fictionality with the turn to futurity. Such reconciliation is heavenly concord, the harmony of

> sweet Societies
> That sing, and singing in their glory move,
> And wipe the tears for ever from his eyes.

The pause between "sing" and "singing" catches time in the moment of arrest. Then, in the next line, sorrow is arrested, and the tears are permanently wiped away, at the same time that the same words suggest everlasting weeping and everlasting motion of comfort. The exquisite reconciliation is the same as that in the caesura and word "move" of the line describing singing. Both lines make momentary arrest and greater movement one. The leisure for fiction, the "meed of some melodious tear," is itself arrested and redeemed (weep no more!) into the pattern that reconciles arrest and ongoingness: "wipe the tears for ever from his eyes." Finally, the two senses of "for ever" unite the two perspectives of comfort: ultimate pastoral fiction, a supernature weeping forever in emotional sympathy with mankind, and the Christian supernature, wiping away the fact of death, putting an end to weeping for all time.

Before approaching the consummate reconciliation of stasis and motion achieved at the end of "Lycidas," the poem comes closer to expressing the present moment than the distance of repeated ground or weighing on an ambiguous word. The bounds fade between time going on and time being gone, giving a perspective that is an extraordinary imitation of actual time:

> Together both, ere the high Lawns appear'd
> Under the opening eyelids of the morn,
> We drove afield, and both together heard
> What time the Gray-fly winds her sultry horn,
> Batt'ning our flocks with the fresh dews of night,
> Oft till the Star that rose, at Ev'ning, bright
> Toward Heav'n's descent had slop'd his westering wheel.

These seven lines apprehend time with a gentle inexorableness that leaves the reader wondering how the poet managed to be so visually exact, to catch and make "present" each picture of the past, and simultaneously to give the sensation of time going by. The subject is time past, but the experience is of time passing. In the second line the eyelids of the morn are "opening," and the extended duration of the present participle belies the fact that the slow sunrise is preceded by darkness in the line before and followed by the activity which we are surprised to find completed: "We drove afield." The caesura strikes like a faint echo of Time's scythe, St. Peter's engine, and the death of Lycidas—which now, in retrospect, seems less like the particular reality of the poem than a metaphor for the passing of time: "For Lycidas is dead, dead ere his prime." That line and all of time have "passed away" more swiftly than could be apprehended; the prime of day, like Lycidas' prime, has been lost. Still more remarkable is the slow-sounding description of noon, the time when the sun seems to stand still, when the moment, like the great moments in *Paradise Lost*, is fixed: "What time the Gray-fly winds her sultry horn." But the very next line introduces evening, "Batt'ning our flock with the fresh dews of night," not only racing the clock through the second half of the day, but assuming in the slow rhythms and extended duration of the participial action, "batt'ning," that those times have not only come but have been going on while we were yet caught at midday, listening to the line before. This is still more startling if we accept the suggestion that "batt'ning" means, not "feeding," but "enclosing." Edgar Daniels notes that the atmosphere of slow time "seems to suggest a prolonged action (like feeding) rather than a brief one (like enclosing)," [23] which makes coming to an awareness of right meaning (enclosing) coming to an awareness of time. The specificity of each image captures and "arrests" the moment, while the swiftness of the whole passage depicts the sensation of time passing turning into time past. Its pastoralism is that of paradise, and the way we know it is that we feel it slipping through our fingers. The only paradise, as Proust recognized, is paradise lost, and we have apprehended that existence outside time when we have experienced it passing away.

The sensation of passing time determines the form of "Lycidas" and makes the poet pass on to something else, a slightly different view, after a few lines have perfectly embodied the single perspective. The duration of "Lycidas," in Bergson's terms, is a series of states of consciousness, and Milton achieves both the sensation of the presentness of each moment and the

moving in time from one "still" to the next. The lines that
follow the swift tour of the hours pause, and pause just when
we have been convinced that any arrest of time is impossible:

> Meanwhile the Rural ditties were not mute,
> Temper'd to th'Oaten Flute;
> Rough *Satyrs* danc'd, and *Fauns* with clov'n heel
> From the glad sound would not be absent long,
> And old *Damaetas* lov'd to hear our song.

"Meanwhile," like the word "while" in "Il Penseroso," line 59,
introduces the arrest of time, for knowing what happens
"meanwhile" identifies the moment and secures it from flowing away down the swift Hebrus to other songs and other
times. It is one of those remarkable words in this poem that
strike us as if we never fully understood what they meant
before.

Perhaps we did not; for "Lycidas" builds its sense of redemption by shattering the normal, seasonal processes of
growth of consciousness according to which we have been
operating. We confront, through continual surprises, our own
inability to estimate duration and significance of time, and
hence our inability to question the death of Lycidas. In contrast to our own impotency, the leaps and turns with which
our consciousness is engaged, the poem asserts the quiet power
of poetry to master time, to endure in that eternal "meanwhile"
after the lines that measured duration have ground the "west-
ering wheel" to a halt. There is all the time in the world when
motion is measured, not by the clock, but in the rhythms of
dance and song. The inexorable pace of time is subdued, and
abortive or jerking movements are "temper'd to th'Oaten
Flute." "*Tempus* in music meant more than mere passing of
events," writes Gretchen Finney; "it indicated measured time

that was given order and proportion." [24] The rural ditties and dance of the Satyrs are free from the threat of premature shattering, of sudden halts at still points that mark unexpected changes of direction. What we find in dance and song that we do not find in the fate of men is, in Bergson's terms, that

every new direction is indicated in the preceding one. Thus the perception of ease in motion passes over into the pleasure of mastering the flow of time and of holding the future in the present. A third element comes in when the graceful movements submit to a rhythm and are accompanied by music. For the rhythm and measure, by allowing us to foresee to a still greater extent the movements of the dancer, make us believe that we now control them. As we guess almost the exact attitude which the dancer is going to take, he seems to obey us when he really takes it: the regularity of the rhythm establishes a kind of communication between him and us, and the periodic returns of the measure are like so many invisible threads by means of which we set in motion this imaginary puppet.[25]

"The periodic returns of the measure" may be the most summary way of explaining how Milton justifies God's ways by turning the story of the Fall into poetry, making the reader feel he is controlling Adam with "invisible threads" and is therefore responsible for his actions. At the same time, musically measured motion explains the way illusion of control makes the dying into the dance, the passing of time, beyond all question. Sartre says, "Strains of music alone can proudly carry their own death within themselves like an internal necessity." Elsewhere Sartre refers to Bergson's concept of duration specifically as "melodic organization." [26]

Bergson's terms help illustrate how intimately the pastoral diversions are connected with the Christian salvation which follows later in the poem. The pastoral and the theological are

two varieties of grace, "of mastering the flow of time and of
holding the future in the present." What happens in the
remembered "rural ditties" is what happens in "Lycidas"
itself, and the invocation of pastoral song becomes one way of
talking about the poem's own triumph over time. That analogy is itself part of the working of grace, for in the graceful,
"we imagine ourselves able to detect, besides the lightness
which is a sign of mobility, some suggestion of a possible
movement towards ourselves, of a virtual and even nascent
sympathy. It is this mobile sympathy, always ready to offer
itself, which is just the essence of higher grace." [27] The "higher
grace" of "Lycidas," at one with the Christian grace it apprehends in the end, is the moving out of each passage from its
particular "fond dream" to talk about the poem itself, the poet,
and us. The apparent subject matter is constantly dissolving
in "sympathy" that reflects back an image of our own problems, a reflection we hardly expected when we were taken out
of an earlier self-confrontation into the pasture of another
passage. What has already begun to happen with the identity
of Lycidas and the "gentle Muse" happens still again in the
line that closes the flight into high lawns. Mrs. Finney notes
"a slowing down of tempo in the last line, 'And old *Damaetas*
lov'd to hear our song.' " [28] What reference there may be to a
figure outside the poem does not diminish our surprise on
encountering someone outside the imagined singing circle into
which we have been led. It is not that Damaetas is to the
singing shepherd as some Cambridge tutor is to Milton, but
that Damaetas is to shepherd as we are to Milton. We were
led into the poetic paradise beyond the domain of time only
to be reminded that we are but auditors whose participation in
timelessness is limited by the length of the song.

The realization that the shepherd's song is past is once more a confrontation of the shattering of experience in time—an unseasonal shattering, since we experience the pastness of the song prematurely, long before the end of "Lycidas." The song is to silence as life is to death, and in analogy to the naïve but undismissable question at the death of the individual—How is it life goes on if he is dead?—one may ask, "How is it the poem goes on if that song has been sung?" If "the rest is silence," one can look at the lines which follow line 36 as analogous to the gathering up of unraveled threads at the close of a Shakespearean tragedy. But the whole poem is a collection of such tangled remains, for death is the fact with which it begins. Though it is difficult to speak of the analogy of poem to life in terms that do not sound simple-minded, nevertheless the poem is built from just this difficulty. To bring the analogy to the surface is to kill it; the poem cannot sustain such self-awareness. On the other hand, parallel to premature arrest in experience is the way the analogy is brought to the surface at still points before the end of the poem. Each still point must remain a point, for suspended stillness is no elegy at all. The ditties of no tone may be the supreme poetic fallacy and the truest analogue to "no life," but the poet's task is not to recapitulate the truth of that demise but to create the fictive comparisons in the interrelations of which new life will be found. The analogy must be, not of a single poem to a single life, but of poetic to life process, so that the repeated breaks and confrontations of "Lycidas" subsumed into the poem will be like individual deaths that are now seen as part of a larger life cycle. To redeem Lycidas the poem must talk about its own silence without itself falling silent.

Part of the way "Lycidas" achieves this is suggested in the lines about rural ditties, bounded as they are by the death of the day on one side and awareness of "the heavy change" on

the other. The interposed little ease of the pastoral song is introduced with a strange negative, "were not mute"—strange because it could suggest, in the process of denying it, something
that would not have occurred to the reader. What is a mute
ditty? Saying that the song was not silent, especially when the
next line describes it as "temper'd," implies more than that
somebody was singing; it suggests that this is not the "riotous
and unruly noise" of Comus' rout but a pastoral approximation of paradisal "unexpressive nuptial song," the ultimate
union of silence and song, death and eternal life. Sartre calls
negation "a refusal of existence," by which a quality "is
posited, then thrown back to nothingness." [29] Such is the
positing of "mute," where quality and its negation momentarily coexist, and the turn between them absorbs denial into
choice, death and negation into song. Such, likewise, is the
fate of the glad song's pastoral simplicity itself, lost in the complexity of this negation as if in sympathy with the loss of the
pastoral singer, yet arrested in song in the lines that state its
loss.

The absorption of silence into song is in a way the manner
of reconciliation of the whole poem, and just as the ditty is
introduced tempered with muteness, Milton previously invoked the Muses, "Begin, and somewhat loudly sweep the
string." "Somewhat" is somewhat like the redemptive reconciliation, the peace that passeth understanding of the "still
small voice" in which God reveals himself and redeems the
moment in time. It is not enough to proclaim the meaning of
Lycidas' death; theological thunder will not do. But the small
echo, "not mute," reverberates in time and reconciles with it
the death of the old self to produce the death which is the
new understanding. The difference between these overstated

critical connections and Milton's tactful lines is itself the best
way of explaining what "somewhat" means when talking
about reconciliation. Later in the poem Milton enacts such
reconciliation when, after the awesome clap of St. Peter's
voice, he quietly beckons Alpheus, and "mild whispers" replace the dread voice. In the end the whole song is one with
the stillness it has caught: "Thus sang the uncouth Swain to
th'Oaks and rills, / While the still morn went out with Sandals
gray." The morn is "still" because the motion of time has
been arrested and because silence has been subsumed into song.

Silence in Song

Great silences, George Steiner tells us, are to be found
wherever there is great literature.[30] But more characteristically
Miltonic is poetry seeming to stand in a silent listening relationship to itself. When Milton closes the song within song of
"Lycidas," he leaves the last lines, like the "still morn" they
describe, going out into silence, carrying, as it were, an echo
of the swain's song. This capacity of the poetic voice to medi-
ate its own relation to the extrapoetic points to the way
Milton makes silence in song an emblem on all levels. From the
smallest verbal effects to the order of the cosmos, it represents
the harmonious relation of creator to creation.

In *Paradise Lost*, Milton describes the peacefulness of cosmic accord as independent of man's theories, Ptolemaic or
Copernican. Both schemes are suggested, and the alternatives
turn on a grammatical "or" like hinges around their still point.
Silence in song is like the pivot's stillness in motion, and both
express the harmony of even the scientific explanation:

> Or Shee from West her silent course advance
> With inoffensive pace that spinning sleeps

On her soft Axle, while she paces Ev'n,
And bears thee soft with the smooth Air along.

[VIII.163–166]

Raphael is of course describing a cosmos as yet unfallen, but in a way, the disruption in the universe that makes necessary the "or," the turn from the first to the modern explanation, is made to represent the disruption of the primeval "or," Adam's choice.

Given the Fall, the great moment when all offensiveness is borne along and accord actualized anew on earth is at the birth of Christ. It too is apprehended in song in the moment of silence. In "Upon the Circumcision," angelic song is borne along "the soft silence of the list'ning night," and in the Nativity Ode, Milton depicts the reign of peace on earth foreshadowed by the stilling of natural sound:

The Winds, with wonder whist,
Smoothly the waters kiss't,
    Whispering their joys to the mild Ocean
Who now hath quite forgot to rave,
While Birds of Calm sit brooding on the charmed wave.

The new reign is marked by the silencing of the sounds of the unchristian attempts to still time. The oracles here, as again in *Paradise Regained*, are mute.

Often silence, in specific contrast to an ungodly and hideous roar, is emblem of God's order. Once fallen, the angels "fled not in silence through the frightened deep" (*PL*, II.994), and characteristically made "clamorous uproar / Protesting Fate supreme" (X.479–480). Wordsworth similarly poses the rebel force against silence when he pictures the "riotous men" in the convent of Chartreuse. The building stands "in silence visible and perpetual calm" (*Prelude*, VI.429), as if to add Milton's influence to the powers of truth and imaginative impulse as saving graces that will preserve the peace of the scene.

If breaking silence is a breaking away, the restoration of silence signals the restoration that is grace. Thus Christ marks Adam's repentance in asking the Father to "hear his sighs though mute" (XI.31). After the Fall prefigured in Eve's dream, the sign of the reconciliation of the first parents is that Eve "silently a gentle tear let fall / From either eye, and wip'd them with her hair" (V.130–131). Each such moment seems to share in the restoration that is God's when he undertakes creation to repair the breach made by the fallen angels: "Silence, ye troubl'd waves, and thou Deep, peace, / Said then th' Omnific Word, your discord end" (VII.216–217). One can almost apprehend the silence in the pause between "deep" and "peace"; the significance of the repeated "p" sound circumscribing a creative moment is emphasized by comparing Bentley's decreation: "Silence, ye troubled Waves, and Peace, thou Deep." [31] If Creation thus imposes silence as order, the return to order is repeated when Satan is "to shameful silence brought" (*PR*, IV.22); when the fallen angels are condemned, "eternal silence be thir doom" (*PL*, VI.385).

The serpent's silence first charms Eve into attention: "His gentle dumb expression turn'd at length / The Eye of *Eve* to mark his play" (*PL*, IX.527–528). If she falls because of his eloquence, it is not without awareness that there is something wrong with speech on the part of a creature which God "created mute to all articulate sound" (IX.557), and the terms of her question, "How cam'st thou speakable of mute" (IX.563), ought to be sufficient to guard against the offensive sound. The very word "mute" comes up five times in the temptation scene, like a reminder of the nature of paradise and the relationship to God it silently stands for. Adam and

the poet himself speak of silence as a condition and emblem
of Eden, reflecting the relationship to God that is heavenly
harmony.[32] After working the destruction of the rebellious
angels,

> *Messiah* his triumphal Chariot turn'd:
> To meet him all his Saints, who silent stood
> Eye-witnesses of his Almighty Acts,
> With Jubilee advanc'd.   [VI.881–884]

One must complete the whole period to understand that the
saints had been silent and are now singing; the verse describing that song does what heavenly song itself does—arrest
silence within song as symbol of the timelessness enjoyed in
heaven. The heavenly harmony is reciprocal, and after Christ
speaks,

> His words here ended, but his meek aspect
> Silent yet spake, and breath'd immortal love
> To mortal men.   [III.266–268]

Susan Sontag says, "As language points to its own transcendence in silence, silence points to its own transcendence—to
a speech beyond silence." [33] The Son's silence is the timelessness of God's relationship to man, the redemption from time
through God's love.

The importance of silence as representation of timelessness
is that it makes the silent moment an apprehension of presentness, the arrest of time in which choice is real. In two central
passages of *Paradise Lost*—one clearly a satanic imitation of
the other—Milton uses silence to represent the moment where
alternatives are "present." Satan asks, "whom shall we send,"

> and expectation held
> His look suspense, awaiting who appear'd

> To second, or oppose, or undertake
> The perilous attempt; but all sat mute.   [II.417–420]

Satan's "look suspense" marks in the physical, spatial world the suspension of time as the alternatives are presented. For the moment it seems that there is choice in hell, and the council members are free to second *or* oppose *or* undertake. He has, of course, already decided, and the moment has been so prepared as to leave no possibility of doubt about where he will pick up after the "deep silence" that seizes hell.

Christ too picks up where he left off after the moment of silence that marks the heavenly choice, and Milton carefully words that resumption of time, "his dearest mediation thus renew'd," so as to prevent the attempt to distinguish the two scenes on the basis that the heavenly one is less determined. The real difference is elsewhere, for the important choice is not who will go, but whether man will be redeemed. God speaks, "but all the Heav'nly Choir stood mute, / And silence was in Heav'n" (III.217–218). This is the silence that the circumcision and nativity poems associate with the birth of Christ. Prefiguring the stillness of Incarnation, it stands for the moment of arrest when God and eternity merge with man and existence in time. The choice in heaven is the alternative offered for all human history: "And now without redemption all mankind / Must have been lost." The word "now" captures the moment that stands for all future moments, the silence of those who "stand and wait."

When half of *Paradise Lost* is yet untold, the poet reaches into silence and finds it less of a threat from this point on. Whatever the dangers to expression of timeless truth for the poet arrested in time, "fall'n on evil days, / On evil days though fallen," he is less threatened by muteness now, because

he is "Standing on earth, not rapt above the Pole." Yet in a
way such rapture is the constant aim of Milton's poetry, as in
the concern of "Il Penseroso" for poetry "that left half told."
D. C. Allen explains the appeal of Chaucer's unfinished
"Squire's Tale" in saying, "Milton was enchanted by the
symbols of intellectual power." [34] More powerful than the
particular symbols (of the conquest of space, the secrets of
nature) is the power implied or put on while standing before
the unfinished tale. Not rushing in where his predecessor
feared to tread, the poet joins angelic company by leaving
might half slumbering on her own right arm. This Wordsworth understands when he speaks of the "power of choice"
mistakingly settling "on some British theme, some old / Romantic tale, by Milton left unsung." [35] In contrast to Spenser,
Milton does not finish the knightly tale, nor does Wordsworth; for both poets, standing before the unfinished tale is
an expression of imaginative independence. Both also apprehend their power when standing before their own unfinished
tales. After the invocation to *Paradise Lost*, Book VII, Milton
will go on to finish the poem, but he achieves at that moment
a power based on contemplating what is yet unsung, what lies
before the poet standing between the world he has created and
the creation yet to be described. In a passage filled with echoes
of Milton, Wordsworth confronts what he himself will leave
more permanently unsung:

> That portion of my story I shall leave
> There registered: whatever else of power
> Or pleasure sown, or fostered thus, may be
> Peculiar to myself, let that remain
> Where still it works, though hidden from all search
> Among the depths of time.   [*Prelude*, V.192–197]

The next word is "yet," which introduces that which lies beyond: the "power" of poets like Milton. This remains an intimation of what would be spoken, remains in the conditional language of "Il Penseroso." The power comes from the "depth of untaught things" (1805 *Prelude*, XIII.310), untaught because the Chaucerian ring and glass are not to be had, untaught because the tale is left unspoken, yet to be achieved.

If the half-silent song is an apprehension of present potential, the reality of alternatives, then silence itself is always one of the options available. Poetry of the sublime demands careful going between the extremes of saying too much, vaunting too loudly, too near heaven, and on the other side, leaving more than half untold, falling silent with "ears / To rapture" before the heavenly theme. The epic poet must half reveal, "by lik'ning spiritual to corporal forms, / As may express them best" (*PL*, V.573–574), where silence best points to the likeness beyond, better than on earth is thought. Half to tell, half to leave to silence is the chosen verse represented by "Il Penseroso," approaching prophetic strain in pointing to a realm of being and meaning beyond the expressable. "These words shalt thou declare, and these shalt thou hide" (II Esdras 14 : 6). As the prophet is to the word of God, so is the penseroso poet to the muse of melancholy,

> Whose Saintly visage is too bright
> To hit the Sense of human sight;
> And therefore to our weaker view,
> O'erlaid with black, staid Wisdom's hue.

This is the wisdom of half-revelation, "sober, steadfast, and demure" in neither falling silent nor hurrying out of rhythm to too full a vision. Aware of the limitations of experience and expression, the poet uses the "ev'n step, and musing gait," like "measured motion," both to keep poetry going, and going at a contemplative pace that arrests the moment in time to the music. The robe of darkest grain worn by Melancholy is the physical emblem of the poetry that absorbs silence into song, the poetry of veiled allusion that, climbing "to something like Prophetic strain," stands in self-conscious awareness of limitation in sight of the paradise beyond.

The poet of veiled words who does not, like Samson, violate the "sacred trust of silence" makes his creation a participation in cosmic creation:

> Before the Heavens thou wert, and at the voice
> Of God, as with a Mantle didst invest
> The rising world.   [*PL*, III.9–11]

Like the mantling with light here, the mantled poetic vision is a means of getting the greater Light "substantially expressed." Such is the distinction between the prophetic voice and the covert language of Satan, "the father of allegory." Behind the diabolic façade is "the crude mechanistic existence of allegorical being"; behind the veiled vision is the glory of God.[36] The Father, who addresses the Son "without cloud, serene" (XI. 45), can only appear to man "in a Cloud" (XII.202), through mediated voice, as the Hebrews find out at Sinai (XII.239–240). The prophetic voice that absorbs silence is a mantled confrontation with God:

And he said, "Go forth, and stand upon the mount before the Lord." And, behold, the Lord passed by, and a great and strong wind rent the mountain, and brake in pieces the rocks before the Lord; but the Lord was not in the wind: and after the wind an earthquake; but the Lord was not in the earthquake: and after the earthquake a fire; but the Lord was not in the fire; and after the

fire a still small voice. And it was so, when Elijah heard it, that
he wrapped his face in his mantle, and went out, and stood in the
entering in of the cave.   [I Kings 19 : 11–13]

The "still small voice" that Elijah hears is the stillness arrested
in song; the dedication to poetry in which that voice is heard
is the invocation to Melancholy to come wrapped in a mantle
of wisdom's hue; and the sign that such a voice has been heard
is the wrapping-up of the revelation of "Lycidas." After the
nakedness of Voice, there remains but the readjustment in the
prophetic or druid garb: "At last he rose, and twitch't his
Mantle blue: / Tomorrow to fresh Woods, and Pastures
new."

Silence and Keats

One of the best commentators on the way Miltonic silence
points to a higher order redemptive of time is Keats, whose
mantled muse take various forms, from Diana in *Endymion* to
Moneta in *The Fall of Hyperion*. One may begin most simply
with "Ode on a Grecian Urn," addressed to the "child of
silence and slow time." The arrest of time which is the basis
for the pun on "still"—"still unravish'd bride"—parallels the
ravishing of silence in *Comus*, "still to be so displac't." The
whole *Comus* passage (ll. 540–580), with its Keatsian "stream
of rich distill'd perfumes" and yearning to "be never more,"
figures the arrest of time between the two poets as though
Keats, with Thyrsis, were "all ear" to Milton's "solemn-
breathing sound."

What suggests Milton in the opening of the ode is the way
silence is linked with Miltonic option, the moment of choice
when alternatives are real. And what Keats does with Miltonic
option can stand for the choice he makes in confronting Milton as a poetic ancestor. Referring to lines like

What leaf-fring'd legend haunts about thy shape
Of deities or mortals, or of both,
In Tempe or the dales of Arcady?
What men or gods are these?

Harold Bloom points to the way "the tale lacks the either /
or referential clarity of language." [37] Such blurring, for Keats,
is of the essence of poetic being. The abstractness of the urn,
the fact that it clearly exists only insofar as it is clearly described, lures the poet to subject matter in which the ideal of
being poised before experience becomes the aesthetic remove
from failures of experience. When tormented by the thought
of his brother's imminent death, Keats wrote of the need to
"plunge into abstract images to ease myself of his countenance
his voice and feebleness—so that I live now in a continual
fever—it must be poisonous to life although I feel well. Imagine 'the hateful siege of contraries.' " [38] Retreat from "the
hateful siege of contraries"—itself a Miltonic phrase—into the
realm of "abstract images" is what one feels in the abandon-
ment of "either/or" clarity for the kind of image, the kind
of poetry that suspends time in the ode. Such is the relationship between writing poetry and what Keats called negative
capability, "when man is capable of being in uncertainties,
Mysteries, doubts." [39] It is in terms of the abstract image that
Keats and reader draw back from the author's life, his literary
ancestors, even the subject of the poem, and confront a silence
that transcends specific objects. De Selincourt cites the
Miltonic tone of a phrase like "wide quietness," which adds
to a landscape "a suggestion of infinite calm—that sense of
distance without which a landscape carries no meaning to our
hearts." [40] Such is the calm in the phrase "bride of quietness."

Keats himself points to this handling of abstraction like a
physical presence as marking the sublimity of Milton. He

notes the lines in *Paradise Lost* in which, with bitterness and irony that do not diminish the grandness of opening up alternatives in hell, Satan addresses the fallen angels:

> Or have ye chosen this place
> After the toil of Battle to repose
> Your wearied virtue, for the ease you find
> To slumber here, as in the Vales of Heav'n? [I.318–321]

"Wearied virtue" becomes a thing in a place, while "Vales of Heav'n" accrues to itself, by its comparative abstractness, all the pathos of the Fall. Perhaps because one hears "veils" behind "Vales," perhaps because the word "Vales" itself seems evocative of romantic distances, the line seems dimly to descry those lands in the very statement of their loss. Keats writes:

It is a sort of delphic Abstraction—a beautiful—thing made more beautiful by being reflected and put in a Mist. The Next mention of Vale is one of the most pathetic in the whole range of Poetry.

> Others, more mild,
> Retreated in a silent Valley &c.[41]

Mentioning a silent valley creates an interposed ease, a "cool pleasure," in Keats's phrase. And calling it silent turns a place into a pleasance. Finally, Milton's suggestiveness in presenting "others," in opening alternative courses, stations the reader in sublime indefiniteness. It is as if there were a moment of choice in which we could follow either those who rend up rocks or those who sing. For that moment the certainty of hell is suspended and we confront possibility. Far from vagueness or imprecision of diction, it is, rather, imaginative richness that creates a sense of freedom.

Keats identifies that freedom again where Milton makes construing the verse seem to participate in the construction of pandemonium (*PL* I.710–730). We encounter "a fabric huge" that "rose like an exhalation" before the certainty of knowing just what that fabric is. "What creates the intense pleasure of not knowing? A sense of independence, of power, from the fancy's creating a world of its own by the sense of probabilities." If one sees such reading of Milton coloring Keats's own verse, it becomes clear why he delights in scenes caught in the process of coming into focus. The moment dramatically fixed at the end of *Hyperion* is often enacted in miniature. In Book IV of *Endymion*, the youth looked—and "Of those same fragrant exhalations bred, / Beheld awake his very dream" (ll. 435–436). His dream, like the devils' architectural plan in *Paradise Lost*, seems to come into being as we move from the misty to the clear line. And the "intense pleasure of not knowing" makes blendings out of focus as attractive as the emergings. In Book II of *Endymion*, Keats retreats from the presence of the lady to the dark Helicon where the "clear fount / Exhales in mists to heaven" (ll. 722–723). Against the background of these long silences and twilight glories, the new poetry dies into life.

Endymion turns his "capable ears" (itself a Miltonism) to apprehend silence as the music of the spheres. The whole poem, we hear in an extraordinary aside, was sung at Phoebus' shrine, and remains still "sounding for those ears / Whose tips are glowing hot." (II.840–841). Keats himself is like the uncouth swain of "Lycidas" whose trembling ears are touched by a higher voice.

It is not just a certain kind of phrase or specific verbal echo that Keats hears. Encountering his dreamy paradises, one senses that the presence of Milton has been absorbed beyond consciousness into the cathexis of desire. Far from being a blocking figure, a covering cherub who must be bypassed to enter paradise, Milton inhabits Keats's imagined

Edens in a way that transforms the natural into the enchanted. There is, in Wordsworth's phrase, "a spirit in the woods," and these bowers are silent because the hovering presence, like God's in Eden, walks quietly in the cool of the day. Keats's poetry is filled with "quiet caves," "holy groves that silent are," arbors "overwove / By many a summer's silent fingering." By themselves, such images convey the richness of consummation, like that of the poet led

> Through almond blossoms and rich cinnamon;
> Till in the bosom of a leafy world
> We rest in silence.   ["Sleep and Poetry," ll. 118–120]

But poetic influence turns the picturesque into the sublime:

> a bowery nook
> Will be elysium—an eternal book
> Whence I may copy many a lovely saying
> About the leaves, and flowers—about the playing
> Of nymphs in woods, and fountains; and the shade
> Keeping a silence round a sleeping maid;
> And many a verse from so strange influence
> That we must ever wonder how and whence
> It came.   [ll. 63–71]

Such silences stand for the awareness of the gap between the self and power—poetic or natural. A wide quietness opens up as one stands (to echo a sonnet echoing Milton, and about confrontation with poetic power) "silent, upon a peak in Darien." Since moments of sublimity bring with them the knowledge that the gap is separation and death, the silent, solitary confrontation can be, not only an escape from the world of fallenness, but a fall individually re-enacted:

> If I do hide myself, it sure shall be
> In the very fane, the light of Poesy:

> If I do fall, at least I will be laid
> Beneath the silence of a poplar shade.
>
> ["Sleep and Poetry," ll. 275–278]

The retreat to pleasant groves and silent confrontation is a "false surmise" of the presentness of paradise, the stasis of the moment when alternatives are real. The romantic lyric, writes Geoffrey Hartman, can be thought of "as a development of the surmise. . . . Surmise expresses the freedom of a mind aware of itself, aware and not afraid of its moods or potentialities." [42] The romantic ode lingers over the Miltonic moment of stillness, as the "ditties that were not mute" become the "ditties of no tone," and the arrested presentness of "Lycidas," the shattering of the leaves, becomes the "silent form" that imitates eternity: "Ah, happy, happy boughs: That cannot shed / Your leaves, nor ever bid the Spring adieu."

Keats's odes do end with an arrest like Miltonic self-consciousness, though since they extend the lulling of the senses beyond the consciously limited Miltonic moments, the break that is awareness of time and death is proportionally more dramatic. "Cold Pastoral"; "the fancy cannot cheat so well / As she is famed to do"; "all the garden Fancy e'er could feign"; "She dwells with Beauty—Beauty that must die"; and, in a way, "Where are the songs of Spring?"—these are all recognitions of what "Lycidas" calls "false surmise." If the poems carry that surmise beyond what Milton considered the province of the poet, they still point in the same direction, to the same kind of attempt to overreach the limits of actuality:

> Heard melodies are sweet, but those unheard
> Are sweeter; therefore, ye soft pipes, play on;
> Not to the sensual ear, but more endeared,
> Pipe to the spirit ditties of no tone.
>
> ["Ode on a Grecian Urn"]

The greater sweetness of unheard melodies is the substance of Miltonic silence. Heard melodies are like the singing of the "allegro" lark and the unreproved pleasures of "sweetest Shakespeare, fancy's child." But beyond the wild warbling of woodnotes are the ditties of no tone, the histing along of "mute Silence" in "Il Penseroso," where the song of Philomel is most profound because it is not heard. There is a shock of recognition like the "unusual stop of sudden Silence" in *Comus*, and the poet, "missing thee," as he says to the bird, confronts a higher reality, an awareness of absence which he absorbs into song.

In "Il Penseroso," such absence is expressed in the way the speaker "walks unseen" in the landscape, as Adam tries to do in the light of God's presence and man's fall. In Keats's version of the serpent and knowledge story, the equivalent awareness—of man's fall from an illusory paradise, and the presence of an external, authoritative reality—is marked by silence:

> A deadly silence step by step increased,
> Until it seem'd a horrid presence there
> And not a man but felt the terror in his hair.
> "Lamia!" he shriek'd; and nothing but the shriek
> With its sad echo did the silence break.
>
> [*Lamia*, II.266–270]

Lamia, like a dream, must vanish, the presentness of the echo prove false, and Lycius (like Adam and Eve clothed with serpentinely shed animal skins) be wound in the serpentine knowledge that is death.

It is the ineluctable accompaniment of death that makes silence so attractive an emblem of aesthetic stasis. Silence as the

mark of the sublime confrontation relates the hypothetical—
in Wordsworth's sense of "something evermore about to be"
—to the paradise that exists only in imaginative creation or
re-creation and must therefore fall or fade. "The Ode to a
Nightingale," writes Harold Bloom, "is the first poem to know
and declare, wholeheartedly, that death is the mother of
beauty." [43] Leaving aside the decision about wholehearted
commitment, we may say that if not directly traceable to a
poetic ancestor, the poem's relationship to death is at least
bound to Keats's relationship with Milton. The stanza most
in love with easeful death opens with the phrase "Darkling I
listen," identifying in word and stance Keats's relationship
to the bird with Milton's relationship to the Muse in the
invocation to Book III of *Paradise Lost*. Like the fading at the
end of "The Eve of St. Agnes" down a "darkling way," the
move to identification with the nightingale is a retreat to
the ground of poetry. Art true to experience finds at the core,
not sweetness and light, but darkness and dangers compassed round.

This consummation in the Nightingale Ode comes after a
passage in which Keats, like the "Allegro" poet who sees
"Such sights as youthful Poets dream / On Summer eves by
haunted stream," is poised before experience: "The coming
musk-rose, full of dewy wine, / The murmurous haunt of
flies on summer eves." The musk-rose is "coming," the summer
is to come, because this passage is outside time in an extraordinary extension of the Miltonic moment of choice. Keats
has been envisioning a Miltonic blindness, where "there is no
light," because the light that matters is inward, unveiled in
ancestral communion, rather than in external reconciliation
with the encompassing darkness. This is not to deny that the
ancestral voice takes the form of a voice of nature, any more

than one could deny that the abstraction from time is marvelously unnegating of time, that it stands before, is open to seasons to come; the romantic poet participates rather than passively absorbs. He "makes it new," as he will shortly make the nightingale song old ("perhaps the self-same song"), thus singing both the continuity of human suffering and the continuity of the poetic voice above it. Both man and bird are timeless, yet forever bound to time and sense. The "embalmed darkness" that brings poet and nightingale together becomes, through awareness of poetic inheritance, the ground of Delphic abstraction, the "melodious plot" in which the sensory image is more real, in which time is momentarily arrested for this embowered poetic meeting.

And it is a meeting, not a negation of self in the presence of power from which the poet will wake in the end. Or if the power of this stanza lies in the transcendence of self, the power is "might half slumbering," for the speaker is very much in control of this semirelaxation of the will. The way the lines use, rather than surrender themselves to, the service of the memory of Milton can be suggested by comparing the Milton sonnet in which vision collapses into dream. Fitzroy Pyle comments on Sonnet XIX:

As he had never actually seen his wife, the picture he forms of her in his dream is featureless. And when he imagines that she bends down to kiss him and so to reveal her face, his fancy cannot cheat so well as one might wish, and he is tolled back from her to his sole self. That we are reminded of the conclusion of Keats's *Ode* is not fortuitous, for both poems are examples of willing surrender to but partially directed idealizations of fancy; yet it is typical of Milton's habitual rectitude of mind that even in the dream state he will not endow the visionary figure with a face supplied by guess-work.[44]

Keats, guessing each sweet, pauses to paint the landscape, while Milton's sonnet affords little time for guesswork. Though the lady's features are not distinguishable, her abstract qualities seem visible: "Love, sweetness, goodness, in her person shin'd." If the substitution of the abstract for the concrete is ordinarily a poetic as it is a perceptual second best, still the sense of substitution conveys the sense of loss in an incomparable way. The longing for more actual vision increases, but the possibility of that unveiling ends the dream and the poem. Keats, on the other hand, holds on to his vision ("Still wouldst thou sing"), carrying it through imagined changes of seasonal and literary landscape, unvanquished till his own echo (self-conscious distance from his own word, while Milton's is imposed distance from his own experience) tolls him back to his sole self.

If beauty implicates death in the turn from such moments of arrested time, the poem that weighs longest on that turn, extending and thus transcending it, is the "Ode to Psyche." The whole ode seems to dally with the false surmise of arrested presentness as though poised between the two meanings of "Psyche"—the goddess of literary tradition, and Keats's own mind, the myth and poem he goes on to make here. Did he dream or did he see "with awaken'd eyes"? Keats stands on the fictive "or," between the verbs emblematic of internality and externality. The extraordinary sophistication of the ode is in its proclamation of its own achievement without any slighting of the past. Confronted with death, Milton had to give up false surmise in "Lycidas"; that fact of externality was overwhelming, and the poet wrote with "forc'd fingers rude." Yet he also himself shattered the leaves, forcing his own way, like Marvell's "forward youth," to the laurel the elegy so justly earned. Keats can acknowledge the full force of that Miltonic equivocation while himself overgoing it. Unlike Milton's elegy, with its "bitter constraint, and sad occasion dear," this poem comes from "sweet enforcement and remembrance dear," for there is no bitterness to the taste of death. Since the only fact of externality the poem encounters is the inheritance of the past, there is only a fading into new life; what is gone is remythologized into what is present. The only death the ode knows is that fancy, "breeding flowers, will never breed the same." Where Milton's flora were plucked or forced to vanish at the awareness of drowned Lycidas, Keats's simply add the pathos of loss to their very much present beauties.

   If an ode must turn, this ode transforms that movement from a turn *away* into a turn *to*. It moves from absence to presence, for where one ordinarily bemoans the absence of what once was, Keats finds only an absent history and replaces it with the present poem. Since there was no era in which the goddess was worshiped, she has had no temple,

>   Nor altar heap'd with flowers;
> Nor virgin-choir to make delicious moan
>   Upon the midnight hours;
> No voice, no lute, no pipe, no incense sweet
>   From chain-swung censer teeming;
> No shrine, no grove, no oracle, no heat
>   Of pale-mouth'd prophet dreaming.

The terms recall those of Milton's Nativity Ode, where the oracles are silenced, but the recall, far from an undoing, is a call to life. The negations are destroyed, in Blake's words, to redeem the contraries. Each negative is part of the silencing that commences creation, like Milton's God silencing the troubled waves. In "Sleep and Poetry," Keats talks of "The silence when some rhymes are coming out; / And when they're come, the very pleasant rout" (ll. 321–322). As if that casual description of artistic creation were grandly mythologized, the routing of the old forms of worship is turned to new poetic service, to the litany that is this ode. The role of the Christ child in Milton's ode is assumed in Keats's poem by a deity who demands no Protestant asceticism of worship, so that in place of a "humble ode" laid "lowly at his blessed feet," Keats offers the luxuriant creation of region, fane, bower, and sanctuary. Milton reconciled fictionality to time with the self-address: "O run, prevent them with thy humble ode." This poem of Keats knows no such limitations, so remaking the old myth, instead of fitting into it, he leaves a shining light and open casement. Defying a poetic closure that implicates death, the openness at the end is the poem's assertion of freedom. The only burden of the past here, as in "To Autumn," is the harvest of its fruits. In this sense the poem is about poetic influence, the waking from "Lycidas"-like unpreparedness to create "in some untrodden region of my mind"—where Milton has not been.

Its subject matter and the fact that it heads the sequence of odes permit the exceptional aesthetic distance of the "Ode to Psyche." Elsewhere the "shadowy thought" that "Psyche" barely acknowledges is given more place, and death, as well as the fever and the fret, is more fully acknowledged. In the Hyperion poems the sleeping Titan images silence, and the sleep of poetic influence is seen as a burden; but beyond this is a more public problem the poet must face, one not to be separated from his relation to poetic tradition. "None can usurp this height," Moneta says,

> But those to whom the miseries of the world
> Are misery, and will not let them rest.

All else who find a haven in the world,
Where they may thoughtless sleep away their days,
If by a chance into this fane they come,
Rot on the pavement where thou rotted'st half.

[*The Fall of Hyperion*, I.147–153]

The poet has not been thoughtlessly asleep up to this point; he has awakened, like Eve after her dream, to the fact of loss. Finding that "The mossy mound and arbor were no more," he turned from that paradise lost to the pandemoniac monument of past human achievement:

I look'd around upon the carved sides
Of an old sanctuary with roof august,
Builded so high, it seem'd that filmed clouds
Might spread beneath, as o'er the stars of heaven.

. . . . .

The embossed roof, the silent massy range
Of columns north and south, ending in mist
Of nothing; then to Eastward, where black gates
Were shut against the sunrise evermore.   [I.61–86]

This "old sanctuary" is modeled on the one under whose "high embower'd Roof, / With antic Pillars massy proof" the "Penseroso" poet envisioned "all Heav'n before mine eyes." Representing what Keats has made out of Milton's myth, and setting the scene for what yet must be made of the new poet, the temple has black gates shut against the sunrise. Not through new revelation, new openness to the chaos out of which more rudimentary art is made—that is not the way. Acknowledging rather what has been shut out, and redirecting himself to the images of the past, Keats progresses along the purgatorial way.

Before touching the lowest stair of spiritual *ascesis* and ascent, the poet's first step must make him share a fall. *The*

Fall of Hyperion begins with the requisite falling to the banquet, where feasting on the fruit of a Miltonic Eden, the poet gleans both the riches of the past and the fact that they are remains, the seeming "refuse of a meal / By angel tasted or our Mother Eve" (I.30–31). With Miltonic pathos, the awareness of loss is subsumed into the description of paradise:

> Still was more plenty than the fabled horn
> Thrice emptied could pour forth, at banqueting
> For Proserpine return'd to her own fields
> Where the white heifers low.   [I.35–38]

The last line has mastered the Miltonic simile and the way imaginative wealth is accumulated from the engendering of new distances, new senses of exclusion from other fields and other groves. Such replacing of paradisal ongoingness with the awe of discovery of loss marks the lines Keats singles out as being "of a very extraordinary beauty in the Paradise Lost": "which cost Ceres all that pain" (IV.271) and "Nor could the Muse defend / Her son" (VII.38–39). Perhaps the most Miltonic thing about Keats is the way poetry does not wait for the drama of loss but subsumes it; death is the mother of beauty, not its matricidal offspring.

Keats characterizes Milton as " 'sagacious of his Quarry,' he sees Beauty on the wing, pounces upon it and gorges it to the producing his essential verse." Keats's poetry describes catching beauty on the wing in phrases consciously Miltonic:

> A drainless shower
> Of light is poesy; 'tis the supreme of power;
> 'Tis might half slumb'ring on its own right arm.
> The very archings of her eye-lids charm
> A thousand willing agents to obey,
> And still she governs with the mildest sway:
> But strength alone though of the Muses born

Is like a fallen angel: tress uptorn,
Darkness, and worms, and shrouds, and sepulchres
Delight it.   ["Sleep and Poetry," ll. 235–244]

The positive terms recall the pastoralism of *Comus;* the negative ones, hell and the war in heaven. Strength alone is like
the angel already fallen, whereas beauty captures the angel in
the act of falling, just as a "shower of light" exists in the falling, not the fallen state. Beauty is born from the new sense in
the engendering of sense, the controlled flight of Mulciber
(caught in the falling, in the turn in time from morn to noon
to eve), the unprecipitous control, in Wallace Stevens' terms,
of leaping from heaven to heaven. The fallen angel, like the
fallen Hyperion, is all too soundly slumbering. The poet's
task is to re-engender the sense of half-slumbering, of the
possible, not the past. He creates, with godlike omnific word,
pronouncing, "let there be"; and the delight is in capturing
the process:

                    and let there be
Beautiful things made new, for the surprise
Of the sky-children.   [*The Fall of Hyperion*, I.436–438]

A moment later all is lost: "Now all was silent." The poet
thinks he has heard "some old man of the earth / Bewailing
earthly loss," for the vitality, the vision, is in the moment of
creating; the death is the creation. Capturing beautiful things
being made new, the capture is the loss.

On Milton's lines describing Satan entering the sleeping
serpent, Keats comments, "Whose spirit does not ache at the
smothering and confinement—the unwilling stillness—the
waiting close?" The anticipation, the potential energy, is the
same as that with which Keats infuses his sleeping Titan, that
with which Keats "possessing soon inspired" Milton. That

influence at its best can be read this way rather than the other
way round is a point better made by T. S. Eliot:

The existing monuments form an ideal order among themselves,
which is modified by the introduction of the new (the really
new) work of art among them. . . . The *whole* existing order
must be, if ever so slightly, altered; and so the relations, propor-
tions, values of each work of art toward the whole are readjusted;
and this is conformity between the old and the new. Whosoever
has approved this idea of order, of the form of European, of English literature will not find it preposterous that the past should
be altered by the present as much as the present is directed by
the past.[45]

Here is Coleridge on the atemporality of poetic influence:

>   the truly great
> Have all one age, and from one visible space
> Shed influence! They, both in power and act,
> Are permanent, and Time is not with them,
> Save as it worketh for them, they in it.
>
>   ["To William Wordsworth"]

Past poets and their things of beauty keep "a bower quiet for
us," and Keats, like Eliot, gives us a sculpture garden where
all is cold pastoral if the past is not altered by the present:

>   Round about were hung
> The glorious features of the bards who sung
> In other ages—cold and sacred busts
> Smiled at each other.   ["Sleep and Poetry," ll. 355–358]

The poet must relate to the existing sculptures; he comes
upon his ancestors as the reader does upon the old order in
the figure of Saturn, "quiet as a stone, / Still as the silence
round about his lair" (*Hyperion*, I.4–5). And in *The Fall*,

Saturn and Moneta are like "sculpture builded up upon the grave / Of their own power (I.383–384). Influence may begin with another voice coming to life, but that is the story of the poet's own awakening to power. Out of the nudging awake of Saturn is born the poetry in which Apollo comes into his own and silences the oracles by speaking in his own voice. The relation between the new god and the old is the relation between the new poet and Milton, and the knowledge of this relationship is put on with the power—indeed, this knowledge is the power:

> Tell me why thus I rave, about these groves!
> Mute thou remainest—Mute! yet I can read
> A wondrous lesson in thy silent face:
> Knowledge enormous makes a God of me.
>
> [*Hyperion*, III.110–113]

The relation between knowledge and power is questionable in political but not in literary or personal history, where knowledge is not focused on things to come but on things past, or more properly, on one's relationship to the past. Only this recognition can silence the old ghosts, whose power is not ignored but "put on"; at the same time, their silence too is put on, for poetry is but the process of coming to one's own quietude. These remarks must be qualified by an awareness of the danger of retreating from interaction into self-absorption, the danger of ignoring the fact that the miseries of the world are misery. The subject matter of poetry must be, not just one's relation to one's literary ancestry, but one's relation to the weight of "the unchanging gloom." Recognizing this is the third path that leads the poet to stand at the crossroads, at the moment of choice. The silencing of a more natural for a more literary self; the silence of the eternal literary monuments; the silent assumption of the burden of the masses of nonpoetic men, who lead lives of quiet desperation—all three are arrested in simultaneous presence as Keats, choosing to bear "the weight of eternal quietude," joins the Miltonic company.

3. A Space Extended

> And when the whirlwinds and the clouds descended
> From the white pinnacles of that cold hill,
> She passed at dewfall to a space extended,
> Where in a lawn of flowering asphodel
> Amid a wood of pines and cedars blended,
> There yawned an inextinguishable well
> Of crimson fire—full even to the brim,
> And overflowing all the margin trim.
>
> Shelley, *The Witch of Atlas*

In Camus's *L'Etranger*, Meursault approaches the Arab as Eve approaches the tree in one of those terrible noon hours in which time stands still as if the whole world bears on the moment of choice: "For two hours the sun seemed to have made no progress, becalmed in a sea of molten steel." Then Camus's hero says something extraordinary, something that places the book in a line of temptation literature but simultaneously identifies it as unmistakably of this century: "It struck me that all I had to do was to turn, walk away, and think no more about it." [1]

Milton's Eve is never struck by such a thought, and it is inconceivable that Milton's epic could incorporate, before it is too late, such an awareness of failure of the will. When already fallen, Satan can consider the alternative of turning back (*PL*, IV.79–80), but only long enough to note its impossibility; and Adam immediately reacts to Eve's fall as though his own were necessitated by it. For Milton the awareness of fall is always of what has passed; protagonist and reader are surprised by sin that is already committed. In Stanley Fish's terms: "We are not warned ('Do not be carried away by this fellow'), but accused. . . . 'I know that you *have been* carried away by what you have just heard; you should not have been; you have made a mistake, just as I knew you would.' " [2]

This sense of closure characterizes the mode of narrative throughout. We read, "thus they relate / Erring" (*PL*, I.746–747), momentarily rapt in that relation till we realize—when it is all over—the error. The epic has no room for the kind of protracted arrest in which Meursault stops along the way to detail each step, to tell us, "I knew it was a fool thing to do," and to describe sensation in language which, because it is metaphoric, seems infuriatingly slow. One may contrast the relative intangibility of a Miltonic moment of fall, especially when it is an imagined, surmised moment rather than one that for Milton was a real moment in history. In Eve's dream the actual moment of eating the fruit is not there. "One expects 'Forthwith' ('immediately after which' or simply 'then') to be followed by 'I reached' or 'I ate' or even 'I decided to eat.' . . . We have missed the deed itself and passed to its effects." [3] Because it is a presentiment and not an actual fall, the dream presents the deed, not in the doing, but imagined as done; the relationship of innocence to the absence of even the imagined arrested moment is in itself part of the preparation of Eve. Kierkegaard says: "*Nil admirari* is therefore the real philosophy. No moment must be permitted so great a significance that it cannot be forgotten when convenient." [4] For Milton the one such moment is the Fall; Camus subjects each episode in his hero's history before his "fall" to the same "admiration," the same concentration of an excruciating self-consciousness. Meursault's murder and arrest by the police are narrative expressions of the random collision of an involuted mind with the external world and the "arrest" of self-absorption.

Self-consciousness in Milton comes only through a fall, through an awareness of having already gone wrong. There can be no prior arrest, because the self confronts itself across a distance identified with the fall, a loss and separation from a prior state of consciousness. One might suspect that sinfulness lurks at the heart of the still moment itself. But granted that some kind of fictional arrest of time is the very condition of the representation of choice, the moral overtones of such fictionalizing need to be more precisely delineated. We may turn to *Comus*, the temptation poem in which the arrest of time is most closely related to the story and its moral valorizations.

Comus and Arrest

In the mask as in the epic, both temptation and arrest are in some way connected with the sensual. Like Satan's temptation of Eve, the poetic process that leads to self-consciousness is entangled with eroticism and fulfills a "consummation" that is knowledge and death. Gusts that blow their fill in "Il Penseroso," ending with "minute-drops from off the Eaves," carry a sensuous suggestiveness, a fragrance of fall. If "shower still" is as immaculate as the "holy passion still" that "L'Allegro" invoked, it is just the holiness and purity of passionate stillness that tempt one to violate their innocence of suggestivity. In *Comus*, Thyrsis describes the song he has heard capture such stillness:

> At last a soft and solemn-breathing sound
> Rose like a stream of rich distill'd Perfumes,
> And stole upon the air, that even Silence
> Was took ere she was ware, and wish't she might
> Deny her nature, and be never more,
> Still to be so displac't.   [ll. 555–560]

It is, in the words of Hamlet contemplating ultimate self-arrest, a "consummation devoutly to be wished." Some of the

ironies of the Shakespearean passage form a mutual interpretation with Miltonic stillness. "Devoutly to be wished" shocks
(and therefore arrests us) in using a religious term for what
would be, if undertaken by Hamlet himself, a hellish termination. "To be wished" restores the projected stasis to its hypothetical status, which therefore does not interfere with time.
The considerations of dreaming which follow act strangely to
integrate the projected death, seen as a still point, back into
time. Then comes the supreme turn when the very process of
dreaming—the thought of ongoingness—"must give us pause."

The pause in action that is ongoingness in song is characteristic of Milton's narrative technique generally. Eve prefers to
hear an account which, like that the poet presents his reader, is
mediated through man:

> hee, she knew, would intermix
> Grateful digressions, and solve high dispute
> With conjugal Caresses.   [*PL*, VIII.54–56]

In a sense the respectful and loving intimacy of the first parents is also the literary relationship in which the poet inter-
mixes grateful digressions and interposes a little ease in dally-
ing with surmises like caresses. Here, as in the passage above
from *Comus*, the mingling of literary and sensual reference is
unquestionably innocent as song "takes in" moments of silence
and is lovingly held "still": "*Thyrsis?* Whose artful strains
have oft delay'd / The huddling brook to hear his madrigal"
(*Comus*, ll. 494–495). In the same way that such strains are
embraced, the orthodoxy in "Lycidas" that shrinks the streams
of Alpheus is encompassed into song, is mixed with grateful
digressions and made (to pursue Milton's metaphor beyond its
legitimate hold on the mind) virilely rather than offensively
aggressive. In the mask, Silence's wish to deny her nature is

the soul's yearning for union with its Creator. Such capacity for re-creation is reflected in Thyrsis' receptivity to the Lady's song. Rapt out of selfhood, he is "all ear," and takes in "strains that might create a soul / Under the ribs of Death" (ll. 561–562). In their various sensuous voices, these strains are all the sounds of grace, redeeming existence in time by seeing death as the displacement of the silent, unquestioning soul into the kingdoms of joy and love. The death of Lycidas is the consummation of that union.

One measure of the resistless power of song that takes in silence is its effect on Comus, who reacts strangely like Thyrsis, having heard, after all, the same song. Comus refers specifically to its effect as "ravishment" and its source as heavenly:

> Can any mortal mixture of Earth's mold
> Breathe such Divine enchanting ravishment?
> Sure something holy lodges in that breast,
> And with these raptures moves the vocal air
> To testify his hidd'n residence.   [ll. 244–248] [5]

A pun is often a means of expressing self-awareness, because consciousness of a second meaning establishes distance from the surface intent. But here Comus' pun on the word "air" does not break his own rapture, for both meanings accord. The phrase about raptures moving the air is a physical description of sound effects at the same time that it explains what keeps the air, or song, going. The air is also moved, emotionally aroused, to express the "something holy" that it has caught. Moving air is here significantly less suspect than the power Marvell, for example, makes pleasure's greatest lure:

> charming Aires;
> Which the posting Winds recall,

And suspend the Rivers Fall.
> ["A Dialogue between the Resolved Soul and
> Created Pleasure"]

The suspended fall contrasts with the way musical-erotic terms in Milton can avoid suggestion of perverse stasis by integrating the temporal arrest of shrunken streams back into musical time. Comus' terms are equally inoffensive and suggest the "divine enchanting ravishment" at the end of "Lycidas," where the soul is entertained by societies "that sing, and singing in their glory move." The pause after "sing" enacts the still point subsumed into the rhythmic motion of the line and the song, the arrest of time now seen as part of a larger movement.

Comus seems to outdo even Thyrsis in the propriety of his response to the Lady's raptures:

> How sweetly did they float upon the wings
> Of silence, through the empty-vaulted night,
> At every fall smoothing the Raven down
> Of darkness till it smiled.   [ll. 249–252]

Where Thyrsis' overwhelming virtue allows him to express the more extravagant auditory response, Comus, here near ravished out of his role of ravisher, expresses the more qualified sensuous effect of the Lady's music. Strains that "float upon the wings / Of silence" are more obviously innocent than Thyrsis' sound that "stole upon the air" (l. 557). And Comus is careful to distinguish the divine song he has just heard from those of his mother and the sirens which "in pleasing slumber lull'd the sense, / And in sweet madness robb'd it of itself." Their song is like the "harmonious madness" of Shelley, who would replace Miltonic "harmonious numbers" with a relationship to a skylark singer who is outside time.

Comus seems to understand precisely the difference between the song that apprehends stillness through a suspect lulling of the senses and the song that redeems existence in time by comprehending stillness in its rhythmic pattern. In contrast with raptures of a blithe spirit that soars higher and higher, raptures that make darkness smile "at every fall" are part of the holy passion still that sees every fall, every loss of the moment, as an echo of the archetypal fall and the beginning of the rising motion of redemption. Like a good musician conducting with his rod, Comus knows that the guiding hand begins to rise at the fall of the downbeat.

While Thyrsis understands that the Lady is in some sense the "hapless nightingale" of which she sings, Comus miraculously adumbrates the saving grace that protects the bird and turns "her sad Song [which she] mourneth well" into a song of universal comfort. Momentarily out of his role as tempter, he hears the nightingale's sorrow as the redemptive song of Philomel we have heard in "Il Penseroso," "smoothing the rugged brow of night." [6] Such images are the caresses of sympathy, in which the sense of personal loss becomes the cry "which universal Nature did lament" for the fall it shares with man.

The close of Comus' soliloquy brings to a climax his own participation in the redemptiveness of song, for in the lines that follow he addresses the Lady in his role as tempter and extols her as a goddess in terms that anticipate Satan's lure of Eve. But meanwhile Comus seems even to have lost some of the perversity of his original purpose. "I'll speak to her / And she shall be my Queen" (ll. 264–265) expresses intent of a different order from what he first announced he would like to do with chaste maidens—stock himself with "as fair a herd as graz'd / About my Mother Circe (ll. 152–153). He shows something like distraction in thinking now that he need but speak, that this Proserpine will be got without violence, but having heard the Lady, he is caught up by the power of the magic that can fall on the human ear. His reaction anticipates his last speech, in which he is almost overcome, even without outside intervention. Comus is momentarily rapt out of character, subject to the Lady's song in just the way the sense is "robb'd of itself" on hearing the song he mentions in order to differentiate the Lady's from it.[7] We are left with the question of how to distinguish the holy passion still from the lulled sense, the perception of paradise that is the arrested moment from the potential sinfulness in it.

One reason Comus is so affected by the Lady's song is that it strikes him as a "home-felt delight," a pleasure that "strikes home" not only because it reminds him of his mother but because it expresses, in song, what he tries to do in action. Translated out of program music into a program of action, the arrest of time when stillness is caught in song becomes the ancient theme of *carpe diem*. The theme is Comus' family inheritance, and he uses the traditional conceits:

> If you let slip time, like a neglected rose
> It withers on the stalk with languish't head.
> Beauty is nature's brag, and must be shown.   [ll. 743–745]

His use of familiar terms is an additional way of arresting time; the magician is doing a little disappearing act with the centuries that intervene between the classical appeal to seize the day and the present one in the modern setting. But he does more than just talk about arrest, and begins his temptation by having the Lady "set in an enchanted Chair." Roy Daniells objects that Comus "begins by the equivalent of tying her up, surely a poor preface to a speech of amorous persuasion." [8]

This is to miss the point, for tying her up is an emblem and partial fulfillment of Comus' symbolic purpose. Northrop Frye moves more easily between the literal and symbolic terms: "It is Comus who represents passion, which is the opposite of action; it is the Lady who holds to the source of all freedom of action." [9] The passion of Comus, like the holy passion of song, is an arrest of action, of ongoingness, of time. What makes one sinister and the other an approximation of heaven is that Comus' is a confusion of art and life, as one knows from his opening words in that scene:

> Nay Lady, sit; if I but wave this wand,
> Your nerves are all chain'd up in Alabaster,
> And you a statue; or as *Daphne* was,
> Root bound, that fled *Apollo*. [ll. 559–562]

Perhaps Comus is overlooking the fact that Daphne was "root bound" not for punishment but for escape. Perhaps we need to modify "the fact that Daphne was 'root bound' " and say that, aware of the nature of myth as fiction, Comus, as arch deconstructionist, suggests that there is no division between levels of being: all "fact" (including his and the Lady's being) is but fiction, and the only choice for her is whether she is to remain mobile or immobile. Perhaps, further than this, Comus is denying that his temptation is symbolic action, and asserting the continuity, rather than the correspondence, between sign and significance. If the Lady refuses to partake of pleasures "That fancy can beget on youthful thoughts" (l. 669), she is refusing by his standard not his allegro for her penseroso mode, but all manner of "begetting." She is denying nature. Since nature and art are really the same, the Lady would be chaining herself to alabaster anyway, turning into a perverse version of the stasis of art because of her perverse attitude toward the genial profligacy of nature.

But for Milton there is a far greater disjunction between sign and significance, and denying Comus would not mean denying nature. On the contrary, accepting Comus would be denying nature and living wholly in the terms appropriate only to art. Comus threatens the Lady with being turned to a statue, and the threat he presents is the threat he represents; his moral stance is stasis, as we can see in the men he has turned to bestial forms. The disjunction between sign and significance is violated in the attempt to interpret temporal arrest "experientially." While still a matter of song, however, arrest is innocent. Though it is morally dangerous for experience to imitate art, art may properly imitate experience. On the most basic level, Milton himself repeatedly imitates suspension in time by grammatically suspending the verse. To take but one example, in the Trinity manuscript Comus tells the Lady:

> if yor stray attendence be yet lodg'd
> wthin these limits I shall know
> ere the larke rouse.

Compare this with the leisured inclusion of alternative as Milton rewrites:

> if your stray attendance be yet lodg'd,
> Or shroud within these limits, I shall know
> Ere morrow wake or the low-roosted lark
> From her thatch't pallet rouse.   [ll. 315–318]

The grammatical extension is an expression of the arrest of the Lady which Comus would like to actualize. The two *ors* allow the poetics of choice to represent the moral problematics of choice.

In a paradox that points to the essence of Miltonic metaphor, symbolic arrest is more real than real arrest—that is,
arrest in song is more in harmony with ultimate reality, heavenly song, than is the necessarily thwarted attempt to actualize
arrest on earth. Thus the Attendant Spirit introduces Circe,
presenting in a poetic parenthesis the whole temptation at
which Circe's son will fail:

> (Who knows not *Circe*
> The daughter of the Sun? Whose charmed Cup
> Whoever tasted, lost his upright shape,
> And downward fell into a groveling Swine.)   [ll. 50–53]

Comus wants to take such arrest out of parenthesis into real
duration, out of the past into a permanent loss of freedom of
the will. He is a mild version of what Northrop Frye calls
Satan: "the power that moves toward the cessation of all
activity." [10]

When it is clearly a musical achievement, moving the vocal
air, that power is not only legitimate but divine. Such is the
power of the Lady's song and of the song of the angels who
"in their glory move." In *Paradise Lost* it will be shared by
Milton's muse: "Then feed on thoughts, that voluntary move
/ Harmonious numbers" (III.37–38). Donald Davie comments:

The eventfulness of the language comes out for instance in "Then
feed on thoughts that voluntarie move," where at the line-ending
"move" seems intransitive, and as such wholly satisfying; until the
swing on to the next line, "Harmonious numbers," reveals it (a
little surprise, but a wholly fair one) as transitive. This flicker of
hesitation about whether the thoughts move only themselves, or
something else, makes us see that the numbers aren't really "something else" but are the thoughts themselves, seen under a new

aspect; the placing of "move," which produces the momentary uncertainty about its grammar, ties together "thoughts" and "numbers" in a relation far closer than cause and effect.[11]

The impression of language's "eventfulness" comes from our awareness of verse's temporality; the "flicker of hesitation" is caught in the moment of arrest between the lines; the "surprise" is the surprise of sin ("wholly fair," justified to man); and the relationship "far closer than cause and effect" is the mark of the disappearance of time. The verse effects produce something like Bergsonian sympathy, in which distance—what Jacques Derrida might call "difference"—between idea and its symbol is dissolved.

Milton then compares his own darkness and song to the nightingale's. But when he continues, "Thus with the Year / Seasons return," the "Thus" seems to be related less to the nightingale song than back to the process of return caught in the verse turn on "harmonious numbers." In the turn from "Year" to "Seasons," enjambment is symbolic of poetic pause integrated back into time. Then, in what seems at first to be more of a parallel action than a distinction, the "Seasons return, but not to me returns / Day. . . ." The metaphoric equation between natural and personal process creates an equilibrium, a lull; yet the awareness that for Milton "day" means, not a unit of time, but daylight shocks us into the realization that time is the meaning we have lost—or rather, that time has been going on, oblivious though we have been, and to time we return.[12] Yet our return coincides with his personal "not to me returns," and we are separated from him by a distance that broadens as we realize that while "Day, or the sweet approach of Ev'n or Morn" focuses our attention on the passing of time, not periods of time but the visual perception of these is missing for Milton. The loss is the gap between poet and us; it is also between these simple words and the multiplicity of sights that could be conjured as images of times of day and the feelings they bring—sparingly and therefore all the more beautifully represented in the lines that follow. The series of absences (no day, or evening, or morn, or sight of bloom, or rose, or flocks . . .) parallels the passage in "Lycidas" after the awareness of "heavy change" and the irretrievability of the past; in both poems, the series of *ors* further marks the vocabulary of loss and its transcendence. Finally (if one can use such a word about a passage that seems to open infinite distances), we recognize that the return of day in the sense of light would be a return like that when the phenomenon greets God's Word: Let there be light, and there was light. Evening, then morn is the order of time that marks the Genesis days; and the progress from light to vegetation to animal life to the "human face divine" is the progress of the hexameron. Having witnessed "Nature's works" being created from line to line, we feel the loss of all in finding, not the fullness of nature, but "a Universal blanc."

There is all the difference between such poetry of loss, imitating experiential arrest in the arrest of song, and, on the other hand, the poetry that lulls, carrying the arrest of song into its experiential equivalent. Circe and her son offer a stasis at best that of sleep: her song "in pleasing slumber lull'd the sense" (l. 260). While the Genius in "Arcades" speaks of the power of music "to lull the daughters of *Necessity*," that is the power, not to violate time, but to accord with it, drawing the low world up "after the heavenly tune." Similarly Adam and Eve are "lull'd by Nightingales" (*PL*, IV.771) to a stasis reconciled with the Fall in that the lines which follow adumbrate it. As long as it remains stasis of song, temporal suspension is not suspect, even in hell:

> Thir Song was partial, but the harmony
> (What could it less when Spirits immortal sing?)
> Suspended Hell, and took with ravishment
> The thronging audience.   [II.552–555] [13]

To show us there is yet a vestige of godly activity, the Muse herself participates; the lines perform grammatically what they assert, suspending "Hell" over the parenthetical line and using enjambment to hold still the attention of the audience.

Stasis in song can be comprehended and looked back upon with an awareness of fall; cut off as it is by a moment of self-consciousness when what we took as present is apprehended as past, it is circumscribed by an awareness of time. When stasis is sought in space, as it is by the plotting and building fallen angels, by Comus turning the lulling of sense into monstrous metamorphosis, what is caught is not the present tense but the present thing, not time passing but time past, and the attempt is bound to fall. Schelling defined space as arrested time, and in that sense David Masson's comment that Milton's is a world of space is significant.[14]

Physical spaciousness is characteristic of chaos and the antithesis of creation—which God begins by circumscribing space. Kierkegaard specifies the relation of limitation to creation, referring to "the principle of limitation" as "the only saving principle in the world." Applying such a principle to *Paradise Lost*, Cope writes, "Contrasting with the order indicated by circumscription, spaciousness is the natural milieu of disorder and evil." [15] What is true of physical expansiveness is true of mental extension, for self-consciousness, if extended beyond the moment, confronts void, fallen space. Uncircumscribed by time, the attempt to hold still mental or material pandemonium is a violation of God's space and out of order.

If we might borrow for the moment Schopenhauer's sense

of will, then that philosopher's separation of music from the other arts can help explain Milton's. The distinction between nonmusical and musical terms is the difference between representation and what, in music, transcends the world for more direct relation with the "thing-itself." In music there is "of necessity no resemblance between its productions and the world as representation, *i.e.*, nature. . . . There must be a distinct *parallelism*." Like the concept of echo in the mask, "parallelism" skips over representation, the attempt to give space to the will for stasis:

The (Platonic) Ideas are the adequate objectification of the will. To stimulate the knowledge of these by depicting individual things (for works of art are themselves always such) is the aim of all the other arts (and is possible with a corresponding change in the knowing subject). Hence all of them objectify the will only indirectly, in other words, by means of the Ideas. As our world is nothing but the phenomenon or appearance of the Ideas in plurality through entrance into the *principium individuationis* (the form of knowledge possible to the individual as such), music, since it passes over the Ideas, is also quite independent of the phenomenal world, positively ignores it, and to a certain extent, could still exist even if there were no world at all, which cannot be said of the other arts. Thus music is as *immediate* an objectification and copy of the whole *will* as the world itself is, indeed as the Ideas are, the multiplied phenomenon of which constitutes the world of individual things. Therefore music is by no means like the other arts, namely a copy of the Ideas, but a *copy of the will itself*, the objectivity of which are the Ideas.[16]

Music is, as it were, a "will more wise" than an attempted objectification of will. Comus' spatial arrest of the lady can stand for a perverse self-assertion of primary will, while the arrest of time in song—especially as echo—expresses the directness of copying "the will itself," the more harmonious reconciliation to a greater order and the more profound expression of what Schopenhauer calls the "will to live." And what is true in moral terms, in terms of the poet's relation to a more authoritative will, is true of poetry, as each false surmise copies the will, not setting its own spatialization to be destroyed by God's order but standing as a secondary expression of the will itself. Moments of stasis leap past imitation or objectification to participate directly in the heavenly music.

In the prolusion "On the Music of the Spheres," Milton finds it credible "that the nightingale passes the night in solitary trilling in order to harmonize [her] songs with that heavenly music." Milton can be playful but not frivolous, and we may, like Thyrsis, recognize the nightingale as the Lady of the mask. The whole poem uses the harmony of song with heavenly music as emblem of the proper apprehension of stasis and fall. The mask is a song writ large, for as song encompasses the still moment, the mask encompasses the stillness represented by Comus. In the end Sabrina is invoked and redeems through song, and the Attendant Spirit sings an epilogue that is a vision of paradise regained. Musical terms thus point to the way Milton treats poetic resolution as an echo of divine resolution of evil. Spenser is his original, and when arrest approaches the stasis of the plastic arts, it must be dissolved back into the order of time. The difference is that in musical, Miltonic terms, nothing is wholly destroyed; the power of music is far from given up when the rout is driven off. The Fall is not the dissolution of a pictorial experience but a discord whose resolution is the very substance of that experience. Comus in the mask becomes, like Satan in the story of the Fall, a counterpoint subsumed into the larger harmony that ends with a world redeemed.

Mephistophelean Arrest

One of the difficulties in talking about the suspect element in stasis is that dwelling on the topic is itself such an arrest. But romantic poets in particular often use terms of stasis and motion with Miltonic import and with characteristic interest in protracting the arrest of time. It may prove useful to turn briefly to a romantic who seems unbound by specific indebtedness to Milton.

Goethe's *Faust* centers about the temptation to hold on to the moment:

> If I to any moment say:
> Linger on! You are so fair!
> Put me in fetters straightaway
> Then I can die for all I care! [17]

Marlowe's *Doctor Faustus*, on the other hand, has little in common with Milton's concept of temptation and is rather about the kind of "tragedy for the imagination" that Wallace Stevens associates with the death of Satan, the irrelevance of the old myths. But Goethe's poem is not only set against a tradition of temptation literature that goes back to Job; it begins with echoes of the biblical material on which *Paradise Lost* is based. Mephistopheles predicts the fate of Faust: "Dust shall he eat, and call it good, / Just like my aunt, the celebrated snake" (ll. 334–335). The statement is related to a theory of human nature that plays with Genesis: man grovels in the dust he was born from; he "sticks his nose in every pile of dung" (l. 292).

As in Milton, some of the greatest appeals to arrest time are erotic. *Faust*, Part I, centers around the hero's involvement with Margaret, and some of the complexity of the psychic battle is indicated by the character's attitudes to the arrest of time when Faust is in love. Simply glimpsing her empty bed, he is enraptured: "Here I could linger on for hours" (l. 2710). And when Faust declares his love, he declares also how he is drawn to fulfilling the terms of the original sanguine pact:

> To yield oneself entirely and to feel
> A rapture that must be everlasting!
> Eternal!—Its end would be despair.
> No! Without end! Without end!
> MARTHA: It's getting dark.
> MEPHISTOPHELES: We must be on our way.
>
> [ll. 3191–95]

As if caught up in the action to the point of forgetting the terms of their original pact, both Faust and Mephistopheles are speaking against the symbolic positions they represent with respect to time. Part of the richness of the poem lies in the way the attractiveness of an episode can momentarily get the better of the characters' allegiance to the philosophic quarrel. In *Comus*, where for very different reasons psychic loyalties are also not tied to absolute positions of good and evil, Comus can get momentarily caught up by the Lady's song; and in *Paradise Lost*, Satan, though carrying hell within him, is for an instant "stupidly good" at the sight of Eve. But "soon / Fierce hate he recollects" (IX.470–471). The difference between Satan and Mephistopheles in this respect is a mark of how much the two authors are committed to absorbing the arrest of time into song. Milton's devil can even pretend to serve mankind only on the brief though wandering path he takes to lead Eve to the tree; the romantic work may be thought of as that journey writ large, itself arrested in time, exemplified in the agreement that Goethe's Mephistopheles serve Faust for what is in fact the duration of the poem.

In Goethe the episode that most entwines the erotic with arrest in time is Faust's love of Helen. Their very meeting is a violation of the inexorable sequentiality of time, though it is significant that Helen is more mythic, Faust a more "historical" being; her duration is that of song, their union that of poetry. The whole episode is imaginative experience in which, Faust says, "day and place grow pale" (l. 9414), and the lovers banish time altogether with a cooperative act of will:

> Past and future, mind may not possess:
> The present only—
> HELEN: is our happiness.   [ll. 9381–82]

In the unity achieved between the parts of the sentence—and, concomitantly, between the lovers—place and time are dissolved.

The antithesis of arrest is activity, and in Goethe's poem "restless doing is the only way for man" (l. 1759). Imitating his master Wagner and *his* master Faust, Homunculus reasons, "I must be active while I am alive" (l. 6888). As *Comus* scales down the temptation of arrest that belongs to Satan in *Paradise Regained*, so *Faust* presents, on the level of its junior protagonist, a smaller version of the central conflict over duration in time. Homunculus could use help from Mephistopheles: "To gird my loins for work would best suit me / Right now, and short cuts are your specialty" (ll. 6889–90). This little spirit of activity is ironically leagued with the arch shortener of ways; but if Homunculus, like Euphorion, chooses romantic destruction, it is in order to bide the slow process of evolution till, in time, he gains human state. Mephistopheles understands no such patience, and on whatever level he picks up the argument, rejects the temporality of creative process. Like Milton's Satan, he must delegate creative acts that lack the instantaneousness of building in hell or between hell and earth. He turns in disgust from slower labors:

> A pretty pastime that! I could put up
> A thousand bridges in the time it takes.
> This work needs skill and knowledge, it is true,
> But it requires some patience too.
> A quiet mind may work for years on end
> But time alone achieves the potent blend.
> And as for what there may be to it,
> There's many an odd ingredient.
> The Devil taught her how to brew it,
> But by himself the Devil cannot do it.   [ll. 2368–77]

The scene here is the witches' kitchen, where the grotesque preparations are relegated to those who add patience to their working skills.

Scene is everywhere a mimesis of the particular kind of stasis, as when the Circean sirens of Part II are set in a rocky cave, at the time of "the moon pausing at the zenith"—an emblem we have seen Milton use for arrested time. The sirens appeal to the moon to tarry, to linger out this night of consummation and ritualistic renewal. The triumphal procession that follows is a triumph of time, climaxing in the approach of Galatea. But she is no sooner arrived than departed, staying only long enough to exclaim, "O father! Delight! / Linger, my dolphins! I cling to his sight!" (ll. 8425–26). Like a Miltonic simile that arrests time in a false surmise of eternal presentness, the vision of Galatea crying, "Delphine, verweilet!" captures the moment that Faust does not mistake: "Verweile doch, du bist so schön!" ("Linger on, you are so fair!") Especially since

Faust regards the hypothetical moment as a visionary sight, and since Galatea's sight is of the moment—when the generations, time past and time future, come together—Galatea's *Blick* is the Faustian *Augenblick*. But the moment does not stay longer than this expression of stasis, and the scene dissolves into harmonies of praise to Process, the working of Eros in time. Like Milton's Sabrina—who also rises Aphrodite-like in an image almost too rich for its context—Galatea too must hasten away. The arrest of time is absorbed into song.

If spatial effects parallel narrative ones, the infringement on space represents the limit of arrest, as it does for Milton's fallen angels who violate earth and bridge the gap from hell. Faust dies while engaged in what is ironically an infringement on space, for he is reclaiming land from the sea. He is imitating God in a way that carries with it the dangers of satanic imitation, creating here "a land like Paradise" (l. 11569). Yet even in his last moment Faust never commits the ultimate arrest of the present that equals damnation. The concept of futurity and choice he reaches is like that taught Adam and the reader at the end of *Paradise Lost:* "Freedom and life belong to that man solely / Who must reconquer them each day" (*Faust,* ll. 11575–76). The very next line recalls Milton directly: the blind Faust envisioning man "umrungen von Gefahr," invoking his vision of a paradise regained, is the blind bard of the invocation in *Paradise Lost,* VII.27, "with dangers compast round." [18] Goethe turns to Milton, poetic father, for his image at this point, as Galatea returns to her father; there is no arrest of time but a vision of what such arrest would be, a moment the poetic sight of which is sufficient to redeem. As Faust recognizes in delineating his plans for posterity, it is not a question of a single but of continued confrontation with the desire for stasis; and the realm of experience of continual choice is the world Adam enters, the world *Faust* has been facing all along. "The sense in which Goethe was right: Continued life means expectation. Death is the abolition of choice. The more choice is limited, the closer we are to death." [19] Existence without expectation is hell, where "hope never comes / That comes to all" (*PL*, I.66–67).

Faust remains open to futurity, open to the experience of option to the very end:

> Such in their multitudes I hope to see
> On free soil standing with a people free.
> Then to that moment I could say:
> Linger on, you are so fair!
> Nor can the traces of my earthly day
> In many aeons pass away.—
> Foresensing all the rapture of that dream,
> This present moment gives me joy supreme.
>
> [ll. 11579–86]

Anticipating that moment appears to be the ultimate arrest in which the bond with the devil is renounced for the bond with mankind. Collapsing futurity in the anticipation, the moment would spell death. But no, the anticipation is the acknowledgment of what is to come, and instead of a denial, there remains this ultimate affirmation of temporality. Faust never says to the moment, "Linger on!" for at the very end he only hypothesizes such a moment, envisioning it in "something like Prophetic strain." His original wager, "werd ich zum Augenblicke sagen," (l. 1699), changes from indicative to subjunctive, "Zum Augenblicke dürft ich sagen" (l. 11581). Faust stands now on Miltonic ground, and as Chiron has told him, "For poets, time restrictions do not hold" (l. 7433). The arrest of time remains technically within the province of poetry, in imagined, rather than infringing, clock time. Not that the unalloyed sublimity that follows has room to argue this technical point; what follows is music, not legalism. Faust ends like the speaker in "Il Penseroso" on a conditional note, and his arrest is absorbed into heaven in song.

Arrest and Shelley

Among English poets perhaps no one has been as personally affected by Goethe's drama of the arrest of time as Shelley. He himself did some translation of *Faust*, and though he claimed to have "only attempted the scenes omitted in this translation [by Claire Clairmont]," [20] the work could not have been undertaken without a sense of how close *Faust* is to his own thought. When the Lord in the "Prologue in Heaven" speaks of a spirit who "seeks unbroken quiet," who provoked by the devil "must create forever," he defines man as Shelley defined himself, as one who goes on until he is stopped and who never is. In Shelley's translation of the Walpurgis Night we can hear the lyrist of the West Wind, the apocalyptic poet whose whole career is a revolt against the orthodoxy of redemption in good time.

> A sound of song
> Beneath the vault of Heaven is blown!
> Sweet notes of love, the speaking tones
> Of this bright day, sent down to say
> That Paradise on Earth is known,
> Resound around, beneath, above.

Toward the end of his life he writes as though Faust's temptation were his own. He describes the arrest of time while boating "under the summer moon, until earth appears another world. Jane brings her guitar, and if the past and the future could be obliterated, the present would content me so well that I could say with Faust to the passing moment, 'Remain, thou, thou art so beautiful.'" He stands, "as it were, upon a precipice . . . content if heaven above me is calm for the passing moment"—terms that must echo Faust's *Augenblick* and the agreement that the cry to the passing moment to stay should be the death knell. Most like *Faust* is the way the passage remains to the end in the conditional; he says, "If the past and the future could be obliterated," [21] in recognition that the unconditional arrest of time is death itself. How and to what extent Shelley figures the arrest of time in his own poetry is related to his confrontation with Milton.

Shelley's own comment on Goethe and poetic influence must seem strange. He wrote to the Gisbornes: "I will only remind you of Faust—my impatience for the conclusion of which is only exceeded by my desire to welcome you—Do you observe any traces of him in the Poem ['Adonais'] I send you.—Poets, the best of them—are a very camaeleonic race: they take the colour not only of what they feed on, but of the very leaves under which they pass." [22] Perhaps the traces of *Faust* in "Adonais" are in the way the Faustian temptation has entered the poetics of the elegy. Let us temporarily label as Miltonic the moment of linguistic option: "He wakes or sleeps with the enduring dead; / Thou canst not soar where he is sitting now." The second line echoes Satan's arrogance to Ithuriel and Zephon (*PL*, IV.829), and might be called Mephistophelean in the way it boasts of assurance and stasis. Now the poet, as it were, sits on his image, for "He wakes or sleeps" turns out to be no Miltonic option, no choice that is fall as we pass from a first to a second more dire awareness. No, "he is not dead, he doth not sleep— / He hath awakened from the dream of life." With an exuberance that has outraged generations of readers, Shelley grasps the fictional moment of arrest, deliberately opting for the equivalent in compositional terms of Faust's temptation to seize the moment. The poem concludes when the rapt poet can say to his fiction—that "the One remains"—"verweile doch! du bist so schön." A Miltonic moment of arrest is enthusiastically embraced and not released into an awareness of fall. Perhaps, like Faust, Shelley has found a technical salvation, one that "works" in poetic terms, for while he seizes this philosophic fiction, the concluding stanzas are all involved with motion *toward* a final stasis. The fiction is bid to linger while the poet addresses himself: "Why linger, why turn back . . . ?" But "Adonais" contains no specific echo of Goethe, and we must proceed more slowly in uncovering the way Shelley is, in his own metaphor, "colored" by his reading.

Most simply, it is as world redeemer that the figure of Faust could appeal to Shelley. The young poet, with his alchemical schemes, his interest in the occult, his "passion for reforming the world" [23] reminds one of the German doctor. James Rieger compares Shelley's science and schemes for a temporal redemption with those of Faust; both were interested in an immediate intervention rather than in laborious involvement with political and social reform. Rieger says about Shelley: "The thought of temporizing with social evil sickened him." [24] Shelley saw himself, though fallen on evil times, as miraculous reclaimer of the land.

On the same level, Shelley was attracted to Milton—or to his own image of Milton as philosophic radical: "The sacred Milton was, let it ever be remembered, a republican and a bold enquirer into morals and religion." [25] The connection between singer and reformer is at the heart of Shelley's *Defence of Poetry* (which defines "authors of revolution in opinion" as poets), and is everywhere the spirit of his Miltonic muse:

Like a Poet hidden
In the light of thought
Singing hymns unbidden,
Till the world is wrought
To sympathy with hopes and fears it heeded not.

["To a Skylark"]

The poet-reformer is differentiated from others who feel "the giant agony of the world" (as Moneta tells Keats) by his dreamy nature and its concomitant sense of isolation. He expresses his feeling of exclusion from the company of the do-gooders in terms that suggest the romantic identification with Milton or his Satan. In the poised "Letter to Maria Gisborne," Shelley saves the Miltonic stand for the worker in the world: Godwin, in London society, can be seen, "Though fallen— and fallen on evil times—to stand / Among the spirits of our age and land," while the poet remains in satanic isolation: "And here like some weird Archimage sit I / Plotting dark spells, and devilish enginery." The Spenserian and Miltonic words are mixed because Shelley is of the giant's faction. Throughout the poetry the passages about rebellion are those that most frequently echo *Paradise Lost:* the speeches of defiance in *Prometheus Unbound*, the end of *Queen Mab*, the opening cantos of *The Revolt of Islam*, the Wandering Jew pieces, the fragments known as "Pater Omnipotens" and "Milton's Spirit."

Shelley relates poetic activity to rebellion in personifying the reigning power as Time. This is not to say that raised to such abstraction his vision becomes apolitical; but it involves politics in the largest sense, for poetry distills the eternal out of quarrels with specific evils. The poet "would do ill to embody his own conceptions of right and wrong, which are usually those of his place and time, in his poetical creations which participate in neither." "As far as relates to his conceptions, time and place and number are not." [26] The poet's work is to arrest "the vanishing apparitions which haunt the interlunations of life," to wrest the moment out of time. Lifting his epistolary style to the height of this great argument, Shelley addresses the Power himself:

Proceed thou giant conquering and to conquer. March on thy lonely way—the nations fall beneath thy noiseless footstep—pyramids that for millen[n]iums have defied the blast, and laughed at lightnings thou dost crush to nought. Yon monarch in his solitary pomp, is but the fungus of a winter day that thy light footstep presses into dust—Thou art a conquerer Time! all things give way before thee *but "the fixed and virtuous will,"* the sacred sympathy of soul, which was when thou wert not, which *shall be* when thou perishest.—summer will come.[27]

The poet's tone, beyond his mixed quotation, captures the "unconquerable will" and "courage never to submit or yield" of Milton's Satan and of the fallen angels who prefer to debate "fixt Fate, Free Will" in hell rather than to submit in heaven. It is the will of Prometheus resisting Jove in the dialogue with Mercury that is filled with Miltonic reminiscence. The Titan is bid to disclose the secret "Which may transfer the sceptre of wide Heaven / The fear of which perplexes the Supreme" (*Prometheus Unbound*, I.373–374). The shadow of secrecy troubles the god with the "fear of change [which] / Perplexes Monarchs" (*PL*, I.598–599). Shelley is thinking of Milton again in *A Philosophic View of Reform* when he speaks of the "rapidly passing shadows which forerun successful insurrection, the ominous comets of our republican poet perplexing great monarchs with fear of change." [28]

Whatever effect Shelley expected Milton's and his own

verse to have on the autocrats of history, he thought poetry should abstract the struggle to that between the tyranny of time and the poetic, the satanic attempt to arrest it. The prophet of the "Ode to the West Wind" relates to the world of time like a Promethean sufferer: "A heavy weight of hours has chained and bowed / One too like thee." He must bear what "Adonais" calls the "weight of the superincumbent hour"—which the true poet turns into a vehicle of freedom of expression, the occasional poem. We might call this weight the burden of the present, in contrast to the literary inheritance of a poem, or the burden of the past. In relation to both, freedom lies in the way the argument of poetry removes conflict from the compromising rule of time; poetry, unlike politics, deals with the internal burden, which is cast off by an act of will when the poet turns from the role of redeemer to that of rebel and rises from his chained position on the lake to create a heaven of hell. The harmony that "suspended Hell" in *Paradise Lost* arrests time in Shelleyan music as well:

> And those are his sweet strains which charm the weight
> From madmen's chains, and make this Hell appear
> A heaven of sacred silence, hushed to hear.
>
> ["Julian and Maddalo," ll. 259–261]

In "Adonais," the relation of Urania to Milton and the morning-star–evening-star identity permit the imaginative act that releases Urania from being "chained to time"; the union of the speaking and the mourned poets becomes an emblem of the triumph over the universe of death.

In *Prometheus Unbound*—the fullest statement of the poetic rebellion against the chains of existence in time—the chains binding the Titan are themselves described in Miltonic terms.[29] More oppressive is the fury who, making Michael's vision by comparison seem like flaccid optimism, offers this vision of the place of the suffering hero in history:

> those who do endure
> Deep wrongs for man, and scorn, and chains, but heap
> Thousandfold torment on themselves and him.
>
> [I.594–596]

She may be mocking not only Prometheus and Christ but the Miltonic God who binds Satan with the false freedom to heap on himself damnation. Shelley's *Essay on the Devil and Devils* makes good fun of the schemes of redemption in time, but for Shelley the necessity for apocalypse to be outside time rather than at a planned moment in it is a profound aesthetic principle. He was sophisticated enough to know the need for reintroducing "chance, and death and mutability" when he first concluded *Prometheus* at the end of Act III. And it was no accident that this grand inclusion, like so much of his urbanity, should realize itself with Miltonic resonance.[30] But the turnings back—to poetic tradition, to the contingencies of experience—only point to the distance of the literary work from the realm of time. Like Milton's God, time may hold "dominion o'er worlds, worms, / Empires, and superstitions," but, Shelley's Ahasuerus asks, "what has thought / To do with time, or place, or circumstance?" (*Hellas*, ll. 800–803). The bold thrust of such timeless vision is expressed in the visionary answer of Demogorgon to Asia, as the single word: "Behold." All of *Prometheus Unbound* in this prophetic sense takes place now, within a single consciousness, so that the moral superiority of Prometheus to Milton's Satan—who enters and spoils created nature—remains untinged by "place or circumstance." The way the timelessness of metaphor escapes the limits of experience is epitomized in Asia's lyric: her soul is *like* a swan, it *seems* to float (II.v.73–74). Being "somewhat like thee" (the singing Voice) in beholding a vision of paradise, she approaches "something like Prophetic strain" without stepping out of song into the object world of fallen nature. The musical terms sustain this Shelleyan arrest of time. In a radical revision of the poetics of choice, not only is the moment kept from collapsing into fallenness; it is extended till it becomes an ocean of sound over which spirit soars, flying backward through time to recapture paradise.

After the Fall, Milton's Adam complains, "But past who can recall, or done undo? / Not God Omnipotent, nor Fate" (*PL*, IX.926–927). Shelley substitutes Jupiter for "God Omnipotent," Demogorgon for Fate, and envisions one who can recall the past—Prometheus. What may not be a legitimate weighing on a word in Milton becomes an extended action in Shelley: the curse is "recalled" in both senses: called back into memory, and revoked. In the romantic attempt to recapture the moment of loss, perhaps no single moment is as dramatic as that when Prometheus declares, "it doth repent me" (I.303). A single stroke wipes away all time between curse and revocation, all time between the statement of problem and the peripeteia, in which classical drama takes place. If we might briefly entertain such a moment as an emblem of poetic influence, it would represent a far more crucial stage than that of verbal indebtedness to Milton's Satan. In psychoanalytic terms, beyond the tension with an authority is the awareness that "nothing can be accomplished without one's having come to terms with the father, or rather, with his image or object representation." [31] And it is characteristic of his interaction with Milton that Shelley's greatest accomplishments are marked, not by language of defiance, but by sophisticated reserve. After the grandly Miltonic phrases of the Phantasm,

Prometheus follows with a line refined because it is banal: "Were these my words, O Parent?" The separation of the response into this question and the simple declarative, "It doth repent me," is like the casualness of the long-suffering Titan saying, "Grief for a while is blind." As when the chorus of *Samson Agonistes* reflects, "Oft he seems to hide his face" (l. 1749), tone is victory.

This arrest of dramatic time is not quite the beginning of Shelley's play. He had to include the original defiance, and we can use the fact that it is spoken by the Phantasm of Jupiter to stand for the modification that is so essential a part of the Freudian model cited above. One comes to terms with the father—"or rather, with his image or object representation." The displacement is crucial, for the imaged representation is very much one's own. We hear not Jupiter's but Prometheus' words, and the father figure stands not outside, but figured within the individual's recreation of psychic battles. Beyond the elementary satanism of verbal echo, the journey to maturity that is poetic process is "satanist" in being independent and imitative, occurring in its own imaginative space and time.

About an analogous journey Wallace Stevens says:

> This is not landscape, full of the somnambulations
> Of poetry
> And the sea. This is my father or, maybe,
> It is as he was,
> A likeness.   ["The Irish Cliffs of Moher"]

"As" here, as so often in Stevens, is the liberating word. If identifying with the father is the necessary step toward maturity, it is a matter of becoming as he is, conceiving one's own creation, not with his muse, but with one like her of one's own literary age. Breaking the identity, "This is my father," into analogy, "It is as he was," is a crucial point in coming to a relationship with an intellectual father. The turning point ("or, maybe," in the Stevens poem) is the word "or," the moment of Miltonic option that unbinds the chains of time and poses the poet at the crossroads of what "may be."

Perhaps the most important task of the psychoanalytic analogue is to suggest why the "or" of freedom is the Miltonic moment of loss. Here is Conrad Aiken: "To be able to separate oneself from one's background, one's environment—wasn't this the most thrilling discovery of which consciousness was capable! And no doubt for the very reason that it is a discovery of one's limits, it is therefore by implication the first and sharpest taste of death." [32] The moment of "or" of poetic influence shares with the moments of "or" throughout Milton's poetry the re-enactment ("The mourning process . . . requires time and repetition") of paradise lost. "The adolescent incurs a real loss in the renunciation of his oedipal parents; and he experiences the inner emptiness, grief, and sadness which is part of all mourning." [33] Such is the burden on the writer of "Adonais," the burden of the muse who accepts no limitation to the process of adolescence but death itself.

In an important study of the "Ode to the West Wind," James Rieger relates the sense of death to the role of the poet through the Orpheus imagery:

Priest, divine victim, and ravenous communicant, Orpheus is first and last a singer of songs. The leaves run before the Wind "like ghosts from an *enchanter* fleeing," and, "by the *incantation* of this verse," the Wind also scatters the evangel of a human spring. Shelley borrowed the pun from Milton:

> What could the Muse herself that *Orpheus* bore,
> The Muse herself, for her enchanting son
> Whom Universal nature did lament . . .

Citing Shelley's poem "Orpheus," Rieger explains the relation of death to poetic presumption: "In the passage last quoted, Orpheus cannot decide whether to take up his lyre or to drown himself. The singer of "Ode to the West Wind" need not so choose, or rather has no choice to make. The trumpet of prophecy will awaken earth *by virtue of* the death he embraces." [34] The wild spirit soars over the moment of Miltonic option, creating an ode that leaves questions of poetic influence far behind. Rieger does not need to explore the way "Orpheus," in contrast, has the singer pause in a moment of choice like some angelic narrator in Milton's epic. The whole poem is in many ways Shelley's most facilely Miltonic. There are no ironic echoes as in the grand, satanist, mythmaking poems, but one finds suspensions, reversals in word order, epic similes, the sense of loss caught in the landscape (from the blasted hell to the "Penseroso" moon), the delicate music of *Comus*. It is a poem about stasis, about loss, about singing, and just as singing suspends hell in Milton and Shelley, it is right that we abandon the clatter of satanist terms in turning to this more harmonious aspect of Shelley's relation to Milton.

One need not give up Urania for the nightingale in speaking of Shelley under the wing of a more benevolent muse. Neville Rogers notes that the "melancholy Mother" in "Adonais" is "the most musical of mourners": "The musical qualities of Urania, not found in Plato, are added from his conception of her in *Paradise Lost* as 'mistress of celestial song.' " [35] Though Shelley is the singer of "Orpheus," the unchallenging acceptance of a higher music may be likened to the nightingale's relationship to the lyrist.

> The birds are silent, hanging down their heads,
> Perched on the lowest branches of the trees

> Not even the nightingale intrudes a note
> In rivalry, but all entranced she listens.
>
> ["Orpheus," ll. 121–124]

Listening, for Milton, is an expression of the arrest of time without the confrontation of loss. Milton could not end a poem or even a descriptive passage (about, say, Orpheus) on the word "listen," for it leaves paradise unlost, the arrest of time not resolved into song. The close of Shelley's "Orpheus" but summarizes the whole effort, for to the chorus question, Does he still sing? Milton's answer would be No, alas; Shelley's is Yes, listen to me. The same assertive timelessness ends "To a Skylark": "The world should listen then—as I am listening now." One might argue that a line like "And singing still dost soar, and soaring ever singest" reconciles the stasis of song with ongoingness, much as do the saints of "Lycidas" who "sing, and singing in their glory move," but the gentle difference is established in Shelley's opening stanza:

> Hail to thee, blithe Spirit!
>   Bird thou never wert,
> That from Heaven, or near it,
>   Pourest thy full heart
> In profuse strains of unpremeditated art.

He may say, "Bird thou never wert," as Harold Bloom suggests, because the skylark is unimaginably far out of sight.[36] But "never" describes the timelessness of poetry, and may be winking at Milton's

> Celestial Patroness, who deigns
> Her nightly visitation unimplor'd,
> And dictates to me slumb'ring, or inspires
> Easy my unpremeditated verse.   [PL, IX.21–23]

The "or" that separates heaven, the realm of Milton's celestial patronness, from somewhere "near it," the more naturalistic poet's metaphor for "high up," is the moment of choice for the romantic's absorption of influence and assertion of freedom.

"To a Skylark" is an unlikely place to look for Milton's influence, but we must be wary of limiting influence to the multiplicity of verbal echoes of Satan and hell. Understatement has its triumphs too, and Shelley is at his best when writing, not as a Reprobate satanist, but as a more urbane artist of the Redeemed. *Prometheus Unbound* starts with satanist defiance, but moves to the sophisticated mockery of Milton's orb and its harmony. And "Julian and Maddalo" recalls the sweet arrest of time in Michael's colloquy with Adam in *Paradise Lost* as though concentrating on that moment were the gentleman's answer to the adolescent's impatience with the course of history. Indeed, it is no accident that "Julian and Maddalo" should so consummately achieve the quietness of poetic arrest; it is about one poet's confrontation with another, and to use Yeats's terms, "Accomplished fingers begin to play." [37] The poet as male initiate leaves behind the hysterical women, picks up "palette and fiddle bow," and measures in equanimity his maturity and independence. In "To a Skylark" it is dubious that Shelley actually thought of Milton when he had the lark sing "from Heaven, or near it"; but the slight sophistication of the qualifier may stand as emblem of the arrest of time as poetic influence. It is an arrest in both senses, for the romantic poet marks the end of more frantic rebellion while he asserts the timelessness of the achieved relation.

The moment of listening at the end of the Skylark Ode does not lose its lyric lightness when it takes on apocalyptic grandeur in *Prometheus Unbound*. Here too the timelessness of listening seems to recount or enact the arrest of time between poets. In Asia's history of the arts,

> music lifted up the listening spirit
> Until it walked, exempt from mortal care,
> Godlike, o'er the clear billows of sweet sound.

[II.iv.77–79]

One may say that in general, when the terms are musical, creative spirit broods "dovelike," without a sense of conflict. Hence even late poems like "To Jane: The Invitation" and "With a Guitar, To Jane" have what Havens calls a "Miltonic lilt" [38] free from discord with their ancestry. Hence also much of *Prometheus* concerns musical sound, for once the Titan has resolved his conflict with Jove, the four acts proceed with increasing aspiration to timelessness.

"What can hide man from mutability?" Prometheus asks, aware as is the whole poem that only song exempts from time and death. In the experiential world it will not do to pretend that "mankind had only to will that there should be no evil, and there would be none." [39] For the revolutionary, however, it is important not to minimize the extent to which social evil could be abolished by men so willing, and for the poetic visionary it is important to connect that willing with the "unconquerable will" that rebels against the tyranny of the Miltonic association of the moment of freedom, of paradisal presentness, with loss and death. Outside the suspended harmony of song the recognition of loss returns to the field of satanist Miltonism. This use of Milton can be playful, as in the "Invocation to Misery," Shelley's answer to the aesthetic remove of both "L'Allegro" and "Il Penseroso." It is less playful, despite the light, ironic tone of the Conclusion, in "The Sensitive Plant."

Shelley echoes Milton's paradise and calls his Lady "an Eve in this Eden" only to mock the celestial time scheme of *felix culpa.*

> And the meteors of that sublunar Heaven,
> Like the lamps of the air when Night walks forth,
> Laughed round her footsteps up from the Earth!
>
> She had no companion of mortal race,
> But her tremulous breath and her flushing face
> Told, whilst the morn kissed the sleep from her eyes,
> That her dreams were less slumber than Paradise:
>
> As if some bright Spirit for her sweet sake
> Had deserted Heaven while the stars were awake,
> As if yet around her he lingering were,
> Though the veil of daylight concealed him from her.
>
> [II.10–20]

One thinks of the dream of Milton's Eve, of the serpent as *ignis fatuus* leading her to the tree, of the wink at Edenic sexuality at the end of Shelley's second stanza, of the courtly humor in the suggestion that a Miltonic Satan fell just for Shelley's Lady. The *as if*s of the last stanza are Stevens-like assertions of freedom. It is all false surmise, in which a choice of poetic fictions replaces the Miltonic, categorical option of fall or no fall. The Spirit does not tempt the Lady but only seems to linger in an "as if." Perhaps that Spirit is meant to be confused with the one in the Conclusion, where the plant or "that / Which within its boughs like a Spirit sat" looks like the traditional tree or the serpent in it. There is no Satan in Shelley's Eden; indeed there are no serpents or worms at all, for such creatures, rather than the protoplasts, are hid in Indian thickets. The characters and events of this story of the Fall can resist alignment with Miltonic equivalents because these are imaginative creations, imagined anew in the new poem. Shelley is radically playful here, replacing a guilty serpent with a possible angel, replacing moral with seasonal fall, confusing man and tree, Lady and God, making "death and all our woe" seem like one more poetic hypothesis. The Lady seems to die, not from some moral necessity, but because one more poetic idea, having been arrested, is now released at the end of Part Second. There follows a long section of paradise lost, where the poet revels in the facts of death and decay.[40] If the parts of the poem seem to embody visions of separate states of being, they can be said to reopen the option Milton closed between "L'Allegro" and "Il Penseroso." It is not that the poet has gone beyond a vision of false paradise to this truer-to-experience view of fallen nature; the destruction is almost as mythopoetic as the paradise, and Shelley has moved, rather, from fiction to fiction. *Prometheus Unbound* had emphasized the lack of destruction at the time of apocalypse as a way of grasping the moment without loss; "The Sensitive Plant" goes further in its revision of the poetics of choice. Instead of drama being arrested at the moment of repentance, where the past is recalled and paradise regained, destruction becomes another in a series of moments, each of which is confronted as a separate fiction. The moment of choice becomes a choice of moments.

The Conclusion carries the Shelleyan arrest of time to its logical conclusion. The poet smiles, as it were, at the way the reader has fallen, has been made to view this poem as if it were a *Paradise Lost*, only to meet a "modest creed" at the end. Ur-

banity is the triumph, and the burden of literary past and the
burden of mortality are conquered by being handled with so
much casual assurance. The poet only needs to send out a *little*
faith to tipple with the giant:

> It is a modest creed, and yet
> Pleasant if one considers it,
> To own that death must be,
> Like all the rest, a mockery.

Maturity here is measured by the fact that the poem presents, after all, only a show of lightness. Shelley knows the
limitations of taking too seriously, as he thought Wordsworth
did, any kind of "faith so mild." But even if death cannot be
shrugged off, one can become more interested in problems of
attitude and perception than in existential angst. By making
the confrontation with Milton part of the subject of the poem,
Shelley confronts the Miltonic moment of arrest and turns the
discontinuity that is fall into the continuity of a series of
imaginative fictions. As in "Adonais," Milton's presence in the
poem allows it, in turning inward to become a poem about
poetry, to save itself (poems can only save themselves, alas,
not their authors) from solipsism or despair. When the Eden
of "The Sensitive Plant" is ravaged, Shelley also destroys the
pathos behind the Adamic cry: "Why am I mockt with death,
and length'n'd out / To deathless pain?" (*PL*, X.774–775).
To own that death, like all the rest, is a mockery, is to pass
from an existential to an interpretive problem. The very label
"Conclusion" announces this change from experience to exegesis. Insofar as the Conclusion is about literary interpretation,
about the way we read the myth of the poem, it is satanist
scorn at our having been taken in by the history as adopted by
the other party. "All things exist as they are perceived—

at least in relation to the percipient. 'The mind is its own place, and in itself Can make a Heaven of Hell, a Hell of Heaven.' " [41]

One may be guilty of critical satanism in diabolically devising Miltonism where it does not exist, or in reducing poems that, on one level, confront Milton to total fixation on the problem of influence. Shelley may not consciously have thought of Milton, or thought of him exactly in the way supposed in the instances examined. But whether as opening move, incidental repartee, or sustained conflict, Shelley's wrestling with Milton, like Jacob's with the angel, is an encounter that does not return to time without conveying benisons. Shelley's Miltonism must be seen as an inheritance that adds, in Yeats's terms, to the multiplicity of meanings that enable highly subjective art to "escape from the barrenness and shallowness of a too conscious arrangement, into the abundance and depth of Nature." [42]

4. A Time to the Space

Ah! lost! lost! lost! for ever!

So Leutha spoke. But when she saw that Enitharmon had
Created a New Space to protect Satan from punishment;
She fled to Enitharmons Tent & hid herself. Loud raging
Thunderd the Assembly dark & clouded, and they ratify'd
The kind decision of Enitharmon & gave a Time to the Space,
Even Six Thousand years; and sent Lucifer for its Guard.
But Lucifer refus'd to die & in pride he forsook his charge
And they elected Molech, and when Molech was impatient
The Divine hand found the Two Limits: first of Opacity,
    then of Contraction
Opacity was named Satan, Contraction was named Adam.

Blake, Milton

The depiction of stasis depends on the awareness of time.
Moments of arrest are measured by some simultaneous ongoingness; turns take place along the distances of time lost; stasis
in song is distinguished from the satanic attempt to carry it
out of time into space; and the temptation to poetic arrest is
woven into the continuity of verse or narrative. One could say
simply that the fallen world is a world of temporality, in
which presentness is apprehended only as it is passing away,
in which choice is realized only as it passes into determinate-
ness. But one would then have to identify Milton with Blake,
finding Creation itself the Fall—a misreading a little more
fallen than creative. We need to turn from fictional arrest to
historicity in Milton's poetics of choice.

Such a perspective is necessitated most plainly by the extent
to which Milton makes time a part of paradise. Were presentness and choice in simple opposition to the awareness of time,
perhaps one could turn to the descriptions of paradise before
the Fall for a longer look at stasis; the moment could have

"extension" without a sense of contradiction. Paradise, the eternal present, would know no time. But Milton deliberately makes Adam and Eve aware of time past, and it is an awareness intimately connected with the concept of choice.

Edenic Time

The account of the Fall does not restrict events to a single day, let alone the day of creation; the first parents have inhabited paradise for some time, long enough to see the rhythmic recurrence of days and nights as a measure of ongoingness. Eve, moderately absorbed in her own being and her own time, questions the reason for the stars shining while she and Adam are asleep, and is answered:

> Those have thir course to finish, round the Earth,
> By morrow Ev'ning, and from Land to Land
> In order, though to Nations yet unborn,
> Minist'ring light prepar'd, they set and rise;
> Lest total darkness should by Night regain
> Her old possession, and extinguish life.
>
> [*PL*, IV.661–666] [1]

The first four lines are rich with awareness of time future; the next two add—not really future possibility, though they are richer for that suggestion—awareness of time past. The exchange occurs after Eve's great lyric in which love becomes man's opportunity to share the divine perspective outside of time: "With thee conversing I forget all time, / All seasons and thir change, all please alike." One can only forget what was once known, and the knowledge of time passed is the basis of the love relationship. Adam and Eve have a little past in common, the awareness they share of days gone by that constitute the remembered, and therefore imaginative, reality that is the realm of love.

In the love lyric preceding Eve's question all nature is consummately praised as if joying in mere being, and then turned and made to be contingent on Adam. In a way the twenty lines form a passage of extended repetition, which, like those discussed in Chapter 2, seems to arrest time, capturing the moment in the turn on "but": "Sweet is the breath of morn . . . pleasant the sun . . . But neither breath of morn . . . nor rising sun . . . without thee is sweet." The extended hold on all of nature is dependent on the pleasure she takes in Adam's company, as though all times, past and to come waited on his presence. The second "but" that introduces her question ("But wherefore all night long shine these?") returns contemplation to time. A remark of Kierkegaard's helps explain how Milton uses the question to emphasize the scene's underlying innocence: "When you begin to notice that a certain pleasure or experience is acquiring too strong a hold upon the mind, you stop a moment for the purpose of remembering." [2]

Eve is not quite aware that her relationship to Adam or to anything in paradise could acquire "too strong a hold upon the mind." In itself the question about the stars seems rather to be the passage closest to expressing her self-absorption, her mistaking the conscious time she shares with Adam for all time. In this it is like the lines that introduce her song ("With thee conversing I forget all time"), slightly suspect because forgetting all time sounds like satanic arrest, the kind of stasis we have associated with Comus and passion. Such overtones remind the reader of the incipient Fall, and help to make the song paradisal. But Eve herself is free from such knowledge;

"I forget all time" turns out to mean, in the next lines, that she forgets what specific time it is, not what existence in time has been, for she goes on to describe exquisitely the times of day. In unfallen speech, what is ignored is not past and future but the fleetingness of the present.

Against this temporal background Eve's question creeps in like a miniature of the moment of choice the serpent presents. The beauty of her exchange with Adam depends partly on our recognition that here are the same problems we face in the fallen world but delicately turned around. While the task of the "uncouth swain" of "Lycidas" is to redeem the sense of the pastness of the past, to make the past "present," Adam's task is to make the present past. It is, in the most humanistic way, an anticipation of the educative function of Raphael and Michael. Adam is talking about the stars shining now, and he explains the present by making it seem a part of Eve's past:

> Millions of spiritual Creatures walk the Earth
> Unseen, both when we wake, and when we sleep:
> All these with ceaseless praise his works behold
> Both day and night: how often from the steep
> Of echoing Hill or Thicket have we heard
> Celestial voices to the midnight air,
> Sole, or responsive each to other's note
> Singing thir great Creator.   [PL, IV.677–684]

Adam reminds Eve of what they oft have heard, giving the new insight—ancestor of Socrates that he is—with the implication that she knew that already.

While Adam speaks to Eve, making the present seem part of their past, Milton makes that past seem present to us, and we read lines like "Millions of spiritual Creatures walk the Earth" forgetting all time between Eden and us till we are recalled by the authorial voice reminding us of the pastness of the past: "Thus talking hand in hand alone they pass'd / On to thir blissful Bower." We are tolled back to poetic time primarily by the reintroduction of the past, narrative tense— "they pass'd"—secondarily by the imagery of hands that must always be read forward and back in this poem ("her rash hand in evil hour"; "from her husband's hand her hand / Soft she withdrew"; "they hand in hand with wand'ring steps and slow"). Lastly, the comparative past is introduced to emphasize the choiceness of this moment: "it was a place [the poet, stepping away, speaks in narrative past] chosen [in some more distant past] by the sovran Planter, when he framed [when was that? further back? no, for Him there is no gap between good intentions and bad choices] all things to man's [we are with Adam here] delightful use."

Narrative attention to lengths of time preceding the temptation, far from diminishing the decisiveness of that moment, augments its significance. The choice of the fruit may be distinguished from the more immediate kind of option which does not gather all the past into it—what Kierkegaard calls "aesthetic choice": "The only absolute either/or is the choice between good and evil, but that is also ethical. The aesthetic choice is either entirely immediate, or it loses itself in the multifarious. . . . When one does not choose absolutely one chooses only for the moment, and therefore can choose something different the next moment." [3] *Paradise Lost* must convince that the first ethical choice, the "absolute either/or," carries with it the psychological impossibility of choosing something different the next moment, and the epic therefore suggests a length of time for Eve's deliberation and a substantial gap between her first taste and Adam's fall. The description of what Adam does "the while" Eve "so long delay'd"

extends that period and points to the new, fallen sense of duration in time as a bane. Suddenly the clock ticks too slowly; or,
more accurately, suddenly there is an intrusion of measured
time in which man is extended where before there was an easy
commerce of old and new. Eve's first fallen words to Adam
describe time with the new and indelible sense of loss:

> Hast thou not wonder'd, *Adam*, at my stay?
> Thee I have misst, and thought it long, depriv'd
> Thy presence, agony of love till now
> Not felt.   [IX.856–859]

Where their past was previously present, where they were
in each other's presence, there is now "the pain of absence," a
dearly bought awareness like the "Knowledge of good bought
dear by knowing ill" (IV.222). The absolute either/or puts
an end to aesthetic or momentary choice and introduces the
pain of irrevocability, the distance between present and past.
An end to immediacy, the new temporality is prepared for by
an awareness of the immediacy of the past in the form of memory. What Adam tells Eve, what Raphael tells them both, establishes the sense of time that is brought to the moment of
the Fall, the sense of time that it will be the task of the last two
books of the epic to re-establish.

Other references to past time in paradise shadow these educative encounters. After Adam answers Eve, the two pass to
their bower, where

> in close recess
> With Flowers, Garlands, and sweet-smelling *Herbs*
> Espoused *Eve* deckt first her Nuptial Bed. . . .
>
> [IV.708–710]

Reading just so much, one might momentarily mistake this approach to the nuptial bed for the first. But the poet goes on:

And heav'nly Choirs the Hymenaean sung,
What day the genial Angel to our Sire
Brought her in naked beauty more adorn'd,
More lovely than *Pandora*.

The syntactical difficulty, the way the sentence restructures itself as it goes on, affects the way the reader shares the experience of time in paradise. It turns out (we already knew, but such passages can make it seem first awareness) that this is not the first day Adam led Eve, that the description is really in the past perfect, another reference to antecedent time. The choirs do not sing about the nuptial day, for "What day" is not the object of "sung" but a prepositional phrase, "on an earlier day, when . . ." Eve was not "more adorn'd" than she is now but "more adorn'd" than Pandora, so that remembered time melts into imaginative time in which Pandora and Eve are one. How does Eve compare with Pandora? or with Delia, Juno, Helen, Pomona, Nausicaa, Proserpina? Associations are poised between the delightful and the damning, and the reader confronts choice in working backward to the associational typology, as well as forward to the moral resonances of a given poetic moment. Literary allusion is less a demystification of a moment's uniqueness than a slight mystification in which the determined strength of the past blurs into an "indefinite abstraction" of choice. Is Eve to be seen as more lovely or more hapless—perhaps more guilty—than Pandora? For the moment the openness of the choice is both ours and hers. In the above passage the real and the imagined coexist in the further abstraction between "What day" and this day, for Eve was presented to Adam by God, and invoking a presentation by a genial angel is an imaginative softening of a perhaps too real "Heavenly Maker" (VIII.485).

Later references to past experience in paradise are specifically about heavenly visitations and heighten the sense of what
has passed by contrasting the visits. The Son greets Adam after
the Fall:

> Where art thou Adam, wont with joy to meet
> My coming seen far off? I miss thee here,
> Not pleas'd, thus entertain'd with solitude,
> Where obvious duty erewhile appear'd unsought:
> Or come I less conspicuous, or what change
> Absents thee, or what chance detains?   [X.103–108]

Ultimately, his mission is grace, and the Son begins by recalling what is gone, because psychologically, "memory plays the
same supernatural role as Grace in Christian thought. It is this
inexplicable phenomenon that comes to apply itself to a fallen
nature, irremediably separated from its origins. . . . Remembrance is 'a succour from on high' which comes to the being
in order 'to draw him from the nothingness out of which, by
himself, he would not have been able to emerge.' " [4] But if
God and memory in the end work to draw man from nothingness, the immediate effect of recalling the past here is to confront its nothingness, to confront loss itself. The relationship of
awareness of loss to redemption is reflected in the experience
of the reader, for when the Son addresses Adam, the reader
awakens with surprise to the realm of what is past, suddenly
seeing that there was duration in paradise, time during which
the Son visited habitually. The change that absents Adam
opens up an imaginative realm precisely when it is seen to be
presently closed.

The sense of loss imbues Eve's reference to past days after
her Satan-inspired dream.

> I this Night,
> Such night till this I never pass'd, have dream'd,
> If dream'd, not as I oft am wont, of thee,
> Work of day past, or morrow's next design,
> But of offense and trouble, which my mind
> Knew never till this irksome night.   [V.30–35]

Describing the effect of this night, Eve makes us aware that there have been previous nights, and enough of them to have established in her mind a pattern of what "I oft am wont." We are not really getting a new piece of information, but as Eve says the words "Such night till this," we perceive the heavy change in a way we did not "till this." The new awareness of the difference, of what has changed, is like a dream of the difference that will be actualized with the Fall. As the Fall turns untroubled experience into a thing of the past, the dream anticipates the Fall by seeing untroubled sleep as past. But more than a foreshadowing, a type of the association of choice, fall, and a sense of the past, Eve's dream creates a past that can be brought, in memory, to the moment of temptation. As such it gives, in terms of "mimic fancy," a sense of things that have been, a sense of history like that which Raphael's rational discourse more overtly presents. Just as Raphael speaks to both parents, so the dream that is recounted by Eve to Adam presents a sense of past to them both; but whereas the angel's reason suits Adam more than Eve, the means of fancy are properly Eve's own.

Eve presents another premonition of the Fall that is associated with an awareness of the past when she recounts to Adam her earliest memory. In innocent outgoingness she is offering love—the attempt to recapture and share one's past— as Adam later expresses his love to Raphael by desiring to detain him with reminiscence. At the same time Eve's memory also intimates the distance between the first parents which later, in spatial and psychic terms, will bring about the Fall. "We all cannot remember the same things. . . . Memory, which allows us by analogy to understand one another, also keeps us apart." [5] Eve begins in the tone of one who has been peacefully living in paradise rather than that of a newcomer there: "That day I oft remember, when from sleep / I first awak't" (IV.449–450). The past gives a sense of continuity, of what is habitual and oft remembered; "that day" implies an intervening period of some time. The whole speech shows to what extent choice is dependent upon an awareness of remembered days and a remembered other self. Eve tells of her first moments when, seeing her image and starting back in surprise and delight, she came close, not only to the self-destructiveness of Narcissus, but to the destructiveness of Satan in love with sin as image of himself:

> but pleas'd I soon return'd,
> Pleas'd it return'd as soon with answering looks
> Of sympathy and love; there I had fixt
> Mine eyes till now, and pin'd with vain desire,
> Had not a voice thus warn'd me, What thou seest,
> What there thou seest fair Creature is thyself.
>
> [IV.463–468]

The repetition in the last two lines grammatically expresses the arrest that is passion. She is drawn out of self-love by a voice that introduces time when it introduces Adam—who is significantly at a spatial remove, just as he is temporally distanced by having been created earlier and by having superior knowledge of the intervening time.

When, after her fall, Eve refers to her new sense of the

"pain of absence," what is new is the pain that accompanies absence rather than the feeling, which she already knew, that someone or some event is not physically or temporally present. Eve's account of her first awakening presents physical absence —her distance from the image in the water—and, in larger terms, her psychic distance from Adam as she first saw him. Telling her story is a recognition of temporal absence, of certain feelings and events as past. It measures her remove from that time in Wordsworthian fashion:

> so wide appears
> The vacancy between me and those days
> Which yet have such self-presence in my mind,
> That, musing on them, often do I seem
> Two consciousnesses, conscious of myself
> And of some other Being.   [*Prelude*, II.28–33]

Eve's history serves in little the purpose of the large historical narrations, creating a sense of "self presence in my mind" as the ground of self-consciousness needed for choice. The conditions of freedom are established when the self sees itself and another, when two identities become simultaneously present rather than "determined" in chronological sequence. The context of the passage from *The Prelude* is particularly relevant to Eve. Wordsworth muses:

> Ah! is there one who ever has been young,
> Nor needs a warning voice to tame the pride
> Of intellect and virtue's self-esteem?
> One is there, though the wisest and the best
> Of all mankind, who covets not at times
> Union that cannot be?   [II.19–24]

Eve originally coveted such union, and the memory of the whole lakeside episode takes the place of the youth she never had. Eve needs such a "warning voice," something Milton cries for, not right before the Fall in Book IX, but at the beginning of Book IV, before the warning which we can hear in Eve's narration.

Her first reaction to Adam is also her first experience of loss. Called away from the image of herself, she follows till she sees him,

> fair indeed and tall,
> Under a Platan, yet methought less fair,
> Less winning soft, less amiably mild,
> Than that smooth wat'ry image; back I turn'd,
> Thou following.   [IV.477–481]

In terms of symbolic sexuality, it seems especially appropriate that Eve should be given this first recognition of loss; in Kierkegaard's categories, "woman explains finiteness, man is in chase of infinitude." [6] Eve recaptures the sense of finitude when, describing Adam as he was then but addressing him now, she faces and turns from her past in recognition of what is present. The original experience of finitude was her impression that Adam was "less fair," for if following him is to represent the first choice, it must involve recognition of something renounced for something else. There is no choice if the rejected alternative does not have an appeal of its own, so the incident is Eve's first lesson that what is immediately more appealing is not necessarily best. Not that there was a real choice at that moment; but looking back, Eve can carry with her the association of alternative with renunciation. "Nonbeing always appears within the limits of a human expectation"; [7] having seen herself first, and expected a form as fair, Eve is aware of the element of negation in turning to a man, "less fair." Many a reader of *Paradise Lost*, as well as Adam himself, has felt the attraction of the chivalric gesture of falling with Eve. Northrop Frye parallels Aeneas' meeting with Dido in hell, pointing to the generalization that a great author polarizes reality, not trivially, but in a way that implicates loss with determination.[8] There is no choice where it is not necessary to say "no" to one alternative, so the first parents are prepared with an awareness of past or hypothetical experience, alternatives to which time has said "no."

Eve herself is not misled about how open her first choice was. She admits, "what could I do / But follow straight, invisibly thus led?" And she notes how Adam wisely gave her little time to make up her mind:

> with that thy gentle hand
> Seiz'd mine, I yielded, and from that time see
> How beauty is excell'd by manly grace.   [IV.489–491]

If yielding does not look like the result of an open option, it does set the background for seeing choice as the alternative to determinacy. Recalling how she was guided then, we can see the difference, see that she herself must choose her fall. Satan, unlike Adam, does not seize but insinuate: "if thou accept / My conduct, I can bring thee thither soon" (IX.629–630). Eve chooses: "Lead then." Once that choice is made, once the Fall takes place, the openness of choice again seems lost. In contrast to her semireluctant yielding to Adam originally is the unself-conscious eagerness with which she responds after the Fall. Adam seizes her hand, and "to a shady bank . . . / He led her nothing loath" (IX.1037, 1039). Reservation is the mark of openness of possibility, of freedom; when feelings are unambiguous, choice seems dead.

In Book V, Raphael comes to create a sense of futurity and possibility, and to create a sense of past and the openness of choice. He provides the memory of the fall of the angels that allows the two alternatives "fall" and "no fall" to be simultaneously present to the choosing consciousness. Providing the material for memory itself acts, not to break continuity, but to establish it. Poulet says, "By remembering, man escapes the purely momentary; by remembering, he escapes the nothingness that lies in wait for him between moments of existence." [9]

Everything about Raphael's visit is designed to make it a confrontation of experience in time rather than a break in continuity. The hour is specified as noon, while Eve "within, due at her hour prepar'd / For dinner" (V.303–304). Laurence Stapleton notes that "the particular indications of days and hours in all the scenes that take place in Paradise are indispensable in creating an effect of continuity"; [10] the description of Eve at a housekeeping task adds to the sense of regularity and ongoingness. In a way time does have to be suspended to give a "picture" of history, and books V through VIII of the epic halt narrative time to make the past "present" to the reader as Raphael makes it present to Adam. Thus Adam sees the coming of the angel as a break in time, "another Morn / Ris'n on mid-noon (V.310–311), just as later he suggests that light "longer will delay to heare thee tell" (VII.101). Eve, on the other hand, is femininely at one with the rhythm of time and serves as the reminder that even heavenly revelation is something absorbed into human history rather than an interruption of it. She reminds Adam that there is little need for preparations or storage when provision is always present, at hand, in season.

In the scene that ensues, the choiceness of the present is related to the concept of choice through the awareness of the linear sequentiality of present moments. Eve is concerned

What choice to choose for delicacy best,
What order, so contriv'd as not to mix
Tastes, not well join'd, inelegant, but bring
Taste after taste upheld with kindliest change.

[V.333–336]

One may be surprised to learn that it is necessary to plan this vegetarian menu, but Eve's experience with fruit is preparation for the choice when one alternative will be the forbidden fruit and the unkindliest change it brings. "Taste after taste" is harmonious experience in time, and such change, "for delicacy best," like the cycle of days in heaven, "for change delectable, not need" (V.629), contrasts with the fallen world where the fullness of daily activity and housekeeping concerns may have to be renounced for the one thing that is needful. Kierkegaard explains, "There is only one situation in which either/or has absolute significance, namely when truth, righteousness, and holiness are lined up on one side, and lust and base propensities and obscene passions and perdition on the other; yet it is always important to choose rightly, even as between things one may innocently choose." Eve's housekeeping involves such little, aesthetic, innocent choices which prepare us, if not her, for the absolute either/or and weave intimations of it into daily experience. "How wide the gulf and unpassable," Blake says, "between simplicity and insipidity." [11]

A familiar "simplicity" is the line "No fear lest Dinner cool" (V.396). There is no hurry and no worry over passing time in the unfallen world, in contrast to the way a line like "Home to his Mother's house private return'd" (PR, IV.639) makes the re-entry of daily time startling. More important, the intrusion of colloquial tone and concern is not felt as an intrusion into the purity of Eden and does not have to be re-

nounced, the way lines which suggested any modulation in the
tone of *Comus* were excised. The line does interject our time,
poet's and reader's, into a description of paradise, but the
poet's mediation turns pedestrian fact into the smallest sorrow
more beautiful than beauty's self. Experiencing the occurrence
of such a turn in the most homey of details, we share the
richness of paradise. But more, when Milton stands between
Eden and us, he establishes a continuity between his reaction
and ours which replaces the discontinuity of paradise lost.

He mediates again in exclaiming over naked Eve minis-
tering to Adam and Raphael:

> O innocence
> Deserving Paradise! if ever, then,
> Then had the Sons of God excuse to have been
> Enamour'd at that sight.　[V.445–448]

Scholars have remarked that Milton enters the controversy
over the meaning of Genesis 6 : 1–2. "And it came to pass,
when men began to multiply on the face of the earth, and
daughters were born unto them, That the sons of God saw the
daughters of men that they were fair; and they took them
wives of all which they chose." [12] Why does Milton bring
that up here? The intervention of the exegetical problem itself
contrasts with the innocence of Raphael's intervention. An unusual turn has taken place in literature's customary position of
being, at best, commentary on the Word, for at this point in
Paradise Lost the problem raised by Genesis and its commentators seems to come from outside, seems to be in marginal relation to the text of the poem. Raphael is not to be tempted, but
the poet captures the indeterminacy of poetry, its implication
of moral choice, in opening the option of introducing commentary into the text. Milton may have known that each of

the kabalistic *sephiroth*, or emanations of God, is associated
with a body of angels as well as a specific archangel; for the
eighth emanation, Splendor, the order of angels is the Sons of
God, and the archangel is Raphael.

The point of such association, whether or not it can legiti-
mately be included in the patristic debate over the Sons of
God, is the renunciation that must be made of its relevance.
The poet's intervention seems to penetrate so much closer to
the center of biblical truth than do the labyrinthine byways
of hermeneutic conjecture. "If ever there were excuse for angels to be tempted by mortals" joins with "If ever there were
reason to bring up the issue of temptation." The "if" is the
conditional in which poet and reader share the indeterminacy
of paradise. "Then" is a word introducing hypothetical consequence, but its repetition (more than a Latin trope) serves
as temporal pointer: "then, / Then"—at that moment, not of
fictional arrest, but of Edenic history. Milton's imagined scene
has become the real truth to point to while we let fade the
Sons of God and the fallen history they inaugurate. We regret realizing that Eve will be more easily tempted by Satan
than Raphael is by her. But sorrow at the loss of innocence is
transcended by the sublimity of the loss of intervening time
as we are rapt beyond logical and theological consequence
into direct perception of unfallen time.

Raphael's visit is one of many events that make historicity
the boon, not the bane, of unfallen man. Careful always to
distinguish the sense of time from the sense of loss, Milton
makes a week elapse between Raphael's visit and Satan's return.[13] For Adam to have freedom of choice, time must elapse
between the guidance and the temptation, alternatives be taken
out of dictated sequentiality into the indeterminate order of
memory. It is as if the first parents were given a push and must

go a way before their motion can be called their own.

The lines that specify the time elapsed describe the voyage of Satan—"The space of seven continu'd Nights he rode. . . . On th' eighth return'd"—and picture his re-entry in terms designed to disentangle the incipient loss from the effect of time:

> There was a place
> Now not, though Sin, not Time, first wrought the change,
> Where *Tigris* at the foot of Paradise
> Into a Gulf shot under ground, till part
> Rose up a Fountain by the Tree of Life.   [IX.69–73]

The period of his wandering (represented in poetic time by the description of place) is the time the first parents spend in uninterrupted presentness before the crucial day. It is their opportunity to contemplate past and future, to recall and re-hearse what Raphael has told them. Memory requires the sense of interim and the chance to forget; "forgetting is the true expression for an ideal process of assimilation by which the experience is reduced to a sounding-board for the soul's own music." [14] About another writer for whom remembrance of things past was crucial, one critic has said that he "wrote at length in order to create within the frame of his novel an interval of *oubli*, the forgetting which would allow the reader a true experience of remembering and recognizing." [15]

A New Perhaps

Many a reader has approached the concluding books of *Paradise Lost* with the weariness of Shakespeare's Richard II, asking, "What more remains?" (IV.i.222). Having seen Adam, like Richard, undo himself, we turn to history as does Richard to a mirror to read "the very book indeed / Where all my sins are writ, and that's myself" (IV.i.274–275). Un-fallen reality appears but a dream beside the historical, fallen world, the world as we know it, and the vision of that world seems a rude awakening:

> Learn, good soul,
> To think our former state a happy dream,
> From which awak'd, the truth of what we are
> Shows us but this.   [V.i.17–20]

If Michael's visions present "the truth of what we are," their purpose is to prepare the first parents and the reader for choosing, for accepting the rightness of that truth. Joseph Summers says they must get Adam, "with his knowledge of the future, to be willing to begin human history." A new choice is opened, and as the poet directs the reader to choose to accept the justice of God's way, the way things are, so Michael comes to direct Adam in choosing things as they are. "Knowing the worst," says Summers, "he must be willing to live, to conceive life as possible and as possibly blest." [16]

The difficulty with such interpretation is that it is hard to see how much choosing Adam can do at the end of the epic. For the reader the Fall is the great moment that Milton makes present, and subsequent history, like the memories of Adam and Eve before the Fall, leave little room for option. Alternatives are real when they are simultaneous, not sequential, but the vision of history seems involved in sequentiality, event following event in a pattern that would seem to be at least as remote from the will of Adam as the first steps of Eve are from her "innate" desires. One might compare the determination that Eve remembers—"with that thy gentle hand / Seiz'd mine"—with the sense that all is now determined in the last angelic act: "In either hand the hast'ning Angel caught / Our ling'ring Parents" (XII.637–638). Neither occasion seems to present much choice, and even the final image, "They hand in hand with wand'ring steps and slow, / Through *Eden* took thir solitary way," though it lets them take their time, does not seem to offer opportunity for alternative. Why not cry out, like Camus's hero, that alternatives "would come to absolutely the same thing. . . . To stay, or to make a move—it came to much the same"? [17] If the choice is between staying in one particular place outside paradise or moving to another, how much choice is there? What matter if "The World was all before them, where to choose / Thir place of rest" when a flaming brand guards the entrance to paradise?

It is against such objections that *Paradise Lost* must reestablish the validity of alternative after the Fall. Every spatial image participates in the symbolic structure that makes the choice of "Thir place of rest" not an indifferent but a symbolic option. In his series of visions Michael makes physical stages into stages in a spiritual progress, and he turns from vision to prophecy as if from more immediate to more remote place. The physical stasis of "resting place" becomes emblematic of the temporal stasis which is the setting of choices, the moments of self-confrontation interposed between the going that is life and the ultimate arrest that Adam learns has been postponed:

> Death,
> Then due by sentence when thou didst transgress,
> Defeated of his seizure many days
> Giv'n thee of Grace.   [XI.252–255]

"Many days" are a period of choice during which man may repent; "Grace" makes existence in time a grace period between the Fall and the final judgment. Death, conceived when man fell but not brought into being immediately, shares in the two-stage creation that is as central to Miltonic theology as it is to human biology; existence in time becomes, not the penalty, but the "interposed ease" between necessitated and actualized finitude. Adam's great option is the option of seeing things thus, and stands as a model for the reader's great option so to view experience and find the justifications of God's ways in the adjustments of perspective toward them. Setting out into history, man is confronted with the choice of viewing historical sequence in the light that all events "rising or falling still advance his praise" (V.191).

Thus the sense of option at the end of the epic is not a vestigial remainder of the Fall but a new attitude toward fallen time. The immensity of one particular choice is replaced by the immensity of futurity; though there is not another tree of knowledge, there is the knowledge of subsequent history to be faced. Future time will provide repeated opportunities to test man, to create a pattern out of his repeated falls. But more important, futurity itself replaces the Fall; standing at the threshold of time replaces the experience of deciding for all time. It may be inadequate to speak of Adam and Eve "accepting" the yoke of wandering, for it is not a new choice they make that takes the place of the wrong choice they made. Adam's education does not involve making one more choice but rather, preparing for the conditions of a world of continual choice. Stevens says:

> He had to choose. But it was not a choice
> Between excluding things. It was not a choice
>
> Between, but of. He chose to include the things
> That in each other are included, the whole,
> The complicate, the amassing harmony.[18]

The paradisal choice "between" is replaced with the choice "of" a world of complete, "amassing harmony"; the eternal presentness of paradise is replaced with the perpetual present-ness of the fallen world which repeatedly presents man with little crossroads, instantaneous options, the continual succes-sion of moments becoming past.

Finding in the last two books, not a new option that Adam takes, but rather a sense of choice to be replacing the choice that was, we find *Paradise Lost* open: the world Adam enters is our own, and reader and hero share, in their own times, the confrontation with futurity. One way of expressing the open-ness of option is by the indeterminate image, in which narra-tive uncertainty about the smallest or most significant detail becomes an expression of redemption as ever present possi-bility. What must appear to be possibility from the perspective of time must be certainty from the perspective of the pattern. For example, through an equivocation about place, the vision of the end of days is clouded in sublime indeterminacy: Christ will come to receive the faithful into bliss, "Whether in Heav'n or Earth, for then the Earth / Shall all be paradise" (XII.462–463). The clouding looks like that of the melan-choly muse approaching something like prophetic strain; but realizing that the reality of the option will be erased—earth and heaven will both be paradise—we realize that this is no likeness to prophetic strain but the thing itself.

Earlier Milton describes the trumpet at God's synod:

> heard in *Oreb* since perhaps
> When God descended, and perhaps once more
> To sound at general Doom.   [XI.74–76]

Expressions of doubt can merely form an intellectual skirmish line when there is a theory open to question or a nondebatable conviction that needs protecting; but concerning apocalyptic vision, uncertainty itself becomes evidence of things unseen. Recalling "Lycidas" helps us see the expression of indefiniteness as anything but needless quibbling:

> Whether beyond the stormy *Hebrides*,
> Where thou perhaps under the whelming tide
> Visit'st the bottom of the monstrous world;
> Or whether thou to our moist vows denied,
> Sleep'st by the fable of *Bellerus* old,
> Where the great vision of the guarded Mount
> Looks toward *Namancos* and *Bayona*'s hold . . .

Great visions are guarded by the hypothetical, because "possibility," in the sense of what might be, and "possibility," with the overtone of what would be wondrous, are one. "Perhaps" is a means of presenting "the idea of the future," which, "pregnant with an infinity of possibilities, is thus more fruitful than the future itself." [19] Wordsworth, who often invokes Milton when conveying the wondrous, speaks of a *possible* sublimity (*Prelude*, II.318). "Perhaps" is fiction's means of fondling time, of providing the sensation of standing before futurity, as in Eve's request for a reconciliation "while yet we live, scarce one short hour perhaps" (X.923). Futurity is wondrous; in Book III, God discusses fate in the past tense ("by me immutably forseen"), the Fall in the present ("they trespass"; "man falls deceiv'd"), and redemption in the future ("man therefore shall find grace"). With no such future the fallen angels are ironically punished with the arrest of the moment, the satanic stasis toward which they aspired.

The climax of the vision of possibility and futurity is the description of the end of days when Michael spoke, "then paus'd, / As at the World's great period" (XII.466–467).

(The "as" is important, for "the World's great period" is just
where Michael is in the narrative; but Adam must learn the
difference between history, the working-out of things in time,
and simile, that which is "as" history is, the "false surmise"
that compresses time and gives the vision he is enjoying.)
Where the angel chooses to pause stands as a model for Adam
of the metaphorical significance of the option left him,
"where to choose / Thir place of rest." There is no "great
period" between the paradise Adam has lost and the one Christ
will establish, when "the Earth / Shall all be Paradise." In the
interim the sense of grand pause is replaced, foreshadowed,
participated in by reading metaphorically all the little resting
places man will find on earth "till we end / In dust, our final
rest and native home" (X.1084–85). Instead of the eternal
present of paradisal pause there are narrative pauses, like the
angel's at the vision of the end of days, and like the one at
the beginning of Book XII:

> As one who in his journey bates at Noon,
> Though bent on speed, so here the Arch-Angel paus'd
> Betwixt the world destroy'd and world restor'd.
> If *Adam* aught perhaps might interpose.

These lines that Milton added to the second edition create a
redemptive analogy between narrative and experiential resting
place, for it is just such pause that Adam learns to make in
the course of Book XII, just such interposition that he brings
to the world he faces outside paradise when left to choose a
place of rest.

At the narrative resting place—the conclusion of the prophecy of the end of days—Adam expresses his most internalized
sense of option. Having absorbed the standard by which temporality is praise, he reacts appropriately in comparing the

final expression of divine goodness to "that which by creation first brought forth / Light out of darkness." If holding in suspension all time between first and last things externalizes the sense of option, holding in suspension two reactions to the pattern of history internalizes choice once more:

> full of doubt I stand,
> Whether I should repent me now of sin
> By mee done and occasion'd, or rejoice
> Much more, that much more good thereof shall spring.
> [XII.471–476]

The option is a miniature of the whole poem. For he does not choose to "rejoice / Much more" instead of repenting; Adam stands where the word "or" is, between past and future, confronting temporality itself as option. He learns to stand in the present, with what is done behind him, what is good before him. One may compare such temporal understanding of the choice between repenting and rejoicing with Adam's expression of sorrow and joy at the end of Book XI:

> Far less I now lament for one whole World
> Of wicked Sons destroy'd, than I rejoice
> For one Man found so perfet and so just.   [XI.874–876]

Between this statement and that at the end of Book XII comes the understanding of duration in time through which the "either/or" of simultaneous alternatives is replaced by the "or" of presentness, with the past preceding, the future following it. To the knowledge of the Fall, the looking back at the past, Michael adds knowledge of the future, re-establishing the sense of alternative lost in Book IX. The concept of choice and the concept of time become one.

The Adam who shares the reader's sense of what it is to live in time stands at a certain mental remove from Adam the creature in paradise, and is conscious of projecting himself at a distance from himself in historical time. Standing full of doubt whether to repent or rejoice the more, Adam is taught an uncertainty principle; he is endowed with the distance which allows him to be both actor and observer, and which therefore establishes the freedom of that actor. An analogue for the relationship between self-consciousness and choice might be the scientific principle according to which the observer, standing in the field of the experiment, interferes with it, so that he cannot both know it precisely and have it work freely. The distance of self-consciousness is the mental distance of observer from actor that is requisite for freedom of choice; that is the freedom Michael's history establishes.

Before the Fall, we have seen, the distance that is self-consciousness was represented by Adam and Eve's relationship to their memories. What it means for a view of future history to replace memory in this way is suggested by Sartre, who calls facing forward "the spirit of adventure": "You suddenly feel that time is passing, that each instant leads to another one, this one to another one, and so on; that each instant is annihilated, and that it isn't worthwhile to hold it back. . . . The feeling of adventure would simply be that of the irreversibility of time." With the Fall, Adam knows that each instant is annihilated, that paradise is lost; but he has yet to accept the renunciation that accompanies choice, the realization "that it isn't worthwhile to hold it back," because a paradise within, happier far, replaces the one that is lost. The choice that remains is whether he will focus back or forward, entering the world with a "spirit of adventure." His experience in the last two books contrasts with the kind Sartre's Roquentin desired: "I wanted the moments of my life to follow and order themselves like those of a life remembered. You might as well try and catch time by the tail." [20] In the last two books history, replacing memory, is teaching that the only order for the moments of life to follow is the order that sees them moving inexorably toward the end of time. To live in a world of continual choice, a world of the possible, Adam must see that it is worth catching at the tail end of time—provided one apprehends the tail not as the moment fled but as the moment to come, the end of days.

A New *Durée*

Besides instructing in eschatology, Michael must educate Adam in the virtue of existing in intervening time that is patience.[21] Throughout Book XI, Adam repeatedly stumbles when he attempts to anticipate history, re-enacting the Fall in miniature. In part Adam must learn to stop intruding himself and not arrest the sequence of events at his present consciousness; he must achieve the impersonality of the epic artist, so that he may stand for and breach the time between himself and Milton, and between himself and the fit audience. On the other hand, the mistakes in apprehension are themselves redemptive rather than just a mark of how far Adam has yet to go; the process is suggested in a Kierkegaard passage about the relationship of the cultivated will to a remembered fall:

If one attempts to dismiss the unpleasant absolutely from mind, as many do who dabble in the art of forgetting, one soon learns how little that helps. In an unguarded moment it pays a little surprise visit, and then it is invested with all the forcibleness of the unexpected. . . . The art in dealing with such experiences consists in taking them over, thereby depriving them of the bitterness; not forgetting them absolutely but forgetting them for the sake of remembering them.[22]

Adam learns, not that he must avoid falling again, but that his own understanding and his offspring's obedience will undergo repeated falls. He learns not to turn away from the Fall absolutely but to "take it over," to remember it in each minor enactment. As a matter of proper seeing, such a perspective provides the godly course of "action" for those who must stand and wait.

After the prophecy of Christ's kingdom comes the final lesson in the series whose object is the understanding that acceptance of futurity must also be tempered. How far Adam has come is measured by the way he anticipates Michael's answer by the question, "will they not deal / Worse with his followers than with him they dealt?" (XII.483–484). The answer is the last look at time as we know it, at the slow pace of events that must work their course between the first and the second coming. Michael's answer is in a similar relationship to the prophecy of second coming as time *anno Domini* is to the Incarnation, and as the concluding books of the epic are to the narrative of the Fall: the expanse that follows the great moment must not seem anticlimactic but rather the dramatic working out in time of what was embodied in the moment. Thus Adam's statement of option made history, "whether I should repent . . . or rejoice," must not end the poem but begin its last prophetic section. Summers comments: "This is the climax. Another poet would have ended the narrative here. But Adam has not yet been brought to know the time between the Ascension and the Judgment, the time which we know. He has not yet been made the reader's equal." [23]

Adam is the reader's equal when he understands not only outcome but duration, when he knows not only the past and its consequences but the experience of enduring in an ever falling presentness. His last speech in the epic describes the difference between prophecy and experience, between collapsible and extended time:

> How soon hath thy prediction, Seer blest,
> Measur'd this transient World, the Race of time,
> Till time stand fixt: beyond is all abyss,
> Eternity, whose end no eye can reach.
> Greatly instructed I shall hence depart,
> Greatly in peace of thought, and have my fill
> Of knowledge, what this Vessel can contain;
> Beyond which was my folly to aspire.   [XII.553–560]

The exclamation "How soon hath thy prediction . . ." is based on the new awareness of how long the race of time has yet to run, and how different participating in that race is from standing on a hill and viewing selected scenes. Adam has come to see two finite spaces as one: the area of time beyond which all is abyss, and the area of human knowledge, beyond which it is folly to aspire. In contrast to serpentine sapience, which would hold the moment or fly into the abyss, knowledge has its right realm in the transient world, in the world of temporal experience. Learning to face futurity in full awareness of the difference between narrative and experience, Adam becomes —to use Summers' phrase—"the reader's equal."

Both the episodes of Michael's history and the dramatics of its narration are chosen to emphasize the difference between prophesying history and experiencing it. Bergson, pointing to the way foreseeing reduces an interval of time by "impoverishing the conscious states which fill it," directs us to a central problem of prophetic utterance in *Paradise Lost*.[24] If foreseeing empties time of the conscious states which fill it, Books XI and XII aim at "filling it," using Adam's reactions to suggest the *durée* absent from an overview of history. Rosalie

Colie describes the need for length in the concluding books "to make the long human experience more real, more actual. . . . Books XI and XII express the long, continuing process of history, the succession of event upon event that is the lot of fallen mankind." [25]

Milton does not need the imitative fallacy of long books to suggest the long process of history, but uses far more dramatic means of expressing extension in time. The difference between receiving sentence and enduring its enactment is the topic of the history Adam learns, the substance of history as man faces it. Parallel to the temporal distinction is the psychic difference between hearing the judgment, "Death denounc't that day / Removed farr off" (X.210–211), and understanding not to ask why God delays "to execute what his Decree / Fix'd on this day" (X.771–773). Ironically even Death, "Sagacious of his Quarry from so far" (X.281), has a better perspective on futurity than have the fallen parents before Michael's lesson. Eve first tries to make the best of what she takes to be a short time, "While yet we live, scarce one short hour perhaps" (X.923), and later moans the loss of paradise of even so short duration,

> where I had hope to spend,
> Quiet though sad, the respite of that day
> That must be mortal to us both. [XI.271–273]

As they have spent the night in paradise, "day" must already be understood metaphorically as the period between the sentence and its final execution. But this is the reader's logic, not Adam's. Sensing God's mercy, he hastily concludes "that the bitterness of death / Is past, and we shall live" (XI.157–158).

Jumping to conclusions is just what is the matter, for in this fallen state they want, like Satan, to have things concluded one

way or the other. Adam hastens history with an impatience
marking the youthfulness to which he tries to hold on. One
might say that Adam addresses Eve with the fervor of an
adolescent who knows no time between first attraction and
final consummation:

> Whence Hail to thee,
> *Eve* rightly call'd, Mother of all Mankind,
> Mother of all things living, since by thee
> Man is to live, and all things live for Man.   [XI.158–161]

No response could be more human than Eve's displeasure and
her feminine suggestion that they live a little first and not rush
things. Between this salute to Eve and (returning to epic tone)
Adam's matured accolade, "Virgin Mother, Hail, / High in
the love of Heav'n, yet from my Loins / Thou shalt proceed"
(XII.379–381), comes the education to experience in time.
About the first of these addresses Summers comments, "The
'Hail' is startling; it embodies both Adam's 'knowledge' and
his ignorance of all the centuries which will ensue before the
second Eve will be so addressed."[26] The second address is
made with the knowledge he has acquired.

If Adam is at first an impatient pupil eager to draw conclusions, it is because he is as yet fixated at the mental state of
the Fall. His crucial conclusion had been made almost paren-
thetically, as if thrown out without stopping while the argument hastened along:

> some cursed fraud
> Of Enemy hath beguil'd thee, yet unknown,
> And mee with thee hath ruin'd, for with thee
> Certain my resolution is to Die.   [IX.904–907]

The two tantalizing words "yet unknown" help direct our
desire to cry out, "Stop a minute!" as distinct from the reac-

tion "Don't stop now!" to Eve's feminine mistake of pausing a while to consider the serpent's argument. If later it is Eve who calls for suicide, her reason is more complex than a desire to have done with it. In contrast, Adam, who first too hastily concluded that death would not trouble them, next too hastily assumes death to be a desideratum:

> Henceforth I fly not Death, nor would prolong
> Life much, bent rather how I may be quit
> Fairest and easiest of this cumbrous charge,
> Which I must keep till my appointed day
> Of rend'ring up, and patiently attend
> My dissolution.   [XI.547–552]

The last phrase almost mocks the ones before, for Adam does not yet understand what patience is and speaks of it like a pupil impatient to please who repeats by rote what he has not yet comprehended. Michael answers him abruptly, not to match his student's sharpness, but to point out how far Adam is still from being able to learn from any verbal formula: "Nor love thy Life, nor hate; but what thou liv'st / Live well, how long or short permit to Heav'n" (XI.553–554). The tone is authoritative and sharp because nothing else, nothing more could be said by way of aphoristic answer; instead, Michael immediately turns Adam's attention away from patterned truths to "another sight," another more direct confrontation with experience, for only experience can prepare the first parents for experience. This potential contradiction is made possible by the device of the visions, in which art becomes, not an antithesis or a short cut, but a kind of experience itself. Adam is made to go through in time what he would know instantaneously, out of time.

It is a mark of thematic unity that Eve approaches the tree

with an argument that turns on just the same mistake about the temporality of knowledge:

> In the day we eat
> Of this fair Fruit, our doom is, we shall die.
> How dies the Serpent? hee hath eat'n and lives,
> And knows, and speaks, and reasons, and discerns,
> Irrational till then.   [IX.762–766]

With a perspective that sees "the day" only as the part of the day already passed, Eve concludes the death decree to be invalid. Her five *and*s represent the thinking process of arrested presentness, in "Allegro" fashion, without consciousness of choice as a process that takes place in time. She knows the truth of the five present-tense verbs that follow "hath eat'n": *lives, knows, speaks, reasons, discerns*—just the sort of knowledge that grows on trees. But she does not know the limits of reason, the limits of human knowledge of the future. She has been told, "In the day we eat . . . we shall die," and nothing else could have been told her about the nature of the transition from conditional to indicative. Only in the first and second visions of Michael does the abstract threat "We shall die" seem converted from formula to fact. Michael's history must introduce a willingness to face futurity as ignorance, to understand the difference between outlined knowledge and the determination of how things will in fact work out.

In Book XI it is relatively simple to distinguish the perception of the moment from the experience in time; Adam is given a vision—by definition a perspective in arrested time—and then the conversation with Michael points to the gap between what can be so seen and what it is to experience history. The change to the prophecies of Book XII is a mark of Adam's progress (not sleepiness), for the difference between outlined and lived history is subtler when all is narrative; the change also brings Adam closer to the reader, for whom the whole poem is narrative. On these two counts the final book must suggest within the narrative process itself two perspectives, foreshortened and endured time.

The model is the exodus from Egypt, a type of fall and redemption, and the biblical experience which is repeatedly accompanied by an injunction to be experienced directly, not as distant history. The Bible asks that every generation recount the story of the Exodus as emotive and ethical experience, redemption felt as personally as Adam learns to see good brought from evil in other times. "Thou shalt show thy son in that day, saying, 'This is done because of that which the Lord did unto me when I came forth out of Egypt'" (Exodus 13 : 8). And beyond this inclusiveness is the vision of the Exodus as involving the son, the student, as directly as his forebear: "We were Pharaoh's bondmen in Egypt; and the Lord brought us out of Egypt with a mighty hand" (Deut. 6 : 21).

Milton's account of the Exodus in Book XII not only itself involves more immediate apprehension of the past, but also points to the technique used throughout for achieving a sense of ongoing experience within the framework of narrative. The whole story is outlined first of how Pharaoh "seeks / To stop their overgrowth,"

> Till by two brethren (those two brethren call
> *Moses* and *Aaron*) sent from God to claim
> His people from enthralment, they return
> With glory and spoil back to thir promis'd Land.
>
> [XII.169–172]

The present tense is part of the magic, especially the parenthetical presentness of Michael talking to Adam, which gives the sense of calling history into being. But it is one thing to talk of redemption, another to experience the trial, the pains, the delays, and the uncertainties of working out an abstract idea in actuality. It is all narrative, of course, but the hundred lines that follow are dedicated to filling in with some of the conscious states whose neglect is the foreshortening that is prophecy. The passage begins with the words "But first" and continues at a slower pace and with a respect for detail that suggests the continuity of experience. All history is here, the images of perverted fertility, storm, locusts, darkness, and most of all the "River-dragon" suggesting the larger domination of Satan. Seeing the larger history in a more particular one is part of the education in experiencing the more particular, in experiencing all the Egypts between the first fall and the final redemption. With petty repetitiveness, Pharaoh submits, then hardens his heart,

> till in his rage
> Pursuing whom he late dismiss'd, the Sea
> Swallows him with his Host, but them lets pass
> As on dry land between two crystal walls,
> Aw'd by the rod of *Moses* so to stand
> Divided, till his rescu'd gain thir shore.   [XII.194–199]

The passage first lets the Israelites pass, then goes back and fills in the detail of the walls divided. It is one thing to see them on the safe shore, another to understand the suspension involved as they pass. H. R. MacCallum calls it "a loop in time," a narrative device which shows that "the ends to be brought about by Providence exist from the beginning." [27]

The technique recalls the reference to the tumult of the drowning "*Memphian* Chivalry":

> While with perfidious hatred they pursu'd
> The Sojourners of *Goshen*, who beheld

> From the safe shore thir floating Carcasses
> And broken Chariot Wheels.   [I.308–311]

First placing the Hebrews on the safe shore, the passage returns to the wreckage, emphasizing the difference between the counterplot of outlined redemption and the experience that catches up people and events propelled in the opposite direction.[28] The difference between foreseen and endured history reaches a climax at the end of Michael's expansion of the Exodus theme:

> at length they come,
> Conducted by his Angel to the Land
> Promis'd to *Abraham* and his Seed: the rest
> Were long to tell, how many Battles fought,
> How many Kings destroy'd, and Kingdoms won,
> Or how the Sun shall in mid Heav'n stand still
> A day entire, and Night's due course adjourn,
> Man's voice commanding, Sun in *Gibeon* stand,
> And thou Moon in the vale of *Aialon*,
> Till *Israel* overcome; so call the third
> From *Abraham*, Son of *Isaac*, and from him
> His whole desent, who thus shall *Canaan* win.
>
> [XII.258–269]

The first lines seem to be bringing to a cadence the long expansion on the return to the Promised Land. Then comes that strange clause, "the rest / Were long to tell," which states that the narrative is putting aside just what it proceeds to tell; the passage points precisely to the difference between such outline narrative and extension in time. In hurrying over the episode of the sun standing still, where even clock time is too fast for working out the events of the day, the packing-in of events in the ten lines before the whole enormous sentence can end comes as close as is imaginable in narrative to convincing the hearer of what is beyond narrative: duration in time.

But Michael is still not quite finished, and in the fifty lines that follow the third statement of arrival in Canaan we are back again before the event:

> And therefore shall not *Moses*, though of God
> Highly belov'd, being but the Minister
> Of Law, his people into *Canaan* lead;
> But *Joshua* whom the Gentiles *Jesus* call,
> His Name and Office bearing, who shall quell
> The adversary Serpent, and bring back
> Through the world's wilderness long wandr'd man
> Safe to eternal Paradise of rest.   [XII.307–314]

In this grand reading of fact as metaphor Adam is confronted both with the facticity of his own exile and its larger metaphoric significance. The Hebrews' wandering in the desert seems but a further reading of the "wandering steps and slow" with which Adam and Eve enter the world of time at the end of the epic, and the arrival at the Promised Land as the safe return to the "paradise of rest." The sentence begins by telling how, not Moses, but Joshua must lead the return, and the rapidity of the change of focus from Joshua to Jesus is the rapidity of schematic rather than incarnated truth. The "meanwhile" that follows the passage establishes once again the difference which Adam must be prepared to face.

One of the details Michael adds to the narrative of wandering in the desert is the people's request to hear the voice of God mediated through Moses. Though one expects the poet to seize on parallels to the universal redeemer, this mediation is a special case of the difference between narrated and unmediated experience. Moses as transmitter of God's word sug-

gests Michael's relationship to Adam, and serves as a reminder
that although Michael tries to indicate within his narrative the
difference between foretelling and experiencing, the real difference is between the pattern revealed by the angel and the
world Adam will himself have to face outside paradise. The
angel as historian is like Moses as lawgiver, presenting a mediated way, in time, as a preparation for more immediate—that
is, incarnated—truth:

> So Law appears imperfet, and but giv'n
> With purpose to resign them in full time
> Up to a better Cov'nant, disciplin'd
> From shadowy Types to Truth.   [XII.300–303]

The veiled muse of "shadowy types" presents "something like
prophetic strain," coming as close as words can to experiential
truth. The difference between the law and the better covenant
parallels the difference between what can be predicted about
history and the actuality, the difference between what the
angel shadows forth and truth. The reason for including Mosaic law in a Christian pattern is always a touchy point, but
Milton dwells on the issue precisely because of that difficulty,
educating the reader, together with Adam, in the existential
fact that the only complete explanation is the existence of the
thing itself.[29] This is not to deny that, for the religious poet,
there are real explanations; but his greatest power is, not in
offering us new explanations or in convincing doubters by
means of the old ones, but in transforming our attitude toward
actuality so that we approach it rather than its reason with the
awe of Adam setting out into the real world.

Perhaps Milton's boldest use of this technique elsewhere is
in the involved and seemingly unnecessary rationalistic

squirming before the pronouncement of judgment on the serpent:

> more to know
> Concern'd not Man (since he no further knew)
> Nor alter'd his offense; yet God at last
> To Satan first in sin his doom appli'd,
> Though in mysterious terms, judged as then best:
> And on the Serpent thus his curse let fall.   [X.168–174]

Northrop Frye comments, "Milton does not know why the serpent was cursed, and it is characteristic of a curious flat-footed honesty in Milton's mind that he should spread so obvious a bewilderment over a dozen lines of blank verse." [30] More than curious, it is an extraordinary confrontation of the limits of perception in time—limits we share, because though literally "Man" is Adam, the idea of the concern of man over the issue of the condemnation of the serpent is more strictly the problem of Milton and reader with the Bible. Unlike poetry, with its indeterminacies and moments of option, the Bible offers no choice. Milton capitalizes on this crux to have poetry look self-consciously at its own limits. Beyond the determined strictness of the sentence is the larger context of Christ's mercy, in which poetry's indeterminacy participates. In this passage we are all participants, included in the parenthetical community of those who "no further knew." Adam, Milton, and reader share that ignorance, establishing an intimacy in face of the awesome voice. The reverence with which the entire poem confronts the sanctity of time is caught in the phrase "judg'd as then best"; the whole passage becomes a lesson in the difference between the explanation and the fact of the curse, and similarly, the difference between the mys-

terious terms of the cursing of the serpent and the terms in
which the curse will be actualized in Christian history:

> So spake this Oracle, then verifi'd
> When *Jesus* son of *Mary* second *Eve*,
> Saw Satan fall like Lightning down from Heav'n.
>
> [X.182–184]

This is half narration, half prophecy, using the limitations of
narrative to point to what is beyond narrative. The anticipations in the poem, far from being undramatic, heighten the
sense of actuality in the fuller accounts. God, spelling out
Michael's charge to him, does not detract from the drama of
Michael carrying out that charge, and there is all the difference in the world between the injunction "So send them forth,
though sorrowing yet in peace" (XI.117) and the actual last
lines of the epic. That difference is what Adam experiences
in the last two books, what the reader experiences throughout
between the prose arguments prefixed to the separate books
and their actualization in poetry.

Paradise Regained further humanizes the problem of time
treated in the last books of *Paradise Lost*. As Adam in the
earlier work must choose not to seek speedy identification
with *adamah*, the earth to which he will, in time, return, so
Jesus in the later poem must choose temporality over easy
identification with the Father. In this epic struggle against
abortive futurity it is Satan who pleads, like Wotan in Wagner's *Die Walküre*, for "das Ende":

> I would be at the worst; worst is my Port,
> My harbor and my ultimate repose,
> The end I would attain, my final good.   [III.209–211]

Arnold Stein says: "The protagonist waits, in perfect resignation to time and God's will, for the worst-best. The antagonist hurries, forcing his resignation to time and God's will, for the best-worse." [31] Satan does not understand, even if he is consciously luring Christ with the question, "If I then to the worst that can be haste, / Why move thy feet so slow to what is best?" (III.223–224). One could contrast such satanic haste with the innocent hurry when Adam and Eve go off to work. There the line "So all was clear'd, and to the Field they haste" (*PL*, V.136) is followed by the words "But first, . . ." and seventy-five lines ensue before Milton picks up where he left off—"On to thir morning's rural work they haste." The acknowledgment of God that is prayer is one with the acknowledgment of time that is the interval between the two occurrences of the word "haste." That acknowledgment, that interval, is what Satan in *Paradise Regained* would have Christ deny. Northrop Frye points to the way the two epic temptations are related: Adam and Christ are both tempted to premature imaginative acts, attempts to force God's hand before the lapse of time his will has decreed.[32]

Christ stands his ground: "My time I told thee (and that time for thee / Were better farthest off) is not yet come" (*PR*, III.396–397). (We identify such use of parentheses as a stylistic expression of the theme; Satan makes ironic use of them in *Paradise Lost*, VI.163.) The quoted parenthesis grammatically suspends God's final judgment of Satan as that judgment is suspended in historical time: the moment is not yet come. Christ tells Satan, "I endure the time, till which expir'd, / Thou hast permission on me" (*PR*, IV.174–175). Satan argues that the time is ripe, "now at full age, fulness of time, thy season" (IV.380), but Christ, like the "Lycidas" poet, knows that unripeness is the human condition, that anticipa-

tion is both pride and despair. So Dante explains the original
fall of Satan: "The first proud spirit, who was the highest of
creatures, fell unripe through not waiting for light." [33] It is
an unripeness Milton echoes again and again in *Paradise Lost*
in the epic similes that play with the relation of Satan to physical light and to God as light. Like the fullness of time in the
natural cycle, Christ will dawn in due time. He, like Samson,
"knows no spells," and must not break out of human time to
assert his godhead. In this light the whole event of the temptation in the wilderness as a break in social and temporal continuity calls for a final re-entry. So *Paradise Regained* ends:

> Now enter, and begin to save mankind.
>   Thus they the Son of God our Savior meek
> Sung Victor, and from Heavenly Feast refresht
> Brought on his way with joy; hee unobserv'd
> Home to his Mother's house private return'd.

No line could more express Christ's humanity than this last,
and the world we re-enter after our absorption in the poem
is a world we experience Christ sharing with us. *Paradise Regained* approaches a real sense of presentness, of ongoing human time.

Blake and the Eternals' Time

When the Son, standing on the temple pinnacle, answers
Satan in *Paradise Regained*, the poem reaches a moment of arrest. Levels of textuality and differences in temporality are
dissolved as the Gospel Jesus interpreting Deuteronomy 6 : 16,
Milton interpreting Luke 4, and the reader interpreting this
line of the poem stand together before the same dispensation
of the Word: "Tempt not the Lord thy God; he said and
stood" (IV.561). Does this answer mean "Tempt not Him"

or "Tempt not me"? Time is arrested in the injunction itself, which does not let one meaning supplant the other but holds both in simultaneous presence. The stasis in which choice can occur is given temporal location in the pause of the mid-line caesura; and the four short words "he said and stood," as though nailing him to the spot, extend the relation of vision to verse. Jesus standing on the pinnacle images prophetic standing on the moment of choice, the moment between the warning word and the alternative interpretations or courses of action that may be taken. Then, moving on from such stasis and opening up like a Blakean vortex, the passage that follows returns us to epic simile and the whole sense of historical time this poem seemed to have abandoned.

The Son, at that moment of scriptural citation, asserts his continuity in the prophetic line. Coming not to destroy the prophets but to fulfill them, he expresses his awareness of the distinction by citing Scripture, by standing in relation to Mosaic dispensation as commentator to text. Milton's Jesus did not put on the knowledge with the power at the instant of a divine shudder in the loins; the self-knowledge he has was gained by studying the old texts, and the self-knowledge he asserts is his proper relation to those texts. Standing by— perhaps we can say *on*—the Word, and resisting to the last the temptation of abortive self-assertion, the Son fulfills his final trial, his final moment of choice. Milton, expanding the account in Luke, but resisting to this point fuller statement of the Son's divinity, likewise fulfills the choice that makes *Paradise Regained* a respectful acknowledgement of, yet independent departure from, scriptural authority.

Literary and divine sons thus confront the moment of choice as the moment of resolution of the generational conflict. It could seem too radical a metaphor to say that standing on the pinnacle, the Son represents the successful resolution of the Oedipal complex; but Milton's previously constrained epic verse suddenly breaks into simile and carries us to just this comparison. Jesus, like him who slew the "Theban monster," knows the nature of man. Referring to Sophocles' version of the myth, we could use the two-pronged stick with which Oedipus blinds himself, like the one with which he struck Laius, and like the forked road at which he encountered Laius, as a figural representation of the moment of choice. The two prongs that merge into one, Thomas Gould has made clear, can serve as an emblem of man's bisexual generation.[34] Recognizing the textuality out of which a moment of choice comes, and standing before alternatives at the moment of choice, the poet presents the successful Oedipal outcome.

All of Blakean myth could be said to be derived from that choice opening out into new imaginative space. As the central identity of the Son (Milton overwhelmingly prefers to call him that) is his humanity, his knowledge of himself as man in relation to God the Father, so for Blake all depends on the recognition of the Eternal Humanity Divine. As the Miltonic moment of choice seems to represent the point at the center of the fork of generation, so in Blake the crucial choice is an integration that will bring the separated sexes together in union with a primal third. In Night the Seventh (A) of *The Four Zoas*, the account of the fall of Albion or primal man given by the Shadow of Enitharmon introduces Urizen as a generated son of Vala. Then, as if returning to and coping with the Oedipal element of disunion, the Spectre tells Los and Enitharmon, "If we unite in one[,] another better world will be / Opend within your heart & loins & wondrous brain" (86.42–43). Blake's dense little poem "My Spectre around Me" represents the forking of the "me" into Spectre and Emanation. The Spectre's speech in Night the Seventh represents a return, then, to the point of division. Disunion is caused by the possessive "female will"; the self-annihilation that leads to reunion is predicated on a new creative will, a second or revised will.

For Blake's Los and his Spectre, the moment of recognition and reintegration is an opening of the center. Inspired by the Divine Mercy, Los recognizes "a world within / Opening its gates" (86.7–8). For Milton's Son and his Satan, the citation of Deuteronomy further opens the interpretation of "Son"— an issue Satan wanted to close—and opens up the text as a whole for the new context and its new temporality. The essential choice to assert identity in relation to an inherited literary line is like the essential prophetic poet's business not to negate but to open up a shadowed world into new imaginative space and time, more than on earth was previously understood. Similarly, in imagining the two-stage conception of Sin by Satan,[35] in recounting at length the separated stories of the fall of the angels and the fall of man, in creating more temporal space between the fall of Eve and the fall of Adam, Milton opens the inherited texts into new space that is his own. Perhaps most important for the composition of *Paradise Lost* and for the implied relation of Milton's poetry generally to an inherited line of biblical exegesis is the view of the two-stage begetting of the Son that Milton expounds in *De Doctrina Christiana*.[36] He denies the necessity of the Son's coeternality and distinguishes the elevation or metaphoric begetting from the inception of the Son at a divinely chosen point in time. The task of distinguishing the times is passed on from Milton's version of the Father (creating the Son), to the Son (creating the cosmos), to Milton (creating the separated Persons and separated times of *Paradise Lost*). It is then passed on to Blake (creating the separation of Milton and his emanation, and the separation and division of Eternal Man). Los, Blake's figure of the prophet-poet, labors in time and creates new temporal spaces, new interposed ease mid the obscuring haste of the old accounts. "Time is the mercy of Eternity; without Times swiftness / Which is the swiftest of all things: all were eternal torment" (*Milton*, 24.72–73). Not losing but recapturing and redeeming the sense of time, the prophet declares that not one moment shall be lost. In a single pulsation of an artery, in a moment when alternatives are real, the prophet finds the opening into new imaginative time.

Satan cannot find that opening moment, for all his haste to have it discovered and delimited. Milton's Satan, crying out at Jesus' slowness in moving toward salvational announcement, may be taken as the prototype of apocalyptic haste, while Jesus, all patience and endurance, is the model of the prophet. We can use the term "apocalyptic," then, to refer to vision as instantaneous and atemporal; "prophetic" implies the creation of new times, and more specifically of new deferrals, intervals between seeing and really seeing, or what we would do better to call change in vision and change in will. New prophetic dispensations seem necessary when the old seem out of date. The new prophet, or the new account concerning the prophet, finds the need for speech by finding insufficient the precursor's sense of "date," of the relation of time present to eternal time. In Blake's *Milton*, Los adjures his sons: "Remember how Calvin and Luther in fury premature / Sow'd War and stern division between Papists and Protestants" (23.46–47). The fury premature must be matched and exceeded by the new prophetic wrath, more accordant with the slow workings of time's mercy, more mature in understanding how knowledge takes place in time.

Looking back at biblical history, and particularly at the account Milton gives in *Paradise Regained*, Blake reviews history, and re-views it, or sees it as it has not been seen before. The separation of the word "re-view" could be taken as emblem of the difference become deferral or new extension in time. In that separation Blake makes room for himself. There must be a new prophetic time, not opened by previous accounts, and there must be a new apocalyptic energy which, like some motion that can retain balance only by going fast enough, goes over the old temporality in a way that turns what was sequence into new ground of option.

In Blake's *Milton*, the recognition of Satan or Selfhood supplies the new apocalyptic energy, and the distinction between Milton's decision to fall and his felt entry into Blake's foot, the distinction between Milton's and Ololoon's descents, instance the new sense of prophetic time. Milton cries, "O when Lord Jesus wilt thou come? / Tarry no longer; for my soul lies at the gates of death" (14.18–19). Urgency and recognition of a larger temporality combine here, and Milton himself takes on the role of the incarnated Eternal. Having heeded the scriptural account (substitute, in Blake, the Bard's Song for Jesus' Old Testament), the savior-poet (substitute Blake's Milton for Milton's Jesus) recognizes, "of whom they spake / I am" (*PR*, I.262–263), and goes forth to redeem the world. At the end of *Paradise Regained* the angelic choir (though we might, at first, mistake the voice as Milton's own, addressing his character) address the Son in their song of victory: "Now enter, and begin to save mankind." It is as if incarnation were taking place there—not at the birth or return from the desert of a historical Jesus but at this point in this prophetic poem; the re-entry is from the literary desert —the liminal status of literature—back to the biblical land

and time. Analogously, Blake's Milton, declaring, "I in my Selfhood am that Satan" (14.30), recognizes his Spectre—an aspect of self which is always there but now newly "assumed" and "entered into," thus reaching the "depths of dirast Hell" (14.40). One remembers Milton's Satan recognizing, "myself am Hell"; Blake's whole poem takes that self-recognition as the redeeming act. With it Milton leaves the deserts of Eternity and re-enters our land and time.

Commenting on Los's recollection of a prophecy that Milton would descend and unchain Orc, Harold Fisch explains, "His arrival is prophesied in Eden; that is, it is biblically motivated and directed." [37] Whatever "biblically motivated" means, Blake is not placing a prior text in causal relationship to Milton's descent, except as a line from which to swerve. The old prophecy is an ironic tribute to the daughters of memory, who can be of help while Los is having a difficult time. But the daughters of inspiration have less to do with accommodation to the old texts, and *Milton* seeks not a reconciliation with history but a revision of it. Blake's epic presents a rewriting of literary history—and a model for the prophetic rewriting of psychic history. Let us suppose (Blake asks of us as readers) that instead of his will to subsume the moment of choice into a pattern of loss, Milton had chosen otherwise. Suppose, taking the idea of the poetry of choice to its logical end, Milton had arrested the moment of choice, and pointed, like Eliot at the end of *Four Quartets*, "Quick now, here, now, always." A supposition is a fiction, but in place of the literary history that has not been, there is the literary history that Blake makes in his own prophetic writing. Blake rewrites the history of Milton's choice by himself arresting the moment of choice in two ways. First, since his use of Miltonic and biblical materials opens up the old stories not only to new readings but to new outcomes, Blake denies historical time which ordinarily interposes between Scripture and literature, between one literary work and another. Second, repeatedly returning to moments of creation and fall, Blake denies ordinary narrative time in which one event can be said to precede another in a definitive and exclusive temporal line.

If there is a family history of the deniers of history, we must return to Milton and recognize in Satan the grand forebear. As the Satan of *Paradise Regained* moves to hasten things to a close, to dissolve futurity, so the Satan of *Paradise Lost* would dissolve the past. Refusing the notion of temporal or hierarchical precedence, he denies both the order of angels and the historical order of angelic experience. "We know no time when we were not as now" (*PL*, V.859). For Blake, the denial of the experience of past history is not quite as serious as the denial of possible history—indeed the muses of memory have to assume second place. But though the rhetoric of revision may demand displacement of memory, psychic reintegration depends on recall of an original state. The Gates of Memory, as the Spectre tells Los, must be unlocked, for if we know no time when we were not as now, and define the self as fixed, then we will know no time when we will not be as we are now. Blake therefore names Satan's class the unchanging Elect, in contrast to those freed from the idea of fixed spiritual state and thus capable of redemption.

Dismissing the dialectic of time, Satan in *Paradise Lost* is fixated at the moment of fall. The fallen angels get just what they ask for, becoming prisoners of the eternal present, without past history, which they do what they can to ignore, and without possible history in the form of hope of regaining their blissful seat, which they refuse more firmly than it is refused to them. For their neglect of history, they are condemned to a repetition compulsion, and have their fall made continually present to them:

> oft they assay'd,
> Hunger and thirst constraining, drugg'd as oft,
> With hatefullest disrelish writh'd thir jaws
> With soot and cinders fill'd; so oft they fell
> Into the same illusion, not as Man
> Whom they triumph'd, once lapst. Thus were they plagu'd
> And worn with Famine long, and ceaseless hiss,
> Till thir lost shape, permitted, they resum'd,
> Yearly enjoin'd, some say, to undergo
> This annual humbling certain number'd days,
> To dash thir pride, and joy for Man seduc't. [X.567–577]

The usual right of fiction to interpose a little ease is taken over by a refreshingly brief truth. Turning irrevocability into positive good, the crisp restatement of man's fall, "once lapst," seems to catch us up in redeemed time, while the fallen angels, having denied the irrevocability of their own fall, now abide in fiction's abstraction from time. It is not enough to make them eat dirt; they could be made to eat dirt all the time, or be simply turned into dirt; but the "certain number'd days" is the divine touch. Irene Samuel, comparing Milton to Dante, notes that "Milton does not exploit the 'torture without end' ";[38] the difference between continuous and continual punishment is the difference between the conception of time and stasis. For Milton, the concept of "number'd days" is precisely what was lacking in the abortive rebellion of the passionate—those absorbed in the moment; the fallen angels neglected history and "right reason," the ability to make a chronology of consequences and hence the ability to choose correctly. Nor is it extraneous that

Milton builds this little tale around the qualifying words, "some say." There is a casualness worse than oblivion to a fate recorded only by what some say. More seriously, here, as when Blake remarks, "some said / 'It is Urizen'" (*The Book of Urizen*, 3.5–6), the indefiniteness of tale-telling is added to the abstraction from time. Fiction involves the suspension of consequences for the indeterminacy of what some say.

"Some say," though not in itself a pointedly Miltonic expression, can stand for the characteristically Miltonic awareness of fictional time. Two brief examples of the way the reader is implicated in the temporality of what "some say" may serve as models for the romantic poet's rereading of Miltonic temporality. One rather precarious model is God's joke about fearing the indeterminacy of his omnipotence. William Empson calls it "the brutal mockery of a much superior force," [39] but the mockery, or more accurately, playfulness, is perhaps less at the expense of Satan than it is for the benefit of the reader, who scans lines in time and has to learn the meaning of waiting for the Son to make clear the tone in which the Father's words are to be taken. The divine patience, suffering the satanic attack, suffering our momentary misreading, is the basis of the humor of the proposed haste: "Let us advise, and to this hazard draw / With speed what force is left" (*PL*, V.729–730). Giving temporal interval to the indefinite tone, God implies that the whole satanic rebellion is similarly extended in time by an act of divine indulgence. Coming to proper reading of the passage becomes an image of coming to proper relationship to the divine pattern of history.

Later God enjoys similar bantering with Adam, and is still more colloquial:

A nice and subtle happiness I see
Thou to thyself proposest, in the choice
Of thy Associates, *Adam,* and wilt taste
No pleasure, though in pleasure, solitary.
What think'st thou then of mee, and this my State,
Seem I to thee sufficiently possest
Of happiness, or not?   [VIII.399–405]

If the exchange with the Son implies a more serious point about
divine temporality, this exchange with Adam is intended to
reveal a more serious point about divine propagation. The
two issues, division of eternity into temporal periods, and the
division of the Eternal into separate persons, are precisely the
issues on which Blake turns most against Milton, reading his
precursor's humanistic modifications as signs of fallenness.
For Milton, however, the passages present opportunities for
the generated Son and generated man properly to image their
creator. Adam, like the Son, "reads" and reacts to the little
text he is given, the manageable portion of divine Word
which requires a little exercise of choice in rejecting the outrageous and clarifying the element of play. It is not really
God's state but time that is in suspension, time in which the
Son and Adam can choose to answer correctly. The freedom
of Adam parallels the freedom of God, the option to suspend
wrong in time, to give alternatives fictional duration in words,
as evil has momentary duration in history. "False surmise"
and the fictional conditions for the presentation of choice become, not poetic perversity, but man's closest approximation
to the Divine. The banter, the war in heaven, the schema of
human salvation are in the same sense "real," for the suspension in time of what is otherwise empty pattern is what makes
them "be." It is the essential creative act: "The paradox of
time and eternity is involved in the Creation itself. In the

mind of God, Creation was instantaneous ('Immediate are the acts of God'; God 'in a moment will create / Another world'), yet it took six days to perform or to be revealed." [40] Similarly, it takes time for what Raphael calls "process of speech," but narrative duration may reflect duration in God's time; what is spoken on earth may be "the shadow of Heav'n, and things therein / Each to other like, more than on Earth is thought" (V.575–576).

For Blake, earth is the shadow of heaven to a far greater extent than Milton thought, and narrative time can obscure the relation of shadowy earth to eternal substance. Blake points to the universal obscuring of that relation by extending the suspension of narrative time, "some say," till the "some" include the majority of men, nonidealists that we are:

Many suppose that before the Creation All was Solitude & Chaos[.] This is the most pernicious Idea that can enter the Mind as it takes away all sublimity from the Bible & Limits All Existence to Creation & to Chaos To the Time & Space fixed by the Corporeal Vegetative Eye & leaves the Man who entertains such an Idea the habitation of Unbelieving Demons[.] Eternity Exists and All things in Eternity Independent of Creation which was an act of Mercy.[41]

If earth is the shadow of heaven in this radical sense, then not only Creation, but every poetic creation, is a fall into temporality. Separating Edenic history into the creation and fall of man is but one mythic representation of our separation from what Blake would call the state of Eden, or full imaginative vision. The more poetic narrative expands its telling of human history, the further it moves from the possible history of imaginative redemption. Milton, perhaps, may be pardoned his expansion of the Genesis story of Adam and

Eve in paradise, since Milton's poetry could be said to create a Beulah-space, a useful guard against further fall into imaginative error. But that pardon should be conditional on the awareness that any extension of time is a spinning out of a web that catches man in the net of history when he should be liberating himself from temporality—especially, the imposed temporal constructs of others' systems.

This rather harsh dismissal of others' vision seems to conflict with the labor of the poet-prophet to create literary space in expansion of a previous closure. But for the purpose of coming to apocalyptic re-vision, we must put aside our vision that time is ultimately redemptive. Literary history is too flattened out by the ironic awareness that one poet simply substitutes his temporality for another's, and we see better if we view the change as a destruction of temporality for the new, atemporal insight. Milton may be said to have taken Shakespearean time as the horizontal, Beulah expanse of "L'Allegro," and seen his own "Penseroso" revision, with its denial of planar inclusiveness, as the vertical, Edenic climb. So Blake may be said to take Miltonic *durée* as that of horizontal, Beulah spaces, and see his own revision as the vertical redemption of the moment. To be sure, this redemption also "takes time"; but it proceeds only by finding the precursor's expansiveness pleasant but not the "better way."

If narrative expansion further lures the reader into the vegetative existence that nonprophetic poetry shares with nonliterary life, then narrative contraction is the new poetry's contribution to visionary redemption. Blake's poems need not be shorter than Milton's, but they must be seen to shorten history. On a small scale, for example, "The Tyger" rewrites Milton's war in heaven and the whole progress from fall to final redemption: "When the stars threw down their spears

/ And water'd heaven with their tears. . . ." We face the compression of history if we ask not "Who?" but "When?" The victorious angels may have thrown down their spears with tears of joy at victory, or tears such as angels weep in sympathy for the fallen. On the other hand, Lucifer and company, thrown out of heaven on the third day of Milton's war, and still lifting their spears in defiance, presumably could weep the tears of repentance at the end of days, if some more generous reckoning were made than Milton or his God had in mind. In *Paradise Lost* the fallen angels remain unrepentant, and God substitutes the creation of man, man's fall, and a long process of redemption till "by degrees of merit raised / [Men] open to themselves at length the way" (*PL*, VII.157–158). For Blake, one can open to oneself the way in a visionary moment, outside any such tedious temporal scheme. Repenting of having misread Milton as outlining a scheme for history, and reading instead a scheme of personal salvation, one chooses that salvation now. The choice may perhaps find an emblem in the question the speaker of "The Tyger" asks: "What immortal hand or eye / Could frame thy fearful symmetry?" Perhaps the fearfulness of a grand scheme of redemption, presided over by the "tyger" of wrath, the God of vengeance and retribution, may lie only in the eye of the beholder of such a scheme; the beholder, or speaker of the poem, is himself moved to change the verb from "could frame" to "dare frame," thus reflecting the Urizenic pattern of creation in response to fear. Perhaps the alternative, "hand or eye," further sums up the alternative between temporal creation and visionary instantaneity. Were one to see the fearfulness of the "tyger" as a tyranny of the eye, that tyranny, and the temporal space between its victorious reign and its final defeat, would be no more.

In the *Book of Urizen*, the contractions of Miltonic temporality are even more radical. Creation is described in terms
that let us see the Satan of *Paradise Lost*, Book II, and God of
Book VII compacted into one, simultaneously reacting against
fallenness, and exhibiting the kind of withdrawal and creative
powers which for Blake less cause than constitute that fallenness:

> First I fought with the fire; consum'd
> Inwards, into a deep world within:
> A void immense, wild dark & deep,
> Where nothing was; Natures wide womb[.]
> And self balanc'd stretch'd o'er the void
> I alone, even I! the winds merciless
> Bound; but condensing, in torrents
> They fall & fall; strong I repell'd
> The vast waves, & arose on the waters
> A wide world of solid obstruction.
>
> [*The Book of Urizen*, 4.14–23]

This is to create the world as Blake said "many suppose" it
was created, out of solitude and chaos. Urizen, like both
Milton's God and his Satan, confronts a void left by a withdrawal into the self, and counters that void by the creation of
a world in it. The dominion over created space is matched by
a temporal tyranny. Withdrawn into a separate holiness,
Urizen is set apart in "stern counsels / Reserv'd for the days
of futurity" (4.8–9). He binds all creation in his temporal
scheme, his "Circle of Destiny," pre-empting futurity under
the hold of his cosmic and moral laws.

As the story of Urizen is expanded in *The Four Zoas*, the
Miltonic tenuousness, "some say," expands to the tenuous
truth of any one version of the fall. But the variant accounts
of the primal fall and the accounts of further falls into dis-

unity are all based on the perception that fear of void leads
to spatial fixation, and fear of futurity leads to temporal
schematization. In commonplace terms, fear of death breeds
jealousy of others' aliveness; possessive jealousy creates schemes
for the undermining of this life to assure valorization of, or
placement in, another one. In more Blakean categories, fear
of a fall from Eternity breeds female will; in Eternity there
is no such thing as female will, and such possessiveness marks
the fall into temporality. Each created space or scheme is designed to protect from fall into "eternal death," and ironically, even the apocalypse itself, as it begins in Night the
Ninth, may seem to come from Los holding on to created
space. When Los seizes the sun and covers the moon, does he
want to grasp or destroy created space? The moment is
apocalyptic because of the collapsed time, the collapsed difference between created and fallen space. More internally, if
the assertion of separate female will marks the fall, redemption lies in turning female will into a second will that, renouncing control over others, regains control of the self. The
separated zoas must subdue their own possessive wills for the
greater will of Albion:

> They must renew their brightness & their disorganized
>   functions
> Again reorganize till they resume the image of the human
> Cooperating in the bliss of Man obeying his Will
> Servants to the infinite & Eternal of the Human form.
>   [*The Four Zoas*, 126.13–16]

Reformation of the will is a long and difficult process, more
difficult than is realized in salvational schemes which can be
overviewed in outline form. Such schemes, like that outlined
to Adam at the end of *Paradise Lost*, seem (in this necessary

misreading) to make the change in will a preliminary conversion, and leave the expanse of historical time outside the self. Blakean myth makes all temporality that of the conversion of the will. Denying real distinction between events of the story as Milton tells it, Blake turns the old temporality into the new temporal arrest where the will, in the process of revision, can "go over" the same events, exercising the power of choice. Every dislocation of an external, outlineable scheme, every break in mythic continuity, every event narrated as another fall thus becomes a contribution to the change in will. If temporal schemes come to be seen as external, then the will can properly be directed further inward, past quarrels with Urizen to more intellectual quarrels with the Spectre. A fall is a fall into disunity, into differences between the persons of composite man; regeneration means a reunification of disparates into alternate selves. Only this return to copresence of alternatives, only this reunion with the Spectre "first as a brother / Then as another Self" can reconstitute human nature, and free the will from the "Domineering lust" (*The Four Zoas*, 85.26–31).

Since the necessary change is a change in will, forcing a change is a hopeless task. In *Jerusalem*, Chapter 2, an attempt is made to bear Albion back "Against his will through Los's Gate to Eden" (39.3). But "the Will must not be bended but in the day of Divine / Power" (39.48–49). Exactly how to express what can be done to take salvation in one's own hands is a problem Blake wrestled with throughout his prophetic poetry. To deny that one takes the initiative oneself is to be cast back into providential schemes like the temporality of a Urizenic divinity; to deny that the problem is a problem of expression is to assert the priority of the scheme to the poetry and thus to be cast, once again, into a Urizenic net. The only way lies in imaginative labor, in the poetic conception, or reconception, of the characters of the myth. In *Jerusalem*, the very imagining of the cities as separate from, working for, Albion expresses the externality, the imposed willfulness of their salvational effort to bring Albion back. In *The Four Zoas*, Albion's address to Urizen in Night the Ninth points to the achievement and limitation of willed redemption.

The "tygers" of wrath are wiser than the plodding horses of temporal salvation. What happens to bring about a second will more wise in Night the Ninth is that Albion gets angry, and addresses Urizen in forceful terms, threatening to cast him out into the permanent indefinite. Urizen is threatened, in other words, by the very fear that originally motivated his possessive usurpation. Is it now fear that brings about a change of mind, or a new clarity of vision that brings about a change of heart? Since Urizen's great decision takes place at this point, Blake leaves the slight ambiguity as an expression of the indefiniteness that marks a moment of choice. However we choose to regard the moment after Albion's speech, the choice, once made by Urizen, clearly involves a change of vision and a change of heart. The change may be taken to represent the way Blake has changed the nature of narrative from a progress along a line of historical continuity to an essentially atemporal progress toward greater clarification. Albion's speech clarifies Urizen's nature as a Miltonic Satan, "dragon of the Deeps"; and the speech appeals to Urizen to clarify for himself the possibility of salvation, the "windows of the morning / Redeemed from Error's power" (120.50–51). Renouncing his will to bind to himself a joy, to seek "for pleasure which unsought falls round the infants path," Urizen takes the major step in reformation of the will: "I cast futurity away & turn my back upon that void / Which I have made[,] for lo futurity is in this moment" (121.21–22).

"If I am not for myself, who will be for me? And if I am only for myself, what am I? And if not now, when?" As if heeding the *Ethics of the Fathers*, the weeping Urizen takes on himself the reassumption of the human, renounces the possessiveness that had made him only for himself, and proclaims the time to be *now*. At this moment of revelation, the veil is rent, and the moment opens up to further temporality —what Urizen, until this achievement of self-knowledge, could not face. Urizen of Night the Ninth has the fullest association with Milton's Satan, and we must recognize in his movement to apocalypse Satan's anxiety for confrontation "Now, at full age, fulness of time, thy season" (*PR*, IV.380). Urizen must then confront what Milton's Son has Satan confront. The time is now, in a visionary sense: now is the time for recognition, for facing the futurity in the moment. But the time is also "not yet," and the apocalyptic hastener must learn a new sense of extension in time. After Urizen speaks, Ahania rises to join him. But the time for reunification is not quite now. "My time," Jesus tells Satan, "is not yet come" (*PR*, III.396–397); Albion tells Urizen, "The times revolve the time is coming" (122.4). The apocalyptic recognition, "time is now," becomes the prophetic cry, "the time is coming." Meanwhile, time is the mercy of eternity, interposing ease between the recognitions to which we are hastened and those for which we are not fully ready. A full reformation of the will, as well as a sudden glance at reformed vision, must take place, and there is imaginative work that lies ahead.

Urizen's recognition in Night the Ninth may be one of Blake's most dramatic representations of visionary recognition, but since poetry is not to be governed by a single tem-

poral scheme, it must proceed, like a horse of instruction
under blinders, ploughing along, putting aside the moment of
insight as an "interposed ease" mid the total labor of apocalyptic renovation. Every moment of self-recognition on the
part of a character or the poet himself must be approached as
such an interposition rather than a terminal point in a single
path which alone is truth. In *Paradise Regained*, Satan tells
Jesus that he hopes for a "shelter and a kind of shading
cool / Interposition" (III.221–222). The plangency of that
moment comes from our awareness that he is fooling himself
(there will be no mercy for mere self-consciousness) and also
from the recognition that the interposition is *here*, not between God's judgment and its execution but now, between
the knowledge Jesus and Satan share and the power Jesus has
yet to put on. The shading cool interposition has no place in
the theological scheme; it can exist only poetically, and is less
descried than actually created at this point in the poem. An
analogous interposition in Blake's *Milton* occurs when Milton,
responding to the Bard's Song, moves to awareness of his own
shadow—and one step further: Blake, as if responding to his
Milton's statement, moves to his own extraordinary self-consciousness:

> Then on the verge of Beulah he beheld his own Shadow;
> A mournful form double; hermaphroditic: male & female
> In one wonderful body. and he entered into it
> In direful pain for the dread shadow, twenty-seven-fold
> Reachd to the depths of dirast Hell, & thence to Albions
>   land:
> Which is this earth of vegetation on which now I write.
>
> [14.36–41]

This last line, in its more relaxed rhythm, simple vocabulary,
and modest self-consciousness, is a shading cool interposition

mid the more taxing labors of private mythmaking; and the break that comes with such a poetic line helps us see the interposition or incarnation of the previous poet (the spirit of the "Humanity Divine") as redemptive of the temporality into which he comes.

Milton's descent into "Eternal Death" makes his stay with the Eternals itself a cool interposition, a vacation from the poet's proper world, the world of ongoing human time. Milton asks, "What do I here before the Judgment? without my Emanation? / With the daughters of memory, & not with the daughters of inspiration?" (14.28–29). To be canonized and stored away is to be condemned to memory, while that poet lives who is being reincarnated as the inspiration for his romantic successors. If Milton had not been "for himself," writing himself into each apocalyptic confrontation, no other poet would have been able to incarnate him. And if he had been only for himself, expressing rather than putting off the selfhood, he would not have been the poet of the second, revised will. And if the time were not now, in the interposed ease of narrative space, when would it be?

5. A Second Will

Yet not the less would I throughout
Still act according to the voice
Of my own wish; and feel past doubt
That my submissiveness was choice:
Not seeking in the school of pride
For "precepts over dignified,"
Denial and restraint I prize
No farther than they breed a second Will more wise.
                    Wordsworth, "Ode to Duty," 1807 edition

In an untitled poem that totters a little under the moral weight which oppressed his later years as a poet, Wordsworth begins by quoting *Samson Agonistes:* "A little onward lend thy guiding hand / To these dark steps, a little further on!" Wordsworth explained, in the Isabella Fenwick note, that he had a recurring eye ailment which "often prevented my reading for months." Yet neither the physiological complaint nor the occasion of being dependent, like Milton's Samson, on youth's guiding hand wholly accounts for the surprise he expresses in the poem at hearing himself recall Milton's lines: "What trick of memory," he wonders, "to *my* voice hath brought / This mournful iteration?"

With these words Wordsworth turns biographical circumstance into the setting for something more surprising than chance similitude. Beyond the curiosity of finding himself in a position that recalls that of a Miltonic character, or even of Milton himself, is the potential awesomeness associated with the sublime in hearing Milton's voice in "*my* voice." Samson's "mournful iteration" is the small, verbal repetition, "a little onward . . . a little further on." Like a human figure perceived beside an object of enormous magnitude, giving

213

a sense of proportionate size, Samson's repetition is seen to stand in relation to the vast spaces between Miltonic utterance and Wordsworthian recall.

Wordsworth takes the Miltonic sublime "a little onward." Perhaps feeling licensed by the natural gap between himself and his daughter, Wordsworth returns to the gap between Miltonic voice and his own. The father is, as he says, "natural leader" of the child, and that commonplace propriety becomes a kind of cover for the poetic act of revisiting a Miltonic paradise in the form of a superior spirit. The role of Eve, herself the fairest unsupported flower, is taken over by Dora, who—though she at first had to be "From flower to flower supported"—now moves with "nymph-like step swift-bounding o'er the lawn." The role of Adam—or is it God himself in relation to Eve?—is taken by Wordsworth. He will be her "happy guide," more happy in himself, more fortuitous in relation to the lady's future, than Adam or a too soon departed divinity proved to Eve. The father-daughter relationship is a step down from either God-Eve or Adam-Eve relations, but through that naturalization or demystification Wordsworth finds his license and his strength. In the gamble of poetic influence, such lowering of the stakes makes for more daring, and it is thus that Milton is advanced a little onward. Besides God and Adam, another guiding spirit hovers in the background of Wordsworth's lines. The guide who requests to "point thy way, / And now precede thee, winding to and fro" poses in the semblance of his serpentine ancestor leading onward to a temptation like that faced by Eve—particularly in the dream version, when the guide shows the way to be freed from earthly confines and at ease in his realm of air.

Secured by his knowledge that his setting is a natural land-

scape, not a theological trial, Wordsworth moves a little further on in the brinkmanship of the Miltonic moment of
choice. Precipitous height "Kindles intense desire for powers
withheld / From this corporeal frame." The desire is to be
airborne—not suicidally plunged; or, perhaps more accurately, the desire itself is for a metaphoric rather than literal
power of flight. This is no sexual fantasy, nor rapture, beyond one's human self, into envy of the state of birds.
Wordsworth himself quotes a Miltonic phrase to indicate
how literary is the temptation, how much other forms of
power are but standing as images of poetic power. The desire
is to be able to plunge into the "abrupt abyss," which he
wants us to recognize as the void in which Milton's Satan did
not fear to tread. The literary echo would point to the satanism of poetic freedom, when a poetic son turns his back upon
Milton-as-God-the-Father and asserts his power, like Wallace
Stevens' angel, freely to leap from heaven to heaven of his
own creation.

The issue of poetic influence will not turn Wordsworth's
poem, interesting though it is, into one of his finest lyrics; but
the poem can illustrate the way Wordsworth achieves some of
his finest moments by turning to Milton. If a discussion of
Blake's relation to Milton can take for its point of departure
Jesus on the pinnacle top—the point from which all either
opens out into infinity or is cast, like every limiting creation,
into a fall—then a discussion of Wordsworth's relation to
Milton can take its point of departure a little onward in Milton's text, after the simile comparisons to Jesus' victory:

> So Satan fell; and straight a fiery Globe
> Of Angels on full sail of wing flew nigh,
> Who on their plumy Vans receiv'd him soft
> From his uneasy station. [PR, IV.581–584]

As if extending the Son's arrest on the pinnacle top, Milton's verse arrests the temporality of the reading process until we realize that the "him" who is "receiv'd soft" is not Satan but the Son; sentence structure is imitating freedom in air by easefully catching proper sense in its pronominal net. Wordsworth's poem imitates that ease. Divided into two sections, one seemingly poised before a plunge, the second, as it were, expressing the Fall as a fall into a lesser sensibility, the poem echoes the *Paradise Regained* passage in the last line of its first section: "Where ravens spread their plumy vans at ease." Imaging as it does flight rather than fall, the line leaves the whole section at ease with the concept of fall, at ease with the implicit fall from Milton's celestial to this natural wingedness.

The Son received full soft on the angelic couch becomes a background image for Milton received softly into the easeful couch of Wordsworth's verse. The higher spirit is entertained in lesser, but no less pleasant, surroundings; indeed the lessening, or naturalizing, of the image is the source of the pleasance. Wordsworth compares his mildly satanic spirit, tempted to dive into the ethereal abyss, to a swimmer impelled to "plunge —dread thought, / For pastime plunge—into the 'abrupt abyss.'" Comparing the spiritual flyer to a simple swimmer is only half the naturalization; as if even that image left too much awe, he extends the pleasance with the qualifier, "for pastime plunge." This is to take the Miltonic hovering over a moment of choice a little further on indeed, as if the dread itself took flight and we were left with the power without the forbidding awesomeness.

Across the gap that separates the two parts of Wordsworth's poem we seem to be left with the sense of the forbidding without the sense of power. The poem steps back from arrested to endured time, the postlapsarian placidness of learning to "calm the affections." Retreating from power that seems too self-prompted, the poet looks forward to milder confrontations with "Heaven-prompted Nature." But it is self-assertiveness in relation to poetic influence, rather than such influence itself, that is renounced. Though he proclaims that the new "reverential awe" will be found "In the still summer noon," we recognize in the images of nuns not an aspect of landscape but an appeal to Milton's penseroso mode; and in the final image of "advancing hand in hand" to learn of paradises within, he makes father and daughter a version of Adam and Eve at the close of *Paradise Lost*, but with the stings of sexuality and unobedient female will removed. Perhaps most important for lightening the burden of influence is the lifting of the blindness originally evoked in the quotation from *Samson Agonistes*. To the "glad eyes from bondage freed" a new receptivity will be granted. Influence will flow from the everlasting gates of the "Fane of Holy Writ" and the temples of classic lore (1827 version). Milton's image of the "everlasting Gates," opened to let in "The great Creator from his work return'd," implies future commerce: God will visit men "and with frequent intercourse / Thither will send his winged Messengers" (*PL*, VII.565–573). So Wordsworth's poem, with or without this particular echo of Milton, looks forward to an easy commerce with the ancient texts. The poem has naturalized and humanized the satanic temptation to rest at ease in the moment of choice. But it retains from Wordsworth's initial reaction to the quotation from *Samson Agonistes* the sense of awe before visitation of higher voice, and the expectation that, for all the discontinuities such intervention may imply, the "trick of memory" that finds Milton's voice now will prove redemptive of the intervening time.

We think of Wordsworth generally as redeeming present vacuity by a turn to the past, a turn of such ritualistic recurrence as to warrant Harold Bloom's calling it the "myth of memory." [1] Wordsworth is not usually looking forward, to "Time / The Conqueror," as in the above poem, but back to time past, time as the medium of distinction between the observed and the perceiving self. Yet in a way the significant apprehension of duration is forward when *The Prelude* begins by looking out for choice of place, and more generally, in the chaos of futurity at each imagined approach to a dark abyss. The "abrupt abyss" Satan confronts in chaos becomes, for Wordsworth, a temporal abyss over which the poet repeatedly hangs suspended, catching from Miltonic echoes the measurement of intervening time. From Milton comes the assurance that the abyss will prove no vacancy but a gap creative of self-consciousness. The intervention of higher strains into the continuity of Miltonic voice stands as a model for apprehending Miltonic voice across the gaps in Wordsworthian continuity.

Authoritative Voice

Milton sets the pattern for the relation of void to voice by raising it to the status of myth in "Lycidas." Though the elegy is filled with shocks of discontinuity, none of the moments caught in the beginning has the intensity of the interruption by Apollo himself. It is an assault on our sense of ongoingness that suddenly shifts everything into the past and simultaneously makes the past present by bringing it all in front of our eyes to be rearranged, reinterpreted in a new light. One cannot say, "Suddenly there is a listener"; rather, "Suddenly there has been a listener," and one seizes the "now" as the point from which the understanding of time has to be changed. Living in time, being reconciled to the pastness of the past, makes the apprehension of the present a kind of revelation that sets all heaven before our eyes. Apollo's speech therefore ends with the equivalence, the simultaneity of seizing the moment and recognizing the irrevocability of experience: "As he pronounces lastly on each deed, / Of so much fame in heav'n expect thy meed." That equivalence is a redemption of death. The famed deed, like the echoed song, is stillness that is motion, simultaneity that is ongoingness, premature arrest that is perennial presence. Wordsworth similarly relates fame to the redemption of time in listening when he speaks of verse that the "Muses shall accept, . . . And listening Time reward with sacred praise" (*Excursion*, I.103, 107).

However strongly the revelation of continuity is put, a break in the conventions of narrator-listener relationship is always in danger of being felt too strongly as a discontinuity to be reconciled with poetic time. One of the remarkable things about such moments in Milton is the way he makes them personal at the same time that they are "wholly other." Precisely when poetic time is broken, a strange continuum is created between the poet and his fictional characters. Phoebus seems to be touching the ears, not only of the uncouth swain, but of Milton himself, as if to say, "You, John, are just the man who can, who *is* testifying to the difference between the life and the praise." Kierkegaard writes of such moments: "The dominant mood in A's preface in a manner betrays the poet. . . . Nor am I surprised that it affected A thus; for I, who have simply nothing to do with this narrative, I who am twice removed from the original author, I too, have sometimes felt quite strange when, in the silence of the night, I have busied myself with these papers." [2] Kierkegaard himself is at third remove from "the original author," but the passage provides one of those strange moments when the barriers between levels of fictionality dissolve and we confront directly the man in each of the authorial levels.

In "Lycidas," the turn that makes speaker into listener redeems a fallen perspective, one generated from private grief and fixated on death. Correction of the voice is a mode of redemption throughout Milton, though the sternness of reproof may momentarily cloud the benignity of intervention.

Perhaps the most familiar example is the reproof of Eve, who, drawn away from self-contemplation, is not immediately—not inherently, that is—aware that the correction of her perspective is for her own good. It is important that the break occur, not through a naturalistic discovery of the false equity of reflected image, but through the intervention of a higher voice. God pronounces:

> What thou seest,
> What there thou seest fair Creature is thyself,
> With thee it came and goes: but follow me,
> And I will bring thee where no shadow stays
> Thy coming, and thy soft imbraces, hee
> Whose image thou art . . . [PL, IV.467–472]

Voice is everywhere the emblem of the distance the recognition of which is creative, the failure of which is fall.[3] Voice separates speaker from listener, author from image, in a way that distinguishes fertile spiritual brooding from the sterility of narcissistic self-confrontation. One may define the distance

that separates Father from Son, Voice from creature, as the
Holy Spirit. To let that distance bespeak Spirit is to hear
Milton's invocations as an appeal for voice, for that power
which will transmute the potentially sterile, self-begotten
poem into a strain of higher mood, leaving the overwhelmed
poet like Job regarding the gap between his own words and
the Voice heard from the whirlwind: "Then Job answered
the Lord and said, I know that Thou canst do every thing,
and that no thought can be withholden from Thee. Who is
he that hideth counsel without knowledge? Therefore have
I uttered that I understood not; things too wonderful for me,
which I knew not" (Job 42 : 1–3). The distance of Job from
his words, of the poet from his own work or the work in
which he stands, is the distance of generation.

In "Lycidas," voice succeeds voice in the most startling
way. The final paragraph is the final shock in a poem that
repeatedly shocks us into better hearing, touching our trembling ears with a voice still higher, a sound still to be expressed. Mourning one who "knew / Himself to sing," the
poem is in danger of self-contemplation as self-destructive as
Eve's inherent, human impulse. But generating distance between Milton and the speaker, and between the speaker and
Lycidas, the poem transforms the fictional equality of the two
shepherds into a generational gap: what separates this poet
from the dead one will separate the next from the present one:

> So may some gentle Muse
> With lucky words favor my destin'd Urn,
> And as he passes turn,
> And bid fair peace be to my sable shroud.

The distance is no less than life itself.

The fact of death is redeemed with a correction in the

voice. We expect, in the face of loss, the comfort of conversation; the "Lycidas" swain calls mourners to say what is due. And no doubt conversation is a comfort. We tend to distinguish it from harsher verbal modes as being that pleasant form of communication, intermixed with grateful digression, in which the self can be lost, in which, at supreme moments, one no longer is conscious of who is saying what. A little ease is interposed in which the "I" steps outside its usual role of exchanging information or asserting itself, of hammering its knowledge or its identity on the head of the "thou." Yet conversation, pleasing intercourse of minds, is no more the aspiration than it is the possible province of poetry. There is, of course—though only at moments in Milton—conversational poetry. That is the mode which comforts by imitating human intercourse; the expression of the poet's feeling compensates for the absence of more direct human communication while the reader reads.

Moments of voice, however, are not limited to what they imitate. If poetry can, at the most—though often supremely —feign conversation, poetry can actualize voice; at such moments the distance of poet from reader is not overcome but felt as the measure of the authority of the voice. In Milton the conversational is sacrificed for the higher mode. Not merely sisters, but "sisters of the sacred well" come, and they do not just talk. There are moments when one hears someone very close, almost, in fact, a friend, as when Camus speaks: " 'Ah! who hath reft' (quoth he) 'my dearest pledge?' " But the personal, helpless line is laid on the altar by a speaker whose rhetorical question is not permitted to become a conversational opener; speechless, he moves on in the procession of mourners to make way for a less genial but more authoritative voice.

The conversational in *Paradise Lost* is likewise hurried by. There are relaxed whispers relieving the omnific rhetoric, but the very lines that establish more genial tone are offered up in measurement of the distance of scene from spectator. Lines like "No fear lest dinner cool" (V.396) and "Nor turn'd I ween / *Adam* from his fair spouse" (IV.741–742) stop just long enough to remind us of Milton as mediator, immediately *there*, between Eden and us.

Conversation is the mode of antihierarchic equality, but in an epic equality does not stand a chance. Milton writes with "answerable style," answerable to his high argument and therefore necessarily above equivocation about authority of voice and above prosaic equity of sign and significance. Eve, looking in the pool, is commanded away from those "answering looks / Of sympathy and love" (IV.464–465). She must be; the reflected image can answer with looks but no voice, and the absence of voice figures the absence of generational distance, the distance she must be told exists between herself and the man she images, and between herself and her watery image. Adam's opening moments similarly involve confrontation with intervening voice. He begins talking to the landscape, first addressing "Thou Sun," not yet knowing that the only "thou" there is the divine "Thou." He is not awake long enough to wonder why nature returns no answer, why he can talk to, but not with, fellow creatures. The possibility of conversation, the pleasing equitable intercourse of "I" and "thou" is overruled in the revelatory sleep that brings ultimate Voice:

> thy Mansion wants thee, *Adam*, rise,
> First Man, of Men innumerable ordain'd
> First Father.   [VIII.296–298]

It is no accident that God's first words to Adam, establishing the distance of Author from creature, are about generation, the distance man will image in his role as author and creator.

The dialogue that ensues approximates conversation between Adam and God, though it always maintains the proper distance between creator and creation, the distance that lets us hear Voice coming from the vision bright even when He replies "as with a smile." The exchange is precisely about the issue of equality and authorship, and at its most conversational raises the question from human to divine generation:

> A nice and subtle happiness I see
> Thou to thyself proposest, in the choice
> Of thy Associates, *Adam*, and wilt taste
> No pleasure, though in pleasure, solitary.
> What think'st thou then of mee, and this my State,
> Seem I to thee sufficiently possest
> Of happiness, or not?   [VIII.399–405]

Though these are remarkably informal lines, raising such a question destroys the ease that makes for conversation by warning Adam and reader to be on their theological toes. But this is not repartee, the mode of equality, so God helps us out even in the posing of the question, revealing more than he is asking about the nature of His "Second":

> none I know
> Second to mee or like, equal much less.
> How have I then with whom to hold converse
> Save with the Creatures which I made, and those
> To me inferior, infinite descents
> Beneath what other Creatures are to thee?
> [VIII.406–411]

We have seen the Father conversing with One which He made, the Son—or perhaps we should hesitate about the word "conversing," for the inequality of divine persons makes even such speech more a matter of authoritative voice than conversational equality. Perhaps one can say that this exchange with Adam comes closer to conversation than the formal talk of Book III, since the distance between speakers here is a matter poet and reader can take more for granted and thus find less an obstacle to conversational intimacy.

Making just the right point about the nature of the Godhead and the nature of conversation, Adam raises his own conversation to the level of divine truth. In the disembodiment of voice from ego to produce depersonalized, pure truth, Adam propounds what one might have thought only God himself could declare:

> Thou in thyself art perfect, and in thee
> Is no deficience found; not so is Man,
> But in degree, the cause of his desire
> By conversation with his like to help
> Or solace his defects. No need that thou
> Shouldst propagate, already infinite.   [VIII.415–420]

Man needs conversation as consolation for the distance that is defect, that will become death. Concerning God, Adam gives what is at once the most casually conversational answer —"no need" (no need to bother)—and the most audaciously theological: the Son is begotten of God's will, not the necessity of God's nature. In Milton's heretical view expressed in *De Doctrina Christiana*, the propagation of the Son is "impelled by no necessity, but according to his own [we may say 'second'] will." "It was in God's power consistently with the perfection of his own essence not to have begotten the Son, inasmuch as generation does not pertain to the nature of the Deity who stands in no need of propagation." [4] Adam also draws the crucial connection between creation and imagistic generation:

> But Man by number is to manifest
> His single imperfection, and beget
> Like of his like, his Image multipli'd,
> In unity defective, which requires
> Collateral love, and dearest amity.   [VIII.422–426]

Man's opportunity to multiply his image is the required recompense for the generational distance that separates man, as image of God, from God. There is no denying the gap Adam experiences in relation to God—the gap his descendants feel in relation to parents when confronting the fact that one is "generated," not author of oneself. But "collateral love," love in which partners are equal, on the same lateral, generational plane, is the comfort and reparation for the vertical, generational gap.

The difficulty with such a notion of "deficience" and recompense is that if distance is divine, establishing an equal love, a woman in the image of a man suffers the narcissistic plight that creation must overcome.[5] Here the Bible provides the principle of a solution on which the poet capitalizes. Eve, created from Adam, leaves Adam in an authorial position like that of God in relation to man. As long as that distance is maintained, grateful intercourse is possible; the collapse of that distance, of Eve recognizing Adam as "author and disposer" (IV.635), is fall.

Besides his relation to Eve, there are two ways Adam spans authorial distance and holds the relation to the visible world that God has to all creation. As "lord of the earth," man images God's dominion, and as namer of the animals (Eve names the plants, we find out in Book XI), he stands in the distance that is voice. All three authorial relationships are brought together in Book VIII, between God's identification of himself as "Author of all this" (l. 317) and Adam's recognition of the "Author of this Universe" (l. 360). In the interim, authoritative voice is delegated from God to man:

> All the Earth
> To thee and to thy Race I give; as Lords
> Possess it, and all things that therein live,
> Or live in Sea, or Air, Beast, Fish, and Fowl.
> In sign whereof each Bird and Beast behold
> After thir kinds; I bring them to receive
> From thee thir Names, and pay thee fealty
> With low subjection; understand the same
> Of Fish within thir wat'ry residence,
> Not hither summon'd, since they cannot change
> Thir Element to draw the thinner Air.
> As thus he spake, each Bird and Beast behold
> Approaching two and two, These cow'ring low
> With blandishment, each Bird stoop'd on his wing.
> I nam'd them, as they pass'd, and understood
> Thir Nature, with such knowledge God endu'd
> My sudden apprehension: but in these
> I found not what methought I wanted still.
>
> [VIII.338–355]

Naming is the process of divine creation: "And God said, Let the earth bring forth the living creature after his kind . . . and it was so" (Gen. 1 : 24). In naming the animals, Adam participates in the Creation, which he further images by giving God's word—"each Bird and Beast behold"—and then, seven lines later, repeating "each Bird and Beast behold." The first "behold" is God's injunction to Adam; the second is not quite Adam's injunction to Raphael ("Look there!" or "You should have seen it!") or Adam's recapitulation of what happened ("I beheld"); it is the language of creation as repetition, perfect enactment of the Word.

Between the repeated phrases Milton does something extraordinary. There is no need to mention the fish; and part of
the charm of the apology is our recognition of Milton's habit
of trying to cope with a difficulty of which we would not
have been aware had he not brought it up. The verbal facility
of the excuse points to the difference between the freedom of verbal creation and the limitations imposed on
created nature. We may think in larger terms of the poet
presuming to soar and draw "empyreal air," who then prays
"with like safety guided down / Return me to my Native
Element" (VII.15–16). This is imaged journey, distinguished
from the suspect attempt of those who, claiming to be of
purer fire, would change their element for one more like
celestial light. Such would be the "high exaltation" of Eve
were she not just dreaming of flight up to the clouds. As
Adam, in naming the animals, comes to an awareness of the
Eve he lacks, so we are made aware of the lack, the loss that
could fall between the acting and the first motion, the line
and its repetition.

Later in the poem Adam, observing the violation of space
in the construction of the Tower of Babel, recalls the original
command for dominion and contrasts its perversion here:

> O execrable Son so to aspire
> Above his Brethren, to himself assuming
> Authority usurpt, from God not giv'n:
> He gave us only over Beast, Fish, Fowl
> Dominion absolute; that right we hold
> By his donation; but Man over men
> He made not Lord; such title to himself
> Reserving, human left from human free.
> But this Usurper his encroachment proud
> Stays not on Man; to God his Tower intends

Siege and defiance: Wretched man! what food
Will he convey up thither to sustain
Himself and his rash Army, where thin Air
Above the Clouds will pine his entrails gross,
And famish him of breath, if not of Bread?   [XII.64–78]

In contrast to the naming of the animals, sign of man's granted dominion, this effort, which heaven "confusion nam'd," is condemned as false dominion. It may seem strange that Adam's condemnation focuses on problems with the tower's kitchen. But if we recall Raphael's speech about a spatially continuous hierarchy in which "of Elements / The grosser feeds the purer" (V.415–416), then the problem of "thin Air" and "entrails gross" becomes, not one of dumbwaiters, but of vociferous uprising. The vain exaltation into the thin air is a violation of geographic and moral space which should be collapsed only by divine intervention.

In this light, the apology in Book VIII about fish, who do not change their element to draw the thinner air, becomes a statement of proper dominion: they represent the respect for distance between named creature and naming creator. They come as a reminder of the space that is not violated between man and prelapsarian animal kingdom, a reminder of the space that should not be violated between prelapsarian man and God. The repeated phrase, "each Bird and Beast behold," represents the actuality that no step has been taken in the direction of violation; we stand at the moment of choice, now beholding both actual innocence and the suggestion of violation. The fish, in between, bring only a suggestion; but then so much of the description of physical paradise is suggestion which, respecting the distance between present attractive grace and potentially ominous connotation (of streams wandering with serpent error or of protoplasts falling to supper fruits) shadows forth the distance that is fall.

If we may violate the distance that separates Wordsworth from Milton, it is possible to hear in the later poet's argument about liberty some of the terms of Adam's address to his sons. Wordsworth may be remembering God's apology about the fish not changing their element when he describes his innocent reaction to Continental strife:

> I seemed to move along them, as a bird
> Moves through the air, or as a fish pursues
> Its sport, or feeds in its proper element.
>
> [*Prelude*, VI.770–772]

It is characteristic of Wordsworth to pose, in the manner of Milton, an option (pursues or feeds) whose freedom from larger concerns expresses an unreproved delight in nature; and it is characteristic of his involvement with Milton to express his freedom in shades of morality ("proper," describing element, has more than the French connotation). But it may be best to put aside such speculative detail, for Wordsworth's relationship to Milton's voice is far more overt. Beside the passage in which heaven laughs at the builders of the Tower of Babel, there is a marginal note in a Wordsworth copy of *Paradise Lost*. Objecting to the impropriety of having "superior beings" laugh at the scene of human folly, he suggests instead that "Shakespear is far more rational & impressive 'Oh! but man proud man – – – – plays such fantastic tricks before high heaven as make the angels *weep*.'" [6] The image from *Measure for Measure* may strike us as being, if possible, more Miltonic than Milton's own. Bypassing the more immediate for the more removed ancestor is a way of being written into the line of poetic tradition; it is as if Wordsworth were overleaping the distance and distaste of Milton's heavenly laughter to assert a greater consanguinity, a closeness of sympathy between heaven and earth, between authoritative voice and his own.

Wordsworth again seems more to bypass or overgo than to echo Milton in *The Excursion*, Book IV. With Adam's address to his sons-to-be in *Paradise Lost*, XII.64–78, we may compare this speech which the Wanderer presents as spoken by Providence:

> Vain-glorious Generation! what new powers
> On you have been conferred? what gifts, withheld
> From your progenitors, have ye received,
> Fit recompense of new desert? what claim
> Are ye prepared to urge, that my decrees
> For you should undergo a sudden change;
> And the weak functions of one busy day,
> Reclaiming and extirpating, perform
> What all the slowly-moving years of time,
> With their united force, have left undone?
> By nature's gradual processes be taught;
> By story be confounded! Ye aspire
> Rashly, to fall once more; and that false fruit,
> Which, to your overweening spirits, yields
> Hope of a fight celestial, will produce
> Misery and shame.   [*Excursion*, IV.278–293]

The Wanderer, like Adam, has undergone a fall, viewed the signs of alienness that nature gave, and heard what Wordsworth calls "That visionary voice." But where Adam reproved the generation to come for their rash aspirations, the Wanderer shares the status of the "inattentive children of the world" thus reproved. Voicing the reproof by Providence, he both assumes his status as generated son and internalizes the higher voice of moral reprobation. If we recognize this "false fruit" and "Hope of fight celestial" as being like the false fruit and false hope of erring angel and man in *Paradise Lost,* we must also recognize how the externality of Milton's account of the Fall has been surpassed. The "reclaiming" here, like that of Goethe's Faust, does not involve a wrong moral direction (as did the building of the Tower of Babel) but a haste in reformation that marks false transcendence of historical time.

As the Wanderer continues his explanation of political and moral aspiration, he focuses proper transcendence outside the realm of time in an achievement of the individual mind: "unless above himself he can / Erect himself, how poor a thing is Man" (IV.330–331). This statement is itself citation (Seneca, by way of Daniel) and suggests the connection between heeding moral law and listening to poetic voice. The connection is not immediately an attractive one, and it is all too easy to dismiss the burden of poetic tradition, like the burden of moral law, as external to the self, indeed as the obstacle to self-transcendence. For Wordsworth, who insists on the connection, the process is far more fertile. He does acknowledge the possibility of conflict between artistic and moral obligations; the sonnet to Milton moves from an awareness of poetic power to the public domain: "and yet thy heart / The lowliest duties on herself did lay." [7] There are places, though, where morality seems only to provide a vocabulary for discussing the soul's power. It will not do to dismiss the moralizing Wordsworth as senility's parody of the prophet of the imagination. Chronology will not account for the problem, any more than will a blanket confusion of moral power with the power he identifies throughout his poetic career as imagination. Moral choice is related in a more central way to the moment of imaginative choice, of choice as arrest of time; from that association we are but a short step to the "spots of time" and the vocabulary we more generally associate with Wordsworth.

The connection between moral vision and imaginative power is taken up by the Wanderer at the close of *The Excursion*, Book IV. Imaginative sympathy, he says, has softened the Solitary's voice, and that softening constitutes both the authority of the voice guiding others and the capacity for the Solitary's own correction of vision. As if in imitation of the role of imaginative play, the Wanderer describes the Solitary's discourse as a Lethean stream that still "has caught at every turn / The colours of the sun" (IV.1125–26). This is not only to say, "There is a little light of truth in what you say," or "There is cause for optimism in such dark vision." The act of metaphor-making itself participates in what he calls "imaginative Will." What accounts for this strange term, this almost violent yoking of imagination and will? Wordsworth could—in fact did at one point—settle for a term as inobtrusive as "inspiration." But "imaginative Will" means more. Beyond a lower faculty that molds opinion is a higher faculty that gradually leads to "divine love, our intellectual soul" (IV.1275), and the progress in that direction can be described as progress toward the coming together of the terms imagination and will. As the spirit grows so does its awareness of itself as a will, free to choose its own imaginative nature:

> Thus deeply drinking-in the soul of things,
> We shall be wise perforce; and while inspired
> By choice, and conscious that the Will is free,
> Shall move unswerving, even as if impelled

By strict necessity, along the path
Of order and of good.   [IV.1265–70]

If the last phrase is a comedown into perhaps too willfully
moral terms, what elevates the lines that precede to loftier
heights is not unlike Miltonic abstraction. There is a seminal
indefiniteness that leaves open the degree to which the lines
are about moral will, the degree to which they describe
imaginative insight into the soul of things. The terms of
freedom and "strict necessity" may specifically echo Raphael's
warning to Adam (*PL*, V.523–543), and relate moral stance
to the elevation of prophetic strain. Yet Raphael is talking
about the will "not over-rul'd by Fate / Inextricable, or strict
necessity" (V.527–528). Wordsworth, turning the necessity
into metaphor, "as if impelled / By strict necessity," revisits
the lost Miltonic moment of choice and carries away new
moral energy that is to be directed to the choice of development of the new imaginative will. One may wish to hesitate
before claiming the phrase "inspired / By choice" as a cardi-
nal imaginative principle; but the inspiration that brings
Wordsworth out of the sterility of versified platitudes comes
from the relation of moral choice to the Miltonic poetry of
choice. On this we need more definite evidence.

Wordsworth's "Ode to Duty" announces in its very title
the concern with the relation of moral to imaginative will,
and in its very first line the concern with the poet's relation
to Milton. "Duty" is necessarily a harsh word, and if the idea
of an ode implies a certain aesthetic elevation, the sternness of
the moral term implies that the special source of elevation
in this poem will involve the poet's claiming for his own
height what others find aesthetically unapproachable. Yet the
notion of moral duty denies a tone of self-aggrandizement

as much as the form of an ode denies self-abnegation. Wordsworth would not have written this ode to duty, any more than
he would have incorporated in moral passages of *The Excursion* deliberate verbal echoes of Milton, had he not recognized
Miltonic strength of will as something other than willful self-
denial. Milton himself drew the distinction, and pointed to
the sterility of curbing the will when not specifically directed
to higher purpose:

In the Gospel we shall read a supercilious crew of masters, whose
holinesse, or rather whose evill eye, grieving that God should be
so facil to man, was to set straighter limits to obedience, then God
had set; to inslave the dignity of man, to put a garrison upon his
neck of empty and over-dignifi'd precepts.[8]

Wordsworth paraphrased from this passage of the divorce
tracts in the 1807 version of "Ode to Duty":

> Not seeking in the school of pride
> For "precepts over dignified,"
> Denial and restraint I prize
> No farther than they breed a second Will more wise.

Making wariness of precepts for their own sake something
of an inherited trait, Wordsworth claims for his own genes,
for his own genius, both the Miltonic wariness and the Miltonic sense of a more valuable restraint. Simple "submissiveness," the naïvely puritanical love of denial, must be
separated from the kind of limitation that is essential to the
creative will, that builds rather than destroys ego. Milton's
presence in this poem and throughout (especially the later)
Wordsworth, provides the voice that distinguishes creative
from stultifying will.

Using direct citation, Wordsworth shows his relationship
with Milton to be a matter of conscious choice, not uncon-

scious influence with its attendant anxieties about discovery and inadequacy. In relation to Milton, as in relation to moral duty, he finds his independent stance in serving "more strictly." The voice that announces debt and obligation will be recognizable as "the voice / Of my own wish" if his own wish is more demanding than that of some external agency. Yet such openness about intentionality belies its own assertiveness, and we tend to read the facility of self-revelation as a mask for a deeper anxiety about the terms in which the problem of independence is being formulated. If Wordsworth can be open about Milton, then it is not the father-poet's authoritative voice he fears but the authorial independence of his own model of authority. Perhaps for this reason Wordsworth was later impelled to cancel this strongest, most assertive stanza. Granted that duty must appear, as Geoffrey Hartman claims it is, "simply the inner strength of voluntarily dedicating oneself to the household bonds of life," [9] then the too voluntary recognition of further meaning must be suppressed. The canceled stanza brings the poem too directly or "willfully" from its ostensible subject (household duty) to its generative subject (imaginative will), confronting the "second Will more wise" as an assertion of power. Without this stanza, the poem retreats into the perhaps more outrageous, but—by virtue of blindness—more secure power of its own fictionality.[10]

Deliberate fiction-making may reach its climax in the stanza that follows, which raises duty to the power of natural law conceived as divine love, able to make the flowers laugh and the stars go right. Yet the flaunting of narrower definition is there all along, implicit in the personification of duty, in the whole attempt to imagine in it a more encompassing, more authoritative power. The first stanza of the poem addresses Duty as "Thou, who art victory and law / When empty terrors overawe." What are these "empty terrors" except fears about the authority of the controlling power? Wordsworth's decision to open the poem by addressing duty as "Stern Daughter of the Voice of God" emphasizes his concern over the authority of the voice.

The phrase "Daughter of the Voice" echoes Milton, himself repeating a rabbinic phrase. Eve, brought to the tree of knowledge, explains to the serpent that she may not eat nor touch: "God so commanded, and left that Command / Sole Daughter of his voice" (*PL*, IX.652–653). It has been pointed out that the "Bath Kol," literally "daughter of voice," is a lessening of the Voice.[11] Eve, repeating the divine injunction, chooses the least authoritative of the forms of revelation, and this fall in the status of the voice implicates the fall of man in violation of the voice. Yet Eve's anxiety is not about the presence of the prohibition but about violating it. She is not consciously concerned to lessen the voice, but concerned lest the command she has received seem lessened, seem less to the serpent than she has taken it to be. Her anxiety concerns the necessary diminution of any direct revelation preserved in back of the minds of God's creatures as a "daughter of the voice," what we may call a "de-generated" voice, one removed from its source of generation. In Genesis, God commands Adam not to eat of the tree; Eve, repeating the command, strengthens herself against it: "God hath said, Ye shall not eat of it, neither shall ye touch it, lest ye die." Adding the extra stipulation, "neither shall ye touch it," Eve (in this rabbinic interpretation) opened up the way to the violation of the voice.[12] Like those Milton condemns in the passage from *The Doctrine and Discipline of Divorce* cited above, Eve sets "straighter limits to obedience, th[a]n God had set."

Denial and restraint thus come to be valued beyond God's word of denial and restraint, deflecting anxiety away from God's word itself. Against this the Bible warns: "Every word of God is pure: he is a shield unto them that put their trust in him. Add thou not unto his words, lest he reprove thee, and thou be found a liar" (Prov. 30 : 5–6). Milton has Eve repeat her addition concerning touch and add also a further statement of law: "the rest, we live / Law to ourselves, our Reason is our Law" (IX.653–654). Milton's serpent then argues that he has "touch'd and tasted"; but more important, he seizes on the statement "Reason is our Law" to argue, to reason his way. His words persuade, being "impregn'd / With Reason, to her seeming, and with Truth" (IX.737–738).

In Wordsworth's poem such independent reasonableness is similarly apprehended as a danger. He appeals in the end to Duty to give "confidence of reason," and thus to govern that faculty Eve left outside the jurisdiction of authoritative voice. Throughout the poem his effort is similarly to aggrandize the power of duty. He fears not duty's awesomeness but the weakness of this conception of awesome authority, and his effort is to make convincing his conscious imaginative investment. To safeguard the authoritativeness of his moral abstraction, he adds sternness to Milton's "daughter of the voice," and pictures himself as having been in something of Eve's situation, coping with "the task imposed from Day to day" (a manuscript line), yet preferring "in smoother walks to stray." [13] If he did not give way to every whim, still he reacted to each external pressure as an imposition on the self. Now nothing seems more sterile than such willful assertion of independence, of "being to myself a guide." Wordsworth, engaged in writing *The Prelude*, knows that the epic, as the supremely guided poem, will only collapse if it degenerates into abortive self-assertion; this knowledge the *Recluse* fragment (addressed to Urania as guide) recognizes, Book I of *The Prelude* confronts. We shall have to look further at the epic concern for voice, but I point to it here to suggest how intertwined the problem of a moral "daughter of the voice" is with the problem of poetic voice. Describing in the "Ode to Duty" the relinquishment of the less certain for the more authoritative guide, Wordsworth is recapturing the new sense of guide at the conclusion of *Paradise Lost*. The first parents accept "Providence thir guide," with all the world before them where to choose. Adam addresses Michael as the "safe guide," by whose direction he will "to the hand of Heav'n submit / However chast'ning" (XI.371–372). Far from simply making a necessary bow to external authority, Adam accepts, in Wordsworth's terms, the chastening voice as that of his own will; he comes to feel, like the "Ode to Duty" poet, that his "submissiveness was choice." The second will, the choice of submissiveness, is the lowly wisdom that replaces the vain attempt of satanic dream, in which Eve, at the flying heights of false wisdom, suddenly realizes that "My Guide was gone, and I, methought, sunk down / And fell asleep" (*PL*, V.91–92). The fruit of such knowledge is a rude awakening; the "Ode to Duty," which glimpses a dreamed Eden in stanza II, turns a more awake eye to the world in which moral knowledge is more painfully purchased. One can thus apply to the Wordsworth ode the kind of comment Harold Toliver makes about the conclusion of *Paradise Lost:* "The soaring hope of the hieratic voice is anchored in human limitations and in an articulate moral program." [14]

Though the vocabulary of morality seems inescapably to be an imposition on the will, it was not, according to Wordsworth, always so:

> Once, Man entirely free, alone and wild,
> Was blest as free—for he was Nature's child.
> He, all superior but his God disdained,
> Walked none restraining, and by none restrained:
> Confessed no law but what his reason taught,
> Did all he wished, and wished but what he ought.
>
> ["Descriptive Sketches," ll. 433–438]

This is Wordsworth's vision of Eden—or perhaps a still more fanciful state, since "Confessed no law but what his reason taught" is like Eve's description of the way the first parents live—"Law to ourselves, and Reason is our Law"—but without any "daughter of his voice" to decree prohibition. Wordsworth's last phrase, "and wished but what he ought," suggests the nagging vocabulary of proscription just enough to mark our distance from such harmony of desire and duty, with the poet standing between the world of morality and the amoral, Adamic realm. "Descriptive Sketches" continues:

> As man in his primeval dower arrayed
> The image of his glorious Sire displayed,
> Even so, by faithful Nature guarded, here
> The traces of primeval Man appear.

One must stop right here, for the next lines intrude with the moral terms that mark the distance of fallen from unfallen man. In Wordsworth, morality serves as mediating distance, keeping out those who cannot see beyond the sense in which duty is an imposition.

The "Ode to Duty" safeguards itself from such an audience less fit, if more numerous, by its surface unattractiveness. Its mask is that of performing household duties, its myth that of son addressing his muse. Though we think of morality as concerning the relations between man and man, this poem's attention is elsewhere. Its very title blocks the way, obtruding the stern face of "duty" in the doorway barred against those who want to argue about freedom and equality between men. The ode is concerned with an internal freedom that transcends conceiving of duty as a set of restrictions on one's sense of identity and finds the sources of freedom in imaginative confrontation with inherited law. We are closest to the poem's idea of freedom when we think in terms of poetic limitation. Wordsworth himself talks about the "republican austerity" of Milton's sonnets,[15] and is impelled to write his own when confronted with the recognition that the limitations of such form are a source of strength that helps create the self it expresses:

> Pleased if some Souls (for such there needs must be)
> Who have felt the weight of too much liberty,
> Should find brief solace there, as I have found.
>
> ["Nuns fret not . . ."]

The weight of too much liberty, like the weight of sin borne by Satan and fallen Adam, is lifted by paying poetic debts to an external source of limitation.

Though one may not finally wish to read the "Ode to Duty" as an allegory of poetic influence, thinking of the source of duty as a poetic authority helps explain something that Wordsworth intends both in terms of morality and poetry: the sense in which the self is not obliterated but indeed re-created by a choice submissiveness. The sonnet on the bounds of the sonnet ends by asserting its own power; when he says that others may "find brief solace there, as I have found," he is referring not only to the sonnet in general but to this particular poem as spelling out its own solace. Such self-assertiveness marks a consciousness and a sense of poetic

power born of the disciplined adherence to a set form. The
"Ode to Duty" ends not only by asserting that its poet, "made
lowly wise," has picked up the Miltonic brand; it addresses
Duty the way a poet does a muse, with the special unity of
supreme submissiveness (the awareness that restoration must
come knocking at the door and is not to be campaigned for)
coupled with supreme self-assertiveness (it is the poet's will;
he himself binds himself in special relationship).

Accepting higher guidance with an act of will, Wordsworth, on a diminutive scale, reacts as does Blake to Milton's
descent. Blake does not take on a brightened world the way
a dutiful Hermes might slip on a winged sandal; the poet is,
after all, binding to himself all the natural world, and his
tone echoes the splendor of that world: "I stooped down &
bound it on to walk forward thro' Eternity" (*Milton*, 21.14).
Blake's action is as assertive as his poem is mighty. The "Ode
to Duty," muted as it is, must be read as involved in a miniature stooping and binding of this kind. When Milton enters
Blake's tarsus, "all the Vegetable World appeared on my left
Foot, / As a bright sandal formed immortal of precious stones
& gold." The stanza of Wordsworth's ode that, in little, attempts such vision transformed by the binding-on of natural
law is just the stanza that provoked most annoyance:

> Stern Lawgiver! yet thou dost wear
> The Godhead's most benignant grace;
> Nor know we anything so fair
> As is the smile upon thy face:
> Flowers laugh before thee on their beds
> And fragrance in thy footing treads;
> Thou dost preserve the stars from wrong;
> And the most ancient heavens, through Thee, are fresh and
>   strong.

The *Edinburgh Review* commented, "The two last lines seem to be utterly without meaning; we have no sort of conception in what sense *Duty* can be said to keep the old skies *fresh*, and the stars from wrong." [16] The "freshness" comes from the fact that as duty is released from a narrower meaning, from being shorthand for a number of prescriptions, it takes on the generative power of a personified being. Faust tells Helen, "Dasein ist Pflicht"; reversing the formula, as it were, in this abstraction from real to literary time, Wordsworth makes duty call into existence the responsive elements. The equivocation between a moral term and a benignant grace makes the suspension that is a moment of choice into an area of free creation.

One imagines Wordsworth sharing the smile on Duty's face, the laughter of heaven overlooking the vain attempts of the mass of men. Involved in the relations between men, we perceive Duty as a "stern Lawgiver"; involved in a special relation to a higher power, the poet perceives Duty as a benignant grace. To the neurotic bind in the chaos of chance desires he contrasts the emancipating power that "from vain temptations dost set free." Coleridge may be paraphrasing this as "from feeble yearnings freed" in the terribly personal poem "Duty Surviving Self-Love." But Wordsworth remains impersonal, in the best sense able to move from an immediate to a universal condition. With a fresh vocabulary he is rephrasing the traditional concept of divine logos keeping the cosmos moving freely. One might be tempted to cite Dante; but here is Milton:

> Confusion heard his voice, and wild uproar
> Stood rul'd, stood vast infinitude confin'd;
> Till at his second bidding darkness fled,
> Light shone, and order from disorder sprung:

Swift to thir several Quarters hasted then
The cumbrous Elements, Earth, Flood, Air, Fire,
And this Ethereal quintessence of Heav'n
Flew upward, spirited with various forms,
That roll'd orbicular, and turn'd to Stars
Numberless, as thou seest, and how they move;
Each had his place appointed, each his course,
The rest in circuit walls this Universe. [*PL*, III.710–721]

Through most of the ode Wordsworth is no doubt referring
to the domestic rather than the cosmic ordering of things, and
this constitutes both the painful individuality of the poem
and the dearly purchased exceptionality of the lines to which
the *Edinburgh Review* objected. The homely quality of the
verse is just what brings it round, like Samson having performed
his duty, "Home to his Father's house." Such is the paradox
of the poetry of voice: its submissiveness (in danger of childlike obedience) is that of a son acknowledging the generated
quality of his own literary being; its assertiveness (in danger
of childish presumptiveness) is that of a son claiming the
hierarchic specialness of that generational line. To claim
literary kinship is to blind oneself to the fact that one has
invested an abstract embodiment of one's own standards with
the power that abstraction is seen to have. To make of Duty
an authorial figure, one who has moral authority, one who
"authors" one's own being, is to see one's second will accordant with an inherited line, a line of those who have suppressed their own voices, their own primary wills, in order
to come into relation with more authoritative voice. Recognizing the generational gap that makes voice wholly other,
the poet himself assumes that voice. Acknowledging the
authorial distance of Milton, Wordsworth borrows Milton's
phrase for authoritative command and addresses his poem to
that generated power: "Stern Daughter of the Voice of God."

Correction of the Voice

The "Ode to Duty" was not consciously inspired by the phrase "Daughter of the Voice of God," or by the need to find doctrinal approval of the desire for subservience. Indeed, Milton's phrase came as an afterthought, though with it Wordsworth turned a lesser poem into one concerned with poetic voice. The poem's own authoritative voice of duty then seems to have directed purging the poem of more willful first ideas. The deletion of the second-will stanza seems a sacrifice to the process of revision; nor is this the only instance in which his most imaginative ideas had to be put aside or veiled. In the first stanza Wordsworth revised his 1807 text which had duty free the soul not only from vain temptations but "from strife and from despair." It was "despair" that bothered him, expressing as it did too much intentionality behind the writing of the poem. He erased first by blurring the image, changing "from strife and from despair" to "from all the weary strife." Then a way of making the line more poetic without returning it to the personal occurred to him; he added an additional verb, turning the last line into an independent clause: "And calm'st the weary strife of frail humanity."

Whether one chooses to call the loss of "despair" a failure of will, or find in "calm'st" a wiser second will, the process of revision asks to be seen in terms that the ode itself discusses. After a poem is written, or after a version is written, the process of revision becomes a correction of voice, and shifts the relationship of the poem to an inherited body of poetry by allowing the poet to stand over his own, more "original" line the way an originator or parent stands over a production or child in need of correction. The concept of originality is thus itself modified, and what the poet first conceived comes to seem less original, less close to its literary origins, than what is produced by a wiser imaginative will. As a step back from a first thought, revision often involves a humbling of the self, a process in which the poet must be made, as he is at the end of the "Ode to Duty," more "lowly wise." But through such self-sacrifice, he rises to higher imaginative achievement. The process of revision is thus a way of writing oneself into the poetic tradition: the relationship of the second will to the first becomes a metaphor for, and to some extent actualizes, the relationship of a more authoritative voice to one's own.

Wordsworth, acknowledging as Milton's the distinction between godly and false restraint, directs us back to Milton's own process of revision. The concept of choice submissiveness to a higher voice can help explain the revision of verse and the revision of attitude so often a subject of Milton's, as of Wordsworth's, poetry. Three examples of Milton's second will in action show the poet confronting the arrest of time in which his poetic choices lie open, and rewriting that temporal arrest as the temporality of his own literary history.

(1) The Muse's Woe

The story of Orpheus is about Pluto's second will, and the Orpheus passage of "Lycidas," with the work of revision preserved in the Trinity College manuscript, demonstrates the poet's second will. The story of Orpheus also appealed to the young Wordsworth, whose translation "Orpheus and Eurydice" from the *Georgics* may use some phrases that relate more to Milton than to Virgil. Two images—"While overhead, as still he wept and sung, / Aerial rocks in shaggy prospect hung," and "Then too upon the voice and faltering tongue / Eurydice in dying accents hung"—contain some of the earliest use of the "indefinite abstraction" caught in the word "hung" that Wordsworth specifically identified with Milton. Hanging over the abyss and hanging suspended in a listening relationship are two of the most central images in Wordsworth's evocation of Milton.

What interested Wordsworth in the image of hovering suspension interested Milton in the larger sense: the story of Orpheus hovers over the moment of death. Whereas death, everywhere but in the realm of this myth, is the one blow that strikes once and strikes no more, the double death of Eurydice images a stasis on the moment of loss. Caroline Mayerson notes: "Milton identifies himself with Orpheus at the moment when the singer was destroyed by the forces of barbarism," and his death is emblem of "the neglect of the true poet by a trivial-minded and mercenary society." Also, "the tradition persisted that Orpheus had been a *theologus,* who had sung and written of the gods and the beginnings of the world." [17] Together these identifications make Orpheus haunt the imagination as the type of the poet, "In darkness, and with dangers compast round" (one further phrase to be added to Wordsworth's most habitual evocations of Milton). The image is that of the artist outside the stream of time, even though finally cast into it. Not only in his relation to society that insists on reintegration rather than fixation on loss, but within the realm of art itself, Orpheus represents the power of stasis: his is the power of song to still nature, and his is the confrontation with the arrested moment of death. On the other hand, his is also the archetypal confrontation with discontinuity, of premature arrest in life and song. In Ovid, Orpheus promises when he asks for Eurydice from Pluto and Proserpine: "She shall be yours to rule when ripe of age she / Shall have lived out her allotted years." [18] His complaint is against unripe death, and her second, like her first passing away, is a prototype of premature arrest. As Gretchen Finney says, "The story of Lycidas is the story of Orpheus." [19]

The reference to Orpheus in the Trinity manuscript was first couched thus:

> ay mee I fondly dreame
> had yee been there, for what could that have don?
> what could the golden hayrd Calliope
> for her inchaunting son
> when shee beheld (the gods farre sighted bee)
> his goarie scalpe rowle downe the Thracian lee.

Comparing this passage with the lines as we now have them, one would not question the revision, though the difficulty with the original is not quite accounted for in the expression of distaste with which Diekhoff greets it. He finds the line with the parenthesis "so bad, so obviously half mere filler, that Milton can only throw it away and rewrite the passage in which it occurs." [20] The danger of the line is its lightness, the way it slights the terrible disparity between enduring and knowing, between being caught up in *durée* and looking on from outside time, from the distance which makes past ("beheld") and future ("rowle downe") one.

The point of the line is undeniable, that whether or not the gods have foresight is irrelevant; Calliope's foresight is a species of the premature arrest that is the subject of "Lycidas," for the parenthesis arrests her time only to find the act accomplished, the terrible tragedy already over in the next line. Bergson says: "All foreseeing is in reality seeing, and this seeing takes place when we reduce as much as we please an interval of future tense while preserving the relation of its parts to one another. . . . But what does reducing an interval of time mean, except emptying or impoverishing the conscious states which fill it?" [21] What is unsatisfactory in what Milton wrote first is not the relation of the parts but the impoverishment, the apparent ease with which the muse stands outside time while her son suffers in it. Such an expression of perspective errs, for, like Sin, it too easily bridges what Wordsworth calls the "froward chaos of futurity" (*Prelude,* V.349). The correction Milton makes in the margin attempts to make that gap more acutely felt:

> what could the golden hayrd Calliope
> for her inchaunting son
> whome universal nature might lament
> and heaven and hel deplore
> when his divine head downe
> the stream was sent . . .

With the word "might" time is suspended and the sense of the pastness of the past forgotten. For the moment, ongoingness seems to be captured and Calliope to share in the same continuum as her son, putting her within it as if there were a choice and nature might still respond to Orpheus' song of lament, with his death depending on how Calliope acts, how the present moment turns out. It sounds like the regretful tone of "Il Penseroso":

> But, O sad Virgin, that thy power
> Might raise *Musaeus* from his bower,
> Or bid the soul of *Orpheus* sing.

These lines are aware of the fall at every point and self-conscious about the premature arrest of Orpheus' achievement, since the granting of "what love did seek" is a story like the one the following line introduces, "half told." We know the other half—what happens after hell conditionally grants Eurydice's return—and that knowledge is the knowledge of death. The way "might" suspends time in "Lycidas" is still closer to the unconditional surmise of "L'Allegro"— "That Orpheus' self may heave his head / From golden slumber on a bed"—or of *Comus:* "strains that might create a soul / Under the ribs of death." In any case "might" in "Lycidas" does correct the too facile parenthesis which was closer to the satanically intrusive suspension of time of Comus himself:

> Some Virgin sure
> (For so I can distinguish by mine Art)
> Benighted in these Woods.   [*Comus*, ll. 148–150]

Having overcome that kind of suspension, the poem might have proceeded, leaving unnoticed the remaining hint of unconsciousness in the process of arrest. But the final version Milton wrote makes other formulations seem irresponsibly negligent of passing time:

> Had ye been there—for what could that have done?
> What could the Muse herself that *Orpheus* bore,
> The Muse herself, for her enchanting son
> Whom Universal nature did lament,
> When by the rout that made the hideous roar,
> His gory visage down the stream was sent,
> Down the swift *Hebrus* to the *Lesbian* shore?

In the revised version the repetition of the words "the Muse herself" is part of the arrest of time, and the change from "might" to "did" makes it an arrest that is knowledge.[22] What could Calliope do? Before the question is completed, nature is described with the words "did lament"; the chance to do something is over, in the past tense. The final version achieves the painful sense of loss as time goes by, the fallen realization that the gory vision is not being foreseen but lamented after the fact. Having read through the line "The Muse herself, for her enchanting son," the reader is caught in the anticipation of the event and is shocked in reading the next lines to find it is already over.

(2) Home-bred Woes

Milton's "At a Solemn Music" is a poem whose ecstatic vision must be carefully controlled. The acceptable sensuousness of the appeal of music could break away from the kind of submissiveness that marks a religious, if not a sexual, passiveness into an assertion of sensual and poetic power. The marriage of voice and verse with which the poem begins is studiously correct, but language is being pushed as far as it will go.

In the manuscript, the line that follows the marriage metaphor, the wedding of divine sounds, extends the power of sound: "dead things wth inbreath'd sense able to pierce." Like the image in "L'Allegro," "Such as the meeting soul may pierce," this could suggest the erotic consummation which is a legitimate image of stasis. Ficino described such power of music: "By the very movement of the subtle air it penetrates strongly: by its contemporation it flows smoothly: by the conformity of its quality it floods us with a wonderful pleasure." [23] But unlike the moments of arrest in "Il Penseroso" and "Lycidas," which are followed by a death, a fall that is knowledge, the lines that follow here, like the "long drawn out" sweetness that follows in "L'Allegro," suggest unbroken continuity: "Whilst yor equall raptures temper'd sweet / in high misterious holie spousall meet." "Whilst," like "meanwhile," stops time "in smoother walks to stray"—to use the terms of the "Ode to Duty." It is a self-assertive stasis, beyond what is permitted in poetic and experiential rhythms. "At a Solemn Music" must, like "Il Penseroso," punctuate the "long drawn out" sweetness of "L'Allegro" with a self-arrest—not a restraint that denies the sensual overtone, but one more wise that images consummation and is thus aware of the knowledge of death. Milton revises in a way that makes the succession of metaphors an expression of submissiveness to a higher order of time. Here the word "pierce" is left at the end of the line while the poem goes on to other matters.

The lines omitted from the final version to make the statement of fantasy follow immediately are the most interesting of all:

> and whilst yor equall raptures temper'd sweet
> in high misterious holie spousall meet
> snatch us from earth a while
> us of our selves & home bred woes beguile.

Heyworth dismisses the omission by saying, "It is clear that with these passages interpolated, the poem was in its early drafts very diffuse, and was to that extent much less effective than it is in the final version." [24] The nature of that diffuseness is worth attention. The more that is said to be going on while something else is taking place, the longer that period seems to be "present." The long "whilst," which suspends time for four lines while those raptures are taking place, carries stasis beyond what is allotted to man. Richard Hooker wrote, "There is also that carrieth as it were into ecstasies, filling the mind with an heavenly joy and for the time in a manner severing it from the body." [25]

For Milton, it is essential that Hooker's qualification, "for the time," be clearly expressed. Musical "ecstasies" are properly qualified in the Nativity Ode, for example, where the

air "With thousand echoes still prolongs each heav'nly close."
The very word which suggests the drawing out of harmonious
sound—"close"—binds duration with termination; "each"
close describes the repeated and therefore individually limited
arrests in music thus reconciled to time. Compare these lines
on the university carrier in which Milton toys with these
serious themes in light verse:

> Rest that gives all men life, gave him his death,
> And too much breathing put him out of breath;
> Nor were it contradiction to affirm
> Too long vacation hast'ned on his term.
>
> ["Another on the Same"]

Whether the music is light or solemn does not alter the de-
leterious effect of such "vacation"; John Hollander may be
said to echo Milton's own uncontradicting affirmation when
he cites as the primary reason for canceling the "and whilst"
passage of "At a Solemn Music" the fact that it "would have
tended to hasten the conclusion of the poem." [26] It is "too
long vacating," prolonging stasis as in the satanic violation of
time.

The canceled verses point to another necessary limitation,
that of the intrusion of self into song. Being beguiled of the
self is something Comus and Thyrsis have made us familiar
with as the limit of song. But the canceled lines go further
and introduce more of "us" into heavenly song than is con-
ceivable without breaking that rapture and returning it to
earth. Gretchen Finney explains that Milton "always avoids
the literalism of lesser poets—a fault that he only narrowly
escaped when he so fortunately eliminated from an early
draft of 'At a Solemn Musick' the line, 'snatch us from earth
awhile.'" [27] But there is more at stake here than literalism.

If the phrase "home bred woes" had been written after Milton's own domestic problems began to create the kind of discord in his life that it could suggest in these lines, we might have had difficulty untying the apron strings of biographical criticism. But no specific event in Milton's personal history is needed to make us see that the image here is breaking out in rebellion against the heavenly order of song; it carries attention out of song into the problem of achieving impersonality of tone. Interpreting "home bred" in another sense, we would need to remark that the soul has but one home, and the attempt to grant permanent status to what must be seen as a wandering place is satanic stasis. Like Comus finding "home-felt delight" in the Lady's song, thus pointing to the way he will try to carry its enchantment out of song into action, the poet is introducing at this point in the song more than can be sustained. He marginally emends "home bred" to "native," but then overcomes the whole temptation and deletes the passage.

What makes phrases like "wed your divine sounds" and "to his celestial consort us unite" accord with the metaphoric world of the poem while "home bred woes" violates it is itself a question related to timing. The poem is about existential analogies to song, so at some point it must carry its statements about the stasis of song specifically into human time. The important question is, when? The long suspended sentence that forms the poem's basic structure suggests grammatically that premature arrest must be avoided in metaphor. Thus the manuscript reads:

> that wee . . .
> may rightly answere that melodious noise
> by leaving out those harsh chromatick jarres
> of sin that all our musick marres

& in our lives & in our song
may keepe in tune wth heaven till God ere long
to his celestiall consort us unite.

"Leaving out those harsh chromatick jarres" is exactly what
Milton does, as if heeding the voice of his own poem. The
passage jars in separating the half steps— "& in our lives & in
our song" [28]—for metaphoric reality depends on not shattering the fiction of that unity till the poem achieves its consummation. In the final version, not a single image, but the whole
poem then steps out of time. The suspended sentence ends
with paradise arrested at its period; the concluding prayer
then forms the break and reconciliation that is stillness in
motion:

> . . . whilst they stood
> In first obedience and their state of good.
> O may we soon again renew that Song,
> And keep in tune with Heav'n, till God ere long
> To his celestial consort us unite,
> To live with him, and sing in endless morn of light.

Unpreceded now by the dichotomies of life and song, the
phrase that kills the analogy by bringing it out in the open
is "And keep in tune with Heav'n." Just at this point we meet
the word that limits the arrest of song, "till," and are reconciled to the fall and the process of salvation that works
through time. This is not to say that the awareness of time
has been suspended for the whole song; as Hollander notes,
" 'as once we did' introduces the historical dimension, and
clearly outlines the reference of the final prayer's 'O may we
soon.' " [29] After reviewing and accepting history as outlined
in the sentence that leads to it, the prayer begins back in the
fallen world and looks forward, making the passing of time

no longer the flaw but the means of redemption: "O may we soon again resume that Song." The rhythms of the next line are faster: "And keep in tune with Heav'n"; having now overcome the temptation of arrest outside time, they move forward in happy acceptance of the ongoingness that is the way toward the ultimate stasis, the union with the divine in song. The poem thus actualizes higher grace that is the movement toward us, dissolving bounds, when *musica mundana* and *musica humana*, subject and execution, are the same. The last line can properly employ both the words "live" and "sing," for in the heavenly music and the music the "measured motion" of the whole poem has made, they are one.

(3) *His Own Woes*

More extended and more self-consciously intended as an arrest of time than the "and whilst" passage of "At a Solemn Music" is the flower passage of "Lycidas." While in "At a Solemn Music" he must delete or temper the arrest of time, in "Lycidas" Milton adds a passage of extended arrest, preserving in the finished poem the temporal process of revision of attitude toward fictional arrest. If we return to the manuscript of "Lycidas," we can observe Milton revising the passage, correcting the voice that calls together the imagined funeral procession. He first wrote:

> bring hither all yor quaint enamel'd eyes
> that on the green terfe suck the honied showrs
> and purple all the ground wth vernal flowrs
> to strew the laureat herse where Lycid' lies.[30]

Between the last two verses he drew a line leading to the marginal words, "Bring the rathe &c," which direct the reader to the trial page preceding "Lycidas" on which he worked out the passage to be inserted:

Bring the rathe primrose that unwedded dies
colouring the pale cheeks of uninjoyd love
and that sad floure that strove
to write his owne woes on the vermeil graine
next adde Narcissus y^t still weeps in vaine
the woodbine and ye pancie freak't wth jet
the glowing violet
the cowslip wan that hangs his pensive head
and every bud that sorrows liverie wears
let Daffadillies fill thire cups with tears
bid Amaranthus all his beautie shed
to strew the laureat herse &c.

The interposed "little ease" expands into a more substantial suspension of actuality, and entwines pastoral arrest of time with the arrest that is death.

Earlier in the poem vegetation reflected the state of desolation at the death of Lycidas: there were harsh berries, wild thyme, gadding vines, cankered roses, and drooping leaves. Now calling for "every bud that sorrows liverie wears," the poem shifts to a less direct, more literary relation between the vegetable and emotional worlds. The change makes nature seem to participate in the arrest of time—or rather, a more fictional nature is participating. The awareness that these flowers are evoked from literary rather than natural gardens only increases the sense that death is the mother of their beauty, so that their presence here seems required by a familial or, in a new sense, "natural" bond to Lycidas. We seem closer to the artifice of eternity, and therefore, magically, closer to truth. For the moment this literariness escapes the easier fiction-making of the beginning of the poem, and presents a perspective in which the poeticizing of grief is a clarifying, not an obfuscating process. Wayne Shumaker, writing about the flower passage of the finished poem, explains this effect: "In the catalogue of flowers Milton says not only, 'There is brilliance as well as dullness in nature,' but also, more indirectly, 'The flowers named here are those poetically associated with sadness. I have made a selection to suit my elegiac theme.' He is not, then, unhinged by his grief. He does not really distort." [31]

The awareness of distortion comes later, when he says, "Let our frail thoughts dally with false surmise." Meanwhile, if there is to be a false surmise, a little ease before fiction is destroyed, he must arrest the excessive self-consciousness that carries fiction beyond pastoral presentness, that makes image come out of song in a bond with man too strong to be broken into a later awareness of the image's fictionality. The primrose, itself emblem of early youth, must lose some of the human suffering Milton ascribes to it. To order the image back into song, he changes "the rathe primrose that unwedded dies / colouring the pale cheeks of uninjoyd love" to "the rathe Primrose that forsaken dies," leaving the story of the flower condensed in the single word "forsaken"—perhaps more plaintive for that word's "indefinite abstraction" of loss—but with the flower less specifically uprooted from a floral to a human condition. He changes "sorrows liverie" to "sad embroidery," which, mingling decorativeness with the awareness of death, is more easily harmonized into the poetic arrangement. With aesthetic stoicism he omits Narcissus that "still weeps in vaine," because the unity of fiction with eternity must not be prematurely arrested and must await the stillness of the song in heaven, where sweet societies "wipe the tears for ever from his eyes." [32]

The most bitter constraint is in striking out "and that sad floure that strove / to write his owne woes on the vermeil

graine." The lines are a mirror of the poet writing his own
woes into the elegy, for the poet, like Apollo in Ovid's *Metamorphoses*, confronts in the hyacinth, "that sad floure," the
premature arrest of time. Apollo mourns: "Fallen before your
time, O Hyacinthus," and such is Milton's plaint about the
death of Lycidas—and about writing the poem. If Hyacinthus
is "defrauded of the prime of youth," mentioning the hyacinth at this point in "Lycidas" would defraud the passage of
its fictional innocence. Self-consciousness is a kind of death
of which the prime of youth must be sweetly ignorant. To be
sure, the elegy sustains more overt shocks of awareness than
this one, but the flower passage is to be the poem's most deliberate fiction, most suspended awareness of actuality. In
the course of that suspension, a delicate change in the relation
of awareness to actuality takes place. More destructive than
the awareness that one has been writing about one's own
death is the awareness of how simple is the fiction covering
that fact, how fragile the poetic figure in which such an
enormous emotional investment has been made. The deliberate fiction of the flower passage requires that the poet overlook the simple fact that his investment is in the poem, not
the occasion for the poem or the experiential awareness that is
the poem's subject. Strangely, the frailty of human life is easier to face than is the frailty of one's literary figure for life's
frailty. Such involution must stop; Milton excises the hyacinth, and leaves in its place the less literary crowtoe.

With this deliberate de-sophistication, he banishes the overtones that would have reached out of song to grasp human
experience with a hold hard to release in a higher reconciliation. "Lycidas" is, in John Crowe Ransom's terms, "a poem
nearly anonymous," so the "poet must suppress the man, or
the man would suppress the poet."[33] The suppression is

choice, to turn a phrase from the "Ode to Duty"; the lines of greatest self-conscious wisdom about the relation between man and poet are suppressed by a wiser second will. Milton thus reserves the hyacinth image, as he originally intended, for the briefest funereal speaker:

> Next *Camus*, revered Sire, went footing slow,
> His Mantle hairy, and his Bonnet sedge,
> Inwroght with figures dim, and on the edge
> Like to that sanguine flower inscrib'd with woe.
> "Ah! Who hath reft" (quoth he) "my dearest pledge?"

The hyacinth reference belongs to Camus because its veiled allusion to the whole poem fits best the mantled, melancholy man. He is all wisdom and eloquence in his ancient appearance and knowing brevity; Perdita herself could not have done better than assign to him alone the flower that in the circumstances of this poem is self-knowledge. His single line, standing apart in self-reflection from the whole poem, says all there is to say.[34] The self-consciousness of the image is the self-consciousness of his question which enacts its theme —a question reft by the uncouth swain's parenthesis, as is the swain by higher voices and Lycidas by heaven.

The gentleness of the Camus passage takes on additional significance when we see it in light of the hyacinth passage Milton excised. Anxiety about inadequate expression is deflected from lines that would have brought the poet himself too much into the poem, and seems diffused when attributed back to this "revered Sire." As a father figure, Camus bears the burden of the anxiety of the poet; but more important, as a weak father, Camus makes the shattering energies of the threat seem dissipated before the threat can touch the speaker of the flower passage. Camus pre-empts the possible response of retreating into the inexpressive, and the poem can move on with assurance that, having adequately—and indeed movingly —couched that alternative, the poem will be able to absorb other voice confrontations into its own temporal progress toward fuller voice. Camus does not even speak the hyacinth reference, which is, rather, written into his garb; when he passes by with his "figures dim," so does the threat of silence, of the poet's own figures dim proving inadequate before those of a more revered Sire.

In the Orpheus passage, the parenthesis "the gods farre sighted bee" made the awareness of fictional time too facile; in "At a Solemn Music," the "and whilst" passage made the use of fictional time too bold; in the hyacinth reference, the expression of the poet's own self-consciousness made the arrest of time too great an independent achievement. Each revision, reordering the relationship of fictional to endured temporality, silences a discordant voice before one more accordant with the poem as a whole. And the poem itself becomes the ground on which this revision in voice can be seen to take place. "At a Solemn Music" becomes a piece of solemn music that resolves its discords to keep in tune with heaven. The opening of "Lycidas" expresses as the shattering of leaves the victory over self-consciousness felt in the canceling of manuscript leaves. The closing of the poem, in destroying the fiction of the speaker, enacts the final correction of the voice; and the last step in temporal reintegration is the last line, in which the poem turns to time outside its own fictional arrest: "Tomorrow to fresh Woods, and Pastures new." Concerning different pastures Geoffrey Hartman asks, "Is there a more archetypal situation of the self-conscious mind than the figure of the halted traveler confronting an inscription, confronting the knowledge of death and startled by it into feeling 'the burden of the mystery'?" [35] Perhaps we may see Milton in poetic process as such a traveler, confronting early in his inscription the knowledge of death; with a second will he shoulders the burden of the mystery and carries it to the end of the poem. We are startled into feeling that the whole song of the uncouth swain has become the inscription over the tomb of the unready poet—an inscription Milton and we, as halted travelers, read and pass by. Milton thus enacts the myth of poetic belatedness: he comes to stand in relation to his earlier voice as does the later poet who, reading Miltonic inscription, must lay to rest the "uncouth swain" in his own voice and go on to pastures new.

Wordsworth and Milton's Voice

If one isolated the major considerations in Miltonic revision of voice as the subduing of self-concern and the timely arrest of stasis, then the former could serve as guide to Wordsworth's revision of his poems, the latter to the dramatization of revision in the well-wrought poems themselves.

Comparing the final text with extant Wordsworth manuscripts gives some simple examples of restraint in expression of self. The opening of *The Recluse* was originally written in first person and later revised, substituting third-person pronouns. The achieved emphasis of the break between the "I" that is and the "he" that was can stand for the separation that is self-consciousness, "conscious of myself / And of some other being" (*Prelude*, II.32–33). A more significant illustration of the way the dramatization of self-consciousness in verse is related to a second will is the Boy of Winander passage of *The Prelude* (V.364ff). Manuscript JJ (transcribed in the Appendix to De Selincourt's *Prelude*) preserves the impulse to collapse verse into self-concern. The boy would

Blow mimic hootings to the silent owls
And bid them answer him. And they would shou[t]
Across the watry vale and shout again
Responsive to my call with tremulous sobs
And long halloes.

If these lines catch the unconscious will to pull down the
fiction into first person, it may be particularly noteworthy
that the change occurs on an assertion of power, in the phrase
"Responsive to my call." Wordsworth's anxiety, like Milton's
in the hyacinth passage of "Lycidas," concerns the adequacy
of "my call" when nature is felt to be alien. As if anticipating
the knowledge of the loss to come, the poet at this moment of
solipsism slips into the first person, for beneath the consciousness of fiction the self feels that nature responsive to a "him"
is as alien as nature not responsive at all. The use of the third
person is consciousness' way of evading or remaining outside
the dialogue between self and scene, and the slip into first
person represents the unconscious evasion of the evasion. Or
perhaps it would be better to say that the slip into first person
produces a text too expressive, too "conscious" of the poetic
problem. Restoring the third person, the poet restores the unconsciousness of the text, its fictional projection of the relation
between the caller and the called. The poet's own, authoritative voice remains at a distance while this "conversation" between boy and birds takes place.

Incorporating the incident into *The Prelude*, Wordsworth
chose to retain the projection onto a third person, and so
made the necessary pronominal changes. Where he wrote in
the manuscript, "pauses of deep silence mocked my skill," he
wrote "his" instead of "my" in the 1805 *Prelude*. In the
1850 text the wording was changed to "a lengthened pause /
Of silence came and baffled his best skill." One could say
that this change concerns alliteration, for the words "silence,"

"baffled," "best," "skill" ironically represent in the chiasmic crossing a perfect responsiveness of the poet's medium to his call. But even considered independently, the change from "mocked" to "baffled" subdues the expression of the poet's own concern with the relation between the artist-as-mocker (imitating nature) and nature-as-mocker (unresponsive to his efforts and thus seeming to scorn them).

The boy finds that nature does not listen, and the boy dies; Wordsworth goes on to relocate the gap that is consciousness, from the difference between the poet and nature, to the difference between the boy that was and the man who stands over the grave, "listening only to the gladsome sounds" of live children. Standing mute for a "long half hour," the poet enacts a reinterpretation of the "lengthened pause / Of silence" that baffled the boy; nature's failure to respond can then be reread as an anticipation of death. The poem thus presents its own capable revision of the incident, and can even image its own nature as revision: the uncertain process of composition is reflected in the image of an uncertain heaven "received / Into the bosom of the steady lake." As product, the poem is just such a receptive holder of the uncertainties, the moments of choice, of the poem-as-process.

Imaging the process of revision, the Boy of Winander episode gains its place in Book V rather than, say, Book II of *The Prelude:* Book V is about books, and the episode dramatizes the rereading of experience. Imaging the process of revisiting the moment of loss, the episode gains its place in the poetry of choice. The experience of the boy, "in that silence while he hung / Listening," is both lost (the birds are silent; the boy dies) and not lost (the poet reworks the failed listening relationship as his listening to the live children). If a premature assertion of the "I" masks an anxiety about power of voice, then the listening relationship, in which one's own voice is silenced before voice more authoritative or more distinctly separated from the self, images the successful resolution of that anxiety. The "indefinite abstraction" of choice finds permanence in the unanxious image of suspension, "hung / Listening," or more substantially, in the way the text is able to enact the listening relationship to itself. If this is epitaph poetry, it belongs most directly to the mode of inscription of "Lycidas," transmuting death into metaphor for the break between the conversational and authoritative voices, between the more uncouth swain and the listening, Miltonic poet.

What happens in *The Prelude*, Book V, happens in smaller ways throughout Wordsworth's poetry when a will to exhibit the "I" is chastened. A second will subdues the "impulse to precipitate my verse" (itself a confession or intrusion of self deleted in revising *Prelude*, Book IX). Suppressing the personal pronoun, Wordsworth subdues authorial voice to give verse a quality of listening, as it were, to the voice of a less self-conscious speaker, one more conversant with nature.

"Simon Lee" is a poem in which such revision of voice transcends manuscript work to become the topic—perhaps one can say the "meaning"—of the text. About "Simon Lee" De Selincourt remarked, "On the text of no other short poem did Wordsworth expend so much labor." [36] The opening stanza of the 1798 version has the line "I've heard he once was tall" where the final text reads, " 'Tis said he once was tall." Compared with the extraordinary turn of stanza VIII in all versions, such variation may seem hardly worth notice. Yet Wordsworth omits the first-person pronoun till that point, and its placement is crucial in a short poem, especially one in a folk idiom. Compare Frost's line "Whose woods these are I think I know" and how easy it would be to disrupt the tentativeness of the pause and the person there by writing, "I think I know whose woods these are"; the "I" must be buried in the woods, as uncertain as the horse.

In Wordsworth's poem the desired effect is not uncertainty but shock. After seven stanzas of description of Simon, the eighth begins:

> Few months of life has he in store
> As he to you will tell,
> For still, the more he works, the more
> Do his weak ankles swell.

At this point it would seem that all there is left to record is further decay and death. Just at this point, and without preparation, the poet intervenes:

> My gentle Reader, I perceive
> How patiently you've waited,
> And now I fear that you expect
> Some tale will be related.

Though Geoffrey Hartman calls such interpolations "Sterne in spirit," more is at stake here than novelistic good humor.[37] If one considers the objection raised to certain manuscript lines in Milton's "At a Solemn Music," that they "would have tended to hasten the conclusion of the poem," then Wordsworth's interruption could be said to assume that risk. He is not stalling but precipitating the end, dropping the fictional convention which we ordinarily expect to be maintained till the end, or till a final statement by the poet when he steps back from a tale and comments upon it. Breaking into his poem before the story is told, Wordsworth makes premature arrest of song a metaphor or replacement for death.

The address to the reader is not poetic "voice" but conversation, the kind of consolation in the face of death that a poem can offer. The poet verbalizes the helplessness of the isolated self and substitutes the communication of this tale for the failure of community with Simon. Not that the old hunter remains literally by himself; but he is isolated from his past, he is singled out for death, he is, like each of us, at a distance from others not easily overcome by offering conversation. More particularly, he is alone because "His Master's dead," and only the occasional sound of hounds' voices is left as reminder of the connection he once had with a source of power, his master's voice.

When Wordsworth addresses the reader, the problem of voice is deflected from Simon's incapacity, past the poet's anxiety about finding voice, to the reader's presumed impatience for poetic voice. Wordsworth's address to the reader, despite its gentleness, seems more a reproof than a consolation: "I fear that you expect / Some tale will be related." Bypassing the poetization of loss by which a failure of story seems a taste of death, the reproof points rather to the possibility of failure of response to the story. As originally written, the poet's apology, "What more I have to say is short, / I hope you'll kindly take it," could be ingratiating; the emendation to "And you must kindly take it," omitting the "I," suggests instead a slight forcing of the matter. From the perspective of the reader, the "must" implies a necessity Wordsworth is asking us to share; from the perspective of the poet, the "must" implies the necessity of deflecting anxiety about voice. In this sense, the poem's last stanza is no confession of inadequacy but a victory over that threat. Simon is profuse in his thanks, which are out of proportion to the deed performed; the poet, like the reader who brings "stores of silent thought," catches in his own more measured speech an authoritative control of voice.

One more change between versions of the poem warrants special attention in this context. Wordsworth adds, at the beginning of the fourth stanza, the line "But, oh the heavy change!—bereft" to separate the Simon that was from the picture of decay and death that follows. Compare Milton's iteration, "But oh the heavy change, now thou art gone, / Now thou art gone, and never must return!" In "Lycidas" the statement of loss, particularly in its repetition, stands for the redemptive reconciliation to ongoing time. Wordsworth's echo not only cuts the line short; it appears abortively, not between death and literary ongoingness, but between the descriptions of young and old Simon. It does not help the man Simon Lee, as it does, say, the mythologized idea of Keats in "Adonais," to be remembered in terms of pastoral elegy; literary allusion only increases the sense of remoteness, of the distance between present experience and the source of past power. As the poem closes, the gap between the speaker's act and Simon's thanks replaces the gap between "Lycidas"-like voice and the more conversational tone that seems so proper to its subject here. These distances, these gaps are transformed from expressions of loss to potentialities for self-consciousness and creative accomplishment.

Like "Simon Lee," the sonnet "Composed after a Journey across the Hambleton Hills, Yorkshire" takes its origin from a need to fill an experiential void. But because the poem is a sonnet, the turn in which setting becomes related to poetic structure has to be all the more sharply defined, and Miltonism must prove a help or be discarded as an excrescence that so dense a poem cannot afford. All too often involvement with a poetic precursor is considered a stultification of a creative impulse rather than an aid in confronting and spanning an abyss of self-consciousness; in this poem vacancy is the starting point, and the process of revision, spread over some thirty or thirty-five years, is Miltonic.

Wordsworth makes genially literal the relation of spatial arrest to the arrest that marks a moment of choice and creative potential. In the Isabella Fenwick note to the sonnet he describes a day on which he, Dorothy, and Mary "were obliged to wait two hours in a severe storm. . . . The spot was in front of Bolton Hall, where Mary Queen of Scots was kept prisoner. . . . To beguile the time I composed a Sonnet. The subject was our own confinement contrasted with hers; but it was not thought worthy of being preserved." Fortunately, the poem he wrote later (how much later is open to question) fared better, and better still because of changes made between the 1807 and 1837 texts. For the purpose of examining the Miltonization, we may collapse the intervening stages and consider these two versions:

> Ere we had reach'd the wish'd-for place, night fell:
> We were too late at least by one dark hour,
> And nothing could we see of all that power
> Of prospect, whereof many thousands tell.
> The western sky did recompence us well
> With Grecian Temple, Minaret, and Bower;
> And, in one part, a Minster with its Tower
> Substantially distinct, a place for Bell
> Or Clock to toll from. Many a glorious pile
> Did we behold, sights that might well repay
> All disappointment! and, as such, the eye

Delighted in them; but we felt, the while,
We should forget them: they are of the sky,
And from our earthly memory fade away. [1807]

Dark and more dark the shades of evening fell;
The wished-for point was reached—but at an hour
When little could be gained from that rich dower
Of prospect, whereof many thousands tell.
Yet did the glowing west with marvellous power
Salute us; there stood Indian citadel,
Temple of Greece, and minster with its tower
Substantially expressed—a place for bell
Or clock to toll from! Many a tempting isle,
With groves that never were imagined, lay
'Mid seas how steadfast! objects all for the eye
Of silent rapture; but we felt the while
We should forget them; they are of the sky,
And from our earthly memory fade away. [1837]

The opening lines of the first version, locating failure between what "we" expected and what encountered, lays heavy stress on the first-person pronoun. Like the first-person singular which we have seen Wordsworth elsewhere suppress, the first-person plural emphasizes self-concern. But where the singular pronoun could point to the concerns of the poet as poet, the plural pronoun here focuses too heavily and too soon on the burden of guilt, the imputation of human inadequacy. The scene seems to reprove the travelers for their lateness—an intrusion of moral terms postponed by the revised text, which saves the nominative pronoun for the twelfth line. The revision gives a more "literary" opening, gently but immediately implicating nature in a failure of response. Now the shades of evening fall with an agency all their own, an otherness emphasized by the passive of the second line: "The wished-for point was reached." There is no increase in personal reference based on the word "dower" and Wordsworth's claim that the poem is set on his wedding day; the marriage is the general one of mind and nature, and the distance at which the revision is written allows for imaginative use of a marriage term where such reference in a first draft might have stultified.[38] The revision is powerfully in command of its tone, using scene with other than personal effect. Human agency is absent here, ominous shades replacing personal aspiration in the first line. When the original continues, "The western sky did recompense us well," it subordinates the scene that follows to a purpose that is egocentric—as opposed to centering on nature as "other" or as void. But when the line is revised to read "Yet did the glowing west with marvellous power / Salute us," the salutation becomes, not a tribute to a human disappointment, but a gesture of farewell, opening up another dimension, as when Adam sees light "More orient in yon Western Cloud" that suggests "something heav'nly fraught" (PL, XI.205, 207).

Wordsworth's sonnet finds no such revelation, and in its absence fancy fills vacancy with shapes of pagan architecture, insubstantial as "straw-built citadels" of Miltonic pandemonium. Wordsworth confronts the mildly satanic overtone of fancy's parody of creation when he revises the description of the tower, "substantially distinct" (which means no more than that this cloud shape impressed the mind), to the extraordinary Miltonism "Substantially expressed." "Distinct" is the word Dorothy used for the tower in her journal, which Wordsworth may have read before writing the poem. "Substantially expressed" is Milton's phrase for the Son (PL, III.140), who without cloud, serene, expresses the Father's glory and man's grace.

Milton's description of the Son comes between God the Father's announcement of the terms of justice and the Son's acceptance of man's guilt. If we ask what Wordsworth's description of the "Substantially expressed" tower comes between, we are directed to the way the revised text captures the process of revision in its completed form. The phrase "Substantially expressed," by expressing the Milton in Wordsworth, and by being the more substantial expression, plays the role in the 1837 text that the choice between "distinct" and "expressed" plays in the process of revision. In the Miltonic moment, in Wordsworth's process of revision toward Miltonism, and in Wordsworth's final text, moral options stand before, imaginative possibilities after, what we can identify as a moment of choice. In Milton, the way the glory of the Son expresses the glory of the Father at the moment of choice stands for the way the choice the Son makes expresses the will of the Father in posing that choice. In Wordsworth's process of revision, the moment at which he conceives of the Miltonism and substitutes it for his own expression stands for the way the choice of words the poet makes expresses a second will of a higher, more authoritative poetic voice. In Wordsworth's revised text, the moment at which an imagined shape seems substantially expressed in nature stands for the way the imagination, expecting a given prospect, confronts in the dark indefiniteness of the natural scene the possibility for more imaginative vision. For the moment, what imagination seizes on must be truth, creative vision redeeming a blank in nature.

Imagination can do no more, so just at this point the vision breaks, returning to time and space with the specification, "a place for bell / Or clock to toll from." This turn is the same in both versions, and marks the division of the sonnet, which we expect to pause between octet and sestet, poised rather in the enjambment on the word "or." The poetry of choice, claiming that revision is the essentially Miltonic creative act, would present a principle too difficult to bear if it insisted on turning every such "or" into a crucial moral and aesthetic choice. Yet the creative power of the principle, like the power of the precursor poet himself, is that of lending to such seemingly indifferent moments some of the vitality of a moment of creation. Following the 1807 phrase "Substantially distinct," the imagined "place" acts further to distinguish the tower: not only could one distinguish a shape of a tower in the clouds, but one could even picture just the place to hang a bell—or, more precisely? more indefinitely?—a clock. Imagination seems to move to more precise definition only to confront the more creative "indefinite abstraction." For one does not pause to consider differences in the facing of clock or bell towers; the point is the towers' sameness and their difference from oneself. The choice suspended on the "or" is a little center of indifference after which time tolls one back to one's sole self. Following the revised phrase "Substantially expressed," the break between parts of the sonnet makes the tolling of clock or bell seem to "express" the image, as if poetic voice could be imagined as transferred from a retiring creator to the "place" or object of imaginative investment.

In the 1807 text, the imagination, once tolled back to self-consciousness, ceases to extend itself beyond time. "Many a glorious pile" marks a failure of imaginative perspicacity, and the scene collapses into the original gap between the expectation of a prospect and the sight of nothing but clouds. What looked like imaginative revelation now seems the work of deluding fancy, the imitative work of Satan building in hell.

A shadow of such terms, at least, governs the generalized scene: "sights that might well repay / All disappointment!" Imaginative specificity retreats to moral specificity, and the poet draws back even from such generalized sights: "and, as such, the eye / Delighted in them." There is too much denial and restraint in the "as such" for the eye to have much delight any longer. A moral will curbs a more imaginative will, and vision retreats behind the community of faith: "but we felt, the while, / We should forget them." It may be impossible to separate the two senses of "should" in "we should forget them," and reserve the connotation of futurity for the revised version, the connotation of moral obligation for the 1807 version; but we do sense the weight of moral imperative as the poem retreats from clouds of fancy to the rock of faith, the empirical, earthly world.

In the revisions that follow the Miltonism "Substantially expressed," vision opens the gap morality had closed between the imagined and the actual. To be sure Wordsworth did make the correction to "expressed" years before the lines that follow were changed; but it is not difficult to imagine that the effect of one Miltonism (perhaps increased by the poet's growing sensitivity to the extrapoetic implications of expressing glory) influenced the less direct Miltonism that followed. After 1820, in any case, "Many a glorious pile" was seen more perspicaciously as "many a tempting isle, / With groves that never were imagined." Such a passage suggests romantic satanism transcending verbal echo. There is no direct recall of Milton's devil, but the new scene is met with awe like that of Satan descrying new groves: "seat worthier of Gods, as built / With second thoughts, reforming what was old" (*PL*, IX.100–101). Beyond description in terms of morality is the moment of abstraction out of self, where the mind remains "stupidly good," blest, as in Wordsworth's

"Nutting," "With sudden happiness beyond all hope." The speaker there, like Satan, is caught by the vision of a bower yet to be destroyed. Or, more properly, it is revision, the product of second thoughts, that produces silent rapture in all these contexts. Satan is surprised to find that the mind is not its own place, that reformation is substantially expressed in the landscape. Romantic satanism consists of an extension that is actually an inversion of these qualities. In "Nutting" the poet waits till fancy takes over the scene. In the sonnet, the mind moves from the failure of actual scene to the imagined Eden, and the surprise is that of a consciousness caught by the power of its own interiority.

The moment of vision is granted additional extension when the isles are described lying " 'Mid seas how steadfast!" Where the 1807 sights were dominated by the overriding sense of disappointment, the vision found here seems in response to the poet's overriding power of substantial expression. Like "the uncertain heaven, received / Into the bosom of the steady lake" (*Prelude*, V.387–388), these imaginative shapes in the sky seem to be given more certain habitation in the image of maternal nature, nature as steadfast *mer*. The sea too is imagined, but the projected relationship of receiver and received leaves the self outside, with added strength, gazing in "silent rapture." At this point the community of human feeling returns with the words "we felt" of line 12, forming a soft turn to futurity after the vision that seemed beyond power of expectation. The closing line of the poem now presents not a reason for turning away but a final acknowledgment of loss, a final awareness of what has been achieved.

Though the Miltonization of the Hambleton Hills sonnet opens new imaginative possibility, one must not read the renewal of the poem's vision as a definitive renewal of the poet's

conception of imaginative power. The substantial expression
of authoritative poetic voice in a generated product is not
a single act or discovery but a myth re-enacted in various
poetic contexts, and each re-enactment is its own revision of
the myth. One cannot, for this reason, assign a date to the
discovery of Milton by a romantic poet, though one can—as
Blake did—reimagine the act of influence as occurring at a
particular moment. Insofar as revision is a process recapitu-
lated in poetic context, the time is always now, in the narrative present of the given poem.

The sonnet "Composed by the Side of Grasmere Lake" is
especially concerned with the temporality of revision, with
the way poetic structure can express the restructuring of
vision. In a way this sonnet begins where Miltonizing left the
other, imagining the extension of the moment in the scene
itself:

> Clouds, lingering yet, extend in solid bars
> Through the grey west; and lo! these waters, steeled
> By breezeless air to smoothest polish, yield
> A vivid repetition of the stars;
> Jove, Venus, and the ruddy crest of Mars
> Amid his fellows beauteously revealed
> At happy distance from earth's groaning field,
> Where ruthless mortals wage incessant wars.
> Is it a mirror?—or the nether Sphere
> Opening to view the abyss in which she feeds
> Her own calm fires?—But list! a voice is near;
> Great Pan himself low-whispering through the reeds,
> "Be thankful, thou; for, if unholy deeds
> Ravage the world, tranquillity is here!"

In the opening line, the lingering of the clouds is a projection
of the mind's lingering on scene as image of the mind's own

power. Like the Hambleton Hills sonnet's imagined groves
that lay " 'Mid seas how steadfast," the imaged stars of his
sonnet find easeful abode in the reflecting water (line 4). If
such calm can already figure metaphor's substantial adequacy
of expression, what more remains? In the image of reflection,
the distance between the stars and their "vivid repetition"
seems substantially to express the distance of the poet from
his image. And is not such distance power, the power of
poetic voice? The sonnet itself seems to evoke these rhetorical
questions by smoothing over objections to so easy a relationship between mind and metaphor. Even the smoothing over
of objections has its emblem—in the waters "steeled / By
breezeless air to smoothest polish," as if the hard surface of
military metal, lending its reflective power to the edge of the
lake, militated against deeper sight.

Perhaps Wordsworth, at this point, could be pictured addressing the stars the way Keats addresses the nightingale:
" 'Tis not through envy of thy happy lot, / But being too
happy in thine happiness . . .'" In any case the "happy
distance" of the stars from the earth makes too fortuitous, too
easy the distance of the poet from the fever and the fret. A
more authentic distance is needed, a distance more private,
more personally related to the source of poetic voice than
the political world of "incessant wars" is related to the vul-
garized classical emblem, "ruddy crest of Mars." In asking,
"Is it a mirror?" the poet questions his own image and in the
distance he thus asserts from it, finds his power: "or the
nether Sphere / Opening." Paul de Man remarks, " 'Nether
Sphere' has an unmistakably Miltonic ring, and the presence
of Miltonic diction in Wordsworth generally indicates a rise
in the pitch of imaginative intensity." [39] The sonnet at this
point enacts a process of revision. The octet gave the original

vision, in which the opening space between a war-tormented
earth and the cosmic peace imaged the distance between nature and the aesthetic detachment of the poet. Then, on the
word "or," the poem turns from vision to revision, from more
easeful powers of "reflection" to Miltonism, and imagination
perceives new distances from the actual. Imagining new
depths nourishes the "calm fires" of creativity—calm in the
poised abstraction of the "nether Sphere" as imagined alternative.

Wordsworth's sonnet turns on a Miltonic "or," the grammatical conjunction standing for the juncture in imaginative
paths, the choice between a ready way and one that has to
be staked out anew. When Milton revised the Orpheus passage of "Lycidas," changing "whom universal Nature might
lament" to "did lament," he caught in grammatical tense
the premature arrest that is fall. Wordsworth in effect restores
the half-slumbering "might" to nature's responsiveness. In
Milton, moments of choice exist only as approached—or
rather, having read further and looking back, one sees that
one must have passed a juncture and taken a turn that is fall.
In Wordsworth the moment of choice seems suspended. "Is it
a mirror?" Most assuredly the lake *is* a mirror, or if "mirror"
is a metaphor based on the lake's reflecting surface, it is a
dead metaphor, one passed over as being language at minimum
distance from physical fact. Suspending such recognition of
factuality, one goes on to the more imaginative possibility,
the fiction that follows. Yet because one knows the lake is a
mirror, that alternative is not dismissed but carried along
as security on the imaginative journey to other spheres. The
recognition of false surmise does not follow and toll us back
but precedes and guards the way. We will not be burned by
the furnaces where new imaginative work is daemonically

forged, only gently warmed and cheered by the "calm fires" of imagery hospitable to the far-traveling mind. The choice between mirror and abyss is thus made without a sense of loss, and this easeful arrest of the Miltonic moment of choice gives rise to the new poetic voice. "Tranquillity," as De Man points out, "is the right balance between the literal and the symbolic vision." [40] Finding this balance where Milton had found precarious temporality and fall, Wordsworth discovers new voice emerging from the relationship with nature that did not have to be renounced: "But list! a voice is near; / Great Pan himself low-whispering through the reeds."

For Milton, voice represents discontinuity, which it is the function of pastoral to bridge. St. Peter speaks, but Alpheus returns, and it is less a matter of pastoral being Christianized than of Christian doctrine being pastoralized. Redemption is in the natural image; Lycidas is to be found "Where other groves and other streams along, / With Nectar pure his oozy Locks he laves." Wordsworth's "groves that never were imagined" are beyond the realm, not only of nature, but of past imaginings. And the "nether Sphere / Opening to view" comes as a world elsewhere, a mildly satanist poet's alternative to the wars in heaven or earth.

Milton's Satan confronts such a nether sphere in his own consciousness when he defines himself as hell: "in the lowest deep a lower deep / Still threat'ning to devour me opens wide" (PL, IV.76–77). But that is to confront a stasis like Wordsworth's "or" without the possibility of imaginative redemption. Satan's "Still threat'ning" threatens more than any definite punishment could, for the torment is that of being always in possibility while excluded from the realm of hope. As the lower deep opens wide, Satan himself undermines his stance; turning physical realms into metaphors of consciousness, he pulls the ground from under himself and makes the fall bottomless. His understanding is decreative, for all space between the cosmic poles of heaven and hell is likewise collapsed into solipsism. His question that follows, "is there no place / Left for repentance?" answers itself in its choice of words, for intervening place is just what Satan denies, creating his own polarity to God. In contrast, Wordsworth's tranquillity, with its equipoise between physical place and metaphor for consciousness, finds place left for repentance, natural "place" for redemptive revision.

On Mount Niphates, Satan overinteriorizes natural place and renounces tranquillity, the ability to remain poised between nature and imagined alternative. Earlier, though, Satan presented a better model for the romantic poet. Freed from the literal space of hell, yet still all involved in external nature, Satan winds his way in a spatialization of imaginative speculation. He wanders

> Amongst innumerable Stars, that shone
> Stars distant, but nigh hand seem'd other Worlds,
> Or other Worlds they seem'd or happy Isles,
> Like those Hesperian Gardens fam'd of old,
> Fortunate Fields, and Groves and flow'ry Vales,
> Thrice happy Isles, but who dwelt happy there
> He stay'd not to enquire.   [*PL*, III, 565–571]

Arresting time with the repetitions, first of "Stars," then of "other Worlds," poetry creates the interval in which other worlds can be perceived. The arrest of time that seems to bring forth imagined realms is an arrest at a moment of choice. For Satan the alternative he must reject is stopping to get a better look; for us, the alternative Milton rejected was not stopping at all to imagine other worlds. We experience the interposed perspective in the extended moment of choice as the substantial expression of "groves that never were imagined."

Earlier in the description of Satan's journey Milton presents another model for the extended moment of choice. Satan stands over the abyss (as does Wordsworth in the sonnet), drawing power from his ability to contemplate new distances, newly conceived nether spheres:

> Into this wild Abyss,
> The Womb of nature and perhaps her Grave,
> Of neither Sea, nor Shore, nor Air, nor Fire,
> But all these in thir pregnant causes mixt
> Confus'dly, and which thus must ever fight,
> Unless th' Almighty Maker them ordain
> His dark materials to create more Worlds,
> Into this wild Abyss the wary fiend
> Stood on the brink of Hell and look'd a while,
> Pondering his Voyage.   [II.910–919]

The repetition of the phrase "Into this wild Abyss" surprises us into realizing that Satan has stalled in the intervening lines; in that arrested interval he confronts the abyss partly as physical space, partly as metaphor for possibility itself, as a chaos of confused elements "unless th'Almighty Maker them ordain / His dark materials to create more Worlds." Like the word that introduces the Son's mercy (III.210), this is a redemptive "unless," not because we need the suggestion that if we fail in this world God could always make another, but because poetry is restoring conditionality to our awareness of time. The formal gracefulness of the passage is experienced as alternative, as counterplot to the chaos described. More than seeing chaos as nature, or the confusion to be replaced by nature, Milton makes the abyss "Womb of nature." And, since we know that nature will bring forth, does bring forth, he adds a phrase that lets us, living in destructible nature, share in the sense of possibility that Satan confronts: "and perhaps her Grave." Seeing creation as precarious increases awareness of the imaginative moment as a moment of choice. At the same time, Satan, able to "look a while," to pause over this gap in nature, asserts no instability, no teetering between imaginative alternatives, but control over them. For the moment he can say, with Wordsworth's Pan, "tranquillity is here"—not in chaos, to be sure, but in the mind's strength of capacity to stand over an "indefinite abstraction."

If Satan pausing over the space of chaos can be taken as an emblem of imaginative strength, Sin passing through space in Book X becomes for Wordsworth an emblem of imaginative failure. In Book V of *The Prelude*, Wordsworth satirizes educators who would too firmly structure the mind's progress to maturity:

> These mighty workmen of our later age,
> Who, with a broad highway, have overbridged
> The froward chaos of futurity,
> Tamed to their bidding; they who have the skill
> To manage books, and things, and make them act
> On infant minds as surely as the sun
> Deals with a flower; the keepers of our time,
> The guides and wardens of our faculties,
> Sages who in their prescience would control
> All accidents, and to the very road
> Which they have fashioned would confine us down,
> Like engines; when will their presumption learn.
>
> [V.347–358]

Havens comments, "Although this passage was suggested by *Paradise Lost* X.229–305, Wordsworth presumably did not intend to imply that the later bridge-builders were like Sin and Death." [41] They are much like Sin and Death and like the builders of devilish enginery of Book VI, too, in mechanizing the process of the imagination and concretizing where there must be freedom to roam the mind's abyss. Wordsworth's phrase "The froward chaos of futurity" pays tribute to the void on which education depends, the gap between what the self is and what it may become if a patterned progress, a pre-established road, does not make escape from the mind's depths too facile, does not too easily naturalize the spirit to this earth.

But it is not only the education of children that he is talking about, or perhaps one should say that primary education here is in part a metaphor for the individual's confrontation with any experiential or poetic "text." Bad educators are like bad poets and overspecify ends, whereas creativity depends on a recognition of an abyss. "The froward chaos of futurity" emphasizes that poetic expression must exist in time, creating the sense of a futurity not yet specified, something evermore about to be. One may contrast the account of Satan's progress through chaos with Wordsworth's description of the "sentiment of Being" that moves

> O'er all that leaps and runs, and shouts and sings,
> Or beats the gladsome air; o'er all that glides
> Beneath the wave, yea, in the wave itself,
> And mighty depth of waters. [*Prelude*, II.406–409]

Unlike the joy of Sin, whose harmony with Satan moves her to earth, Wordsworth's "transport" moves "towards the Uncreated with a countenance / Of adoration." The poet's task is to create that sense of something "uncreated," not to impose but to discover an order. One would regret that the only title Wordsworth ever gave his great poem, "Poem: Title

Not Yet Fixed Upon," has not achieved currency, except that
Prelude gives a similar sense of something not yet fixed upon,
perpetually preluding the way. Throughout *The Prelude*, Wordsworth labors to create
moments where an arrest of time at the "uncreated" opens
into a sense of the re-created, of imaginative alternatives imagined anew. In the opening of Book XII he describes how
finding a "counterpoise" in nature helps the poet confront
moral ambiguities and ambiguities in the self as possibilities
for imaginative revision. Nature knows how to alternate her
seasons, her landscape, her voices, and in the calm continuity
between different states, has lent the poet an image and a
sense of power in facing alternatives:

> Oh! that I had a music and a voice
> Harmonious as your own, that I might tell
> What ye have done for me. The morning shines,
> Nor heedeth Man's perverseness; Spring returns,—
> I saw the Spring return, and could rejoice,
> In common with the children of her love,
> Piping on boughs, or sporting on fresh fields,
> Or boldly seeking pleasure nearer heaven
> On wings that navigate cerulean skies.   [XII.29–37] [42]

So great is the tranquillity, the equipoise between nature and
nature-as-metaphor, that we might miss the moment of arrest
and skip to the indifferent *or*s of the last few lines and their
easy alternations between sporting and bolder seeking, between stasis and continuity. But in expressing a longing for a
voice like that of nature, Wordsworth achieves a moment of
voice: "Spring returns,— / I saw the Spring return." Appealing for poetic voice in the invocation to *Paradise Lost*, Book
III, Milton also expressed the failure of voice when he acknowledged that the seasons return, "but not to me returns /

Day." Wordsworth cannot be said to echo Milton—"spring" is just the word for which Milton could not at that moment find voice. But Wordsworth has the power of sight, the power of relationship with nature, and can gather from that relationship the voice with which to proclaim, and rest on the claim, "Spring returns,— / I saw the Spring return." The return of the word "Spring" makes poetry participate in the renewal, taking on the authority of the natural world.

Earlier in *The Prelude*, Wordsworth derives poetic voice by a more genial relationship with Miltonic verse:

> I would stand,
> If the night blackened with a coming storm,
> Beneath some rock, listening to notes that are
> The ghostly language of the ancient earth,
> Or make their dim abode in distant winds.
> Thence did I drink the visionary power;
> And deem not pofitless those fleeting moods
> Of shadowy exultation: not for this,
> That they are kindred to our purer mind
> And intellectual life; but that the soul,
> Remembering how she felt, but what she felt
> Remembering not, retains an obscure sense
> Of possible sublimity, whereto
> With growing faculties she doth aspire,
> With faculties still growing, feeling still
> That whatsoever point they gain, they yet
> Have something to pursue. [*Prelude*, II.306–322]

The turn in lines 309–310, between the ghostly language and a more natural voice, catches in that "or" an equivocation which needs no resolving, no loss or renunciation to obtain more personal or more authentic relation to voice. The slight obscurity of the soul's own past takes the place of more problematic, more tense relations with the soul's ancestry and the usual Oedipal need to obscure one's origins in asserting the self. In this passage Wordsworth does not need to derive his "visionary power" from a sense of superiority to Miltonic blindness. Instead, darkness is seen as an emblem of possible creation; this is Miltonic darkness that guesses each sweet and coming musk rose. As if humanizing Miltonic repetition, making it more mild, Wordsworth's turn in lines 316–317 involves no taint of death; the only loss is that of specificity: "what she felt / Remembering not." In the gap between the present and a less distinct past lies not vacancy, but the womb of nature, the space of creation. Growing faculties are like the imagination in education, and verbal repetition of that phrase (ll. 319–320) makes verse itself participate in the process, catching the mind in expanding awareness of the unbridged chaos of futurity.

If verbal repetition seems to image the moment of choice expanding into visionary possibility, larger structures of repetition in The Prelude provide opportunities to dramatize that expansion. Book VI turns into narrative episode the experience of going over the ground of choice. The travelers reach "a halting place," linger awhile, start again, meet with a "brief delay," journey on and upward, and learn "that to the spot which had perplexed us first / We must descend" (VI.580–581). Repeating their tracks, they enact geographically the repetition that is moral or memorial return.[43] But the luncheon halt, the postprandial pause, the delay at the stream, and the arrest to listen to the peasant's directions only prepare for the long and leisured break that spreads over twenty-five lines (592–616). Its leisure is its assertion of competence, making the passage an exhibition of the imaginative power it describes. Greatness finds abode, is given a local habitation, in the arrested moment expanded from the Miltonic moment of loss into visionary possibility. In Miltonic fashion, the poet is carried beyond sensuous apprehension of nature, the light of sense going out "with a flash that has revealed / The invisible world." Verbal repetition then imitates the moment that can be gone over without loss: "With hope it is, hope that can never die." The sense of openness is further captured in linguistic effect as individual formulations prove inadequate and verse itself seems to reach forward, waiting on the next word. Abstractions are accumulated because perfectly adequate expression would limit meaning; instead there is approximation toward meaning: "Effort, and expectation, and desire, / And something evermore about to be." Not adequacy—correlation of signifier and significance—but endless possibility. Looking back at the historical moment, the poet can say, "I was lost"; but the present moment—"to my conscious soul I now can say— / I recognize thy glory"—is an eternal present, not a given moment of composition but the duration of poetry itself.

The problem with a break in poetic continuity is that *it* must break off as narrative returns. But Wordsworth has done something extraordinary. Since the specter of imagination, of self-consciousness, rose out of the failure of the mind to confront anything but itself, the return to nature is a return to an already recognized inadequacy. The scene that follows does not turn away in allegro indifference, nor turn with wandering steps and slow, carrying the burden of the penseroso difference. Instead,

> Downwards we hurried fast,
> And, with the half-shaped road which we had missed,
> Entered a narrow chasm. [VI.619–621]

Finding the road not previously taken, the poet finds a third alternative, a naturalization of imaginative vision. The awareness of loss, of nature's not meeting the mind, is not ignored, nor is it simply branded on the pensive brow; it is reimagined. The scene now entered does not retreat from, but re-creates, the still point in "woods decaying, never to be decayed" and "the stationary blasts of waterfalls." Objects of landscape are transmuted to the point where it appears "as if a voice were in them." In "Lycidas" voice intervenes to solve a problem of experiential continuity, only to become itself an emblem of discontinuity that is humanized by poetry. In *The Prelude* voice is absorbed by scene, which instead of proving inadequate, confronting the mind with itself, now comes perfectly to express the mind. Objects combine to appear "all like workings of one mind, the features / Of the same face, blossoms upon one tree." Poetic labor is now blossoming, for one cannot distinguish the separate features of landscape or find in each blossom an inadequate metaphor for the inapproachable tenor, mind. All combine in a series of expressions that culminates in the supreme expression of stasis—supreme because, in citing Milton, mind and nature share the creativity of divinity. Stretching across the temporal gap that separates poet from ancestor, across the spatial gap that separates object from object, across the categorical gap that separates significance from signified and mind from nature, is the uncircumscribed vision of Miltonic eternity, "Of first, and last, and midst, and without end" (VI. 64).[44]

Wordsworth requires us to redefine the poetry of choice because what we have taken as essentially the experience of the moment—or the moment itself—must now be seen as protracted. In discussing choice in Milton, one could point to moments which seem to locate the awareness of loss in the

turn on a line ending, the turn on the word "or," or a pho-
netic gap or creative caesura. In Wordsworth alternatives
may be extended in equilibrium to a point where a new sense
of options opens up. In the climactic scene of Book VI the
new ground is created by widely separating the actual loss
from awareness of it; presumably the Alps were crossed before lunch, and there is a series of arrests, culminating in the
confrontation with the peasant, before expectation is apprehended as over. More generally, Wordsworth pre-empts the
fact of loss, making fall, as in Manuscript JJ, the creative impetus. He *starts* by asking, "Was it for this?" and then con-
trols the arrested process where coming to awareness is a
journey like prelapsarian ongoingness.[45] A sentence of Kierkegaard explains why the poetry of remembered moments opens
the way to new stasis: "Recollection has the great advantage
that it begins with the loss, hence it is secure, for it has
nothing to lose." [46] Under the protection of such security, the
still point expands into a perspective, the moment of arrest
into an adventure in the reimagination of reality.

The last book of *The Prelude* describes one more adventure
with its consummate still point or "breathing-place," and then
climbs further to theoretical statements about the relation of
imaginative prospect to Milton's voice. It is no accident that
the Snowdon incident concludes in a listening relationship.
One of Wordsworth's most profoundly Miltonic poems,
"Nutting," reaches imaginative climax when the poet hears
the murmur of imagined streams. *The Prelude*, requiring that
all stops be played for this supreme climax, calls forth the
fuller harmony of nature and imagination. Beyond vision, the
kind of harmony that can be expressed in a visualized scene,
is a "breathing-place," a visualized moment of arrest, and then

revelation in the form of voice. The waters are there, but now heard in an apocalyptic coming together: "streams / Innumerable, roaring with one voice" (XIV.59–60).

In the section that follows, the distancing and obscuring powers of memory rather than direct presentation allow for the extension of the work of reimagining and internalizing the Snowdon episode. The confrontation with nature's otherness, where scene is met like a single giant with a single voice, leads to the revisionary confrontation with Milton's otherness, where his spirit haunts the depiction of poetic spirit. As Milton is abstracted out of corporeal identity into verbal echo, poetic voice is abstracted as an independent Presence encountered by the poet. Both in the versions of the poem and in the process of revision between them these ghostly encounters stand outside time and achieve the splendor of "indefinite abstraction." One can look upon the 1805 and 1850 versions as expanding that abstraction at the moment of the "or" in the sonnet "Composed by the Side of Grasmere Lake." The octet of the sonnet pictures the lake imaging the sky, giving "A vivid repetition to the stars." The 1805 *Prelude* has scene a "perfect image of a mighty Mind." The sestet of the sonnet then finds Miltonism, finds an abyss opening in which the nether sphere "feeds / Her own calm fires," and finds an image of continuity in the voice of Pan. The 1850 *Prelude* also adds the image of the "dark abyss," increases the Miltonism, and discovers an image of continuity in the voices issuing "In one continuous stream." Wordsworth increases the sense of "indefinite abstraction," seeming to condense all understanding of Milton in two words: "silent light." He also omits from the 1850 version the more definite abstractions, "a genial Counterpart" and "Brother of the glorious faculty." These terms, like the sonnet's "vivid repetition," deflect anxiety from the poet's relation to higher power and find instead too easeful a mirror or sibling relationship. With more restraint, second will more precisely locates the source of tension and power in the individual mind's relationship to "that glorious faculty / That higher minds bear with them as their own."

The 1805 version is already grand; but the increase in power in the changes made over the years is a tribute to the seminal nature of Milton's influence. How do higher minds at their best hold commerce with the "objects of the universe"? (The word "objects" itself is changed to "compass," increasing the indefinite abstraction from the natural world, the sense of power of a godlike mind encompassing a void.) In 1805 such minds

> for themselves create
> A like existence, and, whene'er it is
> Created for them, catch it by an instinct.

In the 1850 version this becomes

> for themselves create
> A like existence; and, whene'er it dawns
> Created for them, catch it, or are caught
> By its inevitable mastery,
> Like angels stopped upon the wing by sound
> Of harmony from Heaven's remotest spheres.

[XIV.94–99]

One could say that the very increase in length is a mark of the power of revision. If Miltonic creativity is expressed in second will, in going over and reinterpreting a primary exclamation, then such "opening" of the text for fuller interpretation marks an increase in imaginative will. One observes the dawning of creative power as the very words "Created for them" seem to share in the protracted moment of choice now opened: "catch it, or are caught / By its inevitable mastery." The first instinct gives way to the second will, the will to extend the moment of confrontation with poetic voice and find oneself—as one ultimately wishes to be—not mastering but mastered, subsumed by a higher power. Out of such will comes the imaginative comparison that follows, capturing arrest in song: "Like angels stopped upon the wing by sound / Of harmony."

Milton's Adam was given power of voice to name the animals, and each bird came, "stoop'd on his wing" (*PL*, VIII.351). In the image of angels "stopped upon the wing" Wordsworth extends the power of voice to envision this more radical, more protracted moment of arrest. The poet proves a more capable Adam, one of those higher "Powers" who does not lose, with a fall, his capacity "To hold communion with the invisible world." In the 1850 version this becomes

> To hold fit converse with the spiritual world,
> And with the generations of mankind
> Spread over time, past, present, and to come,
> Age after age, till Time shall be no more.   [XIV.108–111]

Such is the power Adam wished to retain in being able to address his sons, exercising superiority of voice through the generations to come. The arrest of time "till Time shall be no more" expresses the power the poet wishes to hold in relation to fit audience of all generations. Turning then to overt Miltonism, Wordsworth gives the stamp of authority to this passage of voice by having it echo a passage of higher voice in Milton. Paradise is where one feels no need for fruitless self-assertion, where knowledge can be gained without loss of power, where one can listen to a higher voice discoursing on the growth of the soul. Wordsworth echoes Raphael's description of the soul receiving reason, "Discursive or intuitive" (*PL*, V.488). As the 1850 text makes clearer, in such moments the soul is "by communion raised," finding in relation to divine word a repose never approached by mere self-expression. In a way Milton's Raphael is discussing what we could call a process of sublimation, whereby a more primary instinct is redirected to more satisfactory means of expression; indeed, the very word occurs in the description of the corporeal turned incorporeal, "by gradual scale sublimed" (V.483). In turning to Milton, Wordsworth finds an emblem for the education of the soul, "drawn out," sublimed into the realm of timeless voice.

Poetic voice restores the continuity of the sublimating process, the process of turning corporeal nature into the more incorporeal nature of metaphor. Each pause over a "dark abyss" or gap in nature allows mind to project voice. In Book VI, envisioning the scene in Miltonic "silence visible," the poet hears the voice of Nature: "I heard it then and seem to hear it now" (VI.432). In Book XIV, envisioning the "silent sea of hoary mist," the poet hears the voice of the waters, and reimagines the "breathing space" as the abyss with "voice issuing forth to silent light" (XIV.73). The fear is that these projections will prove inadequate, that imagination will confront only itself as unfathered vapor rising from the mind's abyss. Reimagining those projections as coming from outside the self, Wordsworth finds new ground for the continuity of the mind's engagement with nature. Each arrest at a moment of choice, each imagining of an abyss adds new momentum, new sense of "wholesome separation" between perceiving and perceived consciousness. Voice becomes not a moment of confrontation to be overcome, but the principle of continuity itself by which the stasis of any moment widens to create self-consciousness from the separation of voice and listener. Even when most caught up,

> I said unto the life which I had lived,
> Where art thou? Hear I not a voice from thee
> Which 'tis reproach to hear? Anon I rose
> As if on wings, and saw beneath me stretched
> Vast prospect of the world which I had been
> And was; and hence this song, which like a lark
> I have protracted, in the unwearied heavens
> Singing.   [XIV.377–384]

To a primary will which, being so caught up, can only be surprised, Wordsworth presents a second will, one that puts on knowledge with power and not only asks but conjures voice: "Where art thou?" Fall here is humanized into a myth for the separation of a present from a previous sense of being. As both Adam and God, the secluder in secret groves and the discerning intellect, the poet hears reproach as the voice of his own previous being. The quarrel is, in Yeats's terms, with the self, and thus the very material of poetry. The terms of morality have not been abandoned but assumed, reproach not reacted against but absorbed into second will. Hence the confidence of the image that follows, a putting on of divinity like that of Eve's dream. This is not easy transcendence, on the model of the allegro poet who, "like the lark at break of day arising / From sullen earth, sings hymns at heaven's gate." Nor is this a sudden stop of silence when the penseroso nightingale is apprehended as "missing," when reproved poet is shocked into recognition of absence. Here is a reimagining of the unimagined lark, whose power is the continued arrest of the moment, the *protracted* song.

One of Wordsworth's duties in closing *The Prelude* is to

pay tribute to his patron Calvert, and one must see duty here, too, not as a stumbling block but as a further voice absorbed into song. He calls Calvert's bequest that which "enabled me to pause for choice, and walk / At large and unrestrained" (XIV.360–361). The "pause for choice" has been protracted over the length of the poem, or more accurately, over the length of a lifetime of choice revision of the poem. One may dismiss the choice of phrase here as lowly wisdom, yet it is not less but more heroic because of that. The wing that is not "damped too soon" is that which soars to epic heights, as the will that walks at large is that which takes the whole newly conquered earth as its domain. *The Prelude* begins, as *Paradise Lost* ends, with the problem of where to choose a resting place. The journey becomes, like that of Milton in Wordsworth's tribute "At Vallombrosa," a choice of inspirational springs, among heights where "he would choose / To wander." *The Prelude* suggests that each actualization of such choice is of epic concern. Willful self-confidence first asserts, "I cannot miss my way," and willful self-assertion first proposes "nothing better than a wandering cloud" to replace the biblical image of the guidance of Jehovah. Both in the course that the poem describes and in the course of evolution of the poem, the wandering cloud becomes the poet himself as he assumes the power of his divine and poetic fathers. He finds a better way; comparing his course to that of a "home-bound laborer" beneath "the mellowing sun, that shed / Mild influence," he admits Miltonic influence to the poem. When he describes misjudging his theme to be "some old / Romantic tale by Milton left unsung," he recognizes the misapprehension as a consequence of "the ambitious Power of choice, mistaking / Proud spring-tide swellings for a regular sea." This is to confront his own proud swellings—the first will—and to transmute concern into what his own revision calls the "power of choice," the chastened second will of a "regular sea." Steady choice singles out a theme that appears to be of more lowly wisdom than some old romantic tale, but it is the more heroic argument.

At the end of the poem Wordsworth recognizes the "genuine liberty" of the second will, not unchecked desire, but the checking of error turned into the means of continued progress, a regular sea, protracted song.

> A humbler destiny have we retraced,
> And told of lapse and hesitating choice,
> And backward wanderings along thorny ways.
>
> [XIV.136–138]

As the work of poetic revision, these lines themselves are the product of second will; they also summarize the reimagining of the myth of fall into lapse of time, of archetypal choice into protracted choice, of Miltonic repetition into "backward wanderings." The line that follows—"compassed round by mountain solitudes"—revises a favorite Miltonism, revises an earlier version into Miltonism, and revises the Miltonism into the poet's own image for himself, echoing his poetic father but speaking in his own voice. In a sense the poet of mind and nature is threatened by the darkness of solipsism—the lure of mind—and the dangers of the weight of what he calls, quoting Milton, "a universe of death"—the lure of nature. The power of choice is reconceived as that which holds alternatives in protracted arrest and creates, out of the abyss between them, out of the will to encounter the abyss, a second will more wise.

Afterword

The nothingness was a nakedness, a point

Beyond which thought could not progress as thought.
He had to choose. But it was not a choice
Between excluding things. It was not a choice

Between, but of.

Wallace Stevens, "Notes
toward a Supreme Fiction"

George Poulet has said that Bergson's originality lay "in his affirmation that duration is something other than history or a system of laws; that it is free creation."[1] I have been arguing that such is Milton's originality: his poetry conveys a sense of duration "so to interpose a little ease" in historical sequentiality; on the basis of this freedom he establishes an intimacy between poetry and its subject matter, between poetic process and the processes of free creation—the Father's creation of the Son, the Son's creation of the cosmos, man's creation of history, the poet's creation of moments of choice in which the reader can share the sense of potentiality.

Bypassing the contingencies of time, the poetics of choice itself seems to draw later poets into the circle of these analogies. Beyond "history or a system of laws," the romantic poet, turning to Milton, finds a source of "free creation." Not that a shared poetic denies literary history; Milton is not, like fallen Adam, to be "brought down / To dwell on even ground now with thy Sons" (*PL*, XI.347–348). The distance remains; only it can be consciously turned from a matter of temporality into a metaphor for imaginative space. The distance is thus "willed" in both directions, both senses: decreed by Milton's historicity, desired by the romantic seeking poetic voice. If we think in terms of a bequest rather than a burden, we open ourselves to discover both the salubriousness of the relation to the past and the element of volition in entering that relationship. The emphasis must be both on second *will*, the conscious, controlled turning to a Miltonic way, and on *second* will as the matured submissiveness to a voice that must seem to come from outside. At moments, volition itself seems to be held in indefinite abstraction between poets: not only does a romantic reach back, but authoritative voice seems to reach forward, arresting time, to touch the trembling ears of the listener in another life and another time.

A poet's distance from voice is measured by the uneasy resemblance of voice to moral prohibition; his closeness, by the feeling that literary history has this dimension of family history. In "Lycidas," Milton invokes the angel of prohibition, and achieves poetic voice in the grand domestication of that angel's concern: "Look homeward Angel now, and melt with ruth." In "To William Wordsworth," Coleridge finds "the Angel of the vision" in Wordsworth's hopeful spirit; he recounts how *The Prelude* sang "Of Duty, chosen Laws controlling choice," and turned Miltonic sublimity, "summoned homeward," into the egotistical sublime. Awe at the uncanny and attachment to the canny, the *heimlich*, are brought together in these spiritual homecomings, and in similar encounters, from Adam's with Michael to Stevens' discovery of the necessary angel.

Looking at Stevens makes us see Michael's bequest as poetry's estate:

> Yet always there is another life,
> A life beyond this present knowing,
> A life lighter than this present splendor,

Brighter, perfected and distant away,
Not to be reached but to be known,
Not an attainment of the will
But something illogically received,
A divination, a letting down
From loftiness, misgivings dazzlingly
Resolved in dazzling discovery.
There is no map of paradise.[2]

If we let frail thought dally with the false surmise of Milton's presence behind these lines, we can hear not an imitation but an echo, not an attainment of the will—at least not primary will—but something illogically received. In Stevens' terms, one apprehends an order not imposed but discovered; it is not a discovery by horizontal, "Allegro" exploration—"Straight mine eye hath caught new pleasures"—but by a vertical, "Penseroso" descendentalism, making poetry capture the fallen Adam and Eve's new knowledge of "A life beyond this present knowing." Lingering a moment longer, one discovers the arrest of the present through structured repetitions, and the silence arrested in song between the conclusion of the long sentence and the quick expression of the awareness of what cannot be written in poetry, cannot be turned into structure: "There is no map of paradise." One cannot lay out in space what is so essentially experienced in time, what is apprehended only as it is being lost, "a letting down / From loftiness."

Such is the "letting down" with which Milton too expresses the dazzling experience when visionary poetry re-enters ongoing time:

Let us descend now therefore from this top
Of Speculation; for th' hour precise
Exacts our parting hence. [*PL*, XII.588–590]

The first enjambment keeps us poised, looking back to the root meaning of "Speculation" as "outlook," looking forward as we descend from the pointedness of "top" down the syllabic steps of the longer word. Another way: for the moment, we catch the elegant Latinate word as the grandness of the past—and, simultaneously, the "degeneration" in the descent out of Eden caught in this Anglo-Saxon "top"—and the awareness that higher voice is now looked back upon as mere speculation. The second enjambment captures in its precision all the pathos of the "parting hence." "We do not know what 'the hour precise' is, but the fact that it has been determined helps us to return to a different scale of experience." [3] The passing of time marks the new awareness of human life; one shares with the poet the descent from artistic splendor to dazzling discovery of experience beyond pattern, beyond second-hand representation as narrative past. The real resolving of "misgivings" is not in any statement, however angelic, of the justice of God's ways, but in the awareness of the difference between pattern and life, an awareness it is Milton's greatest achievement to express in such verse.

The "letting down from loftiness" within Miltonic verse is a model for experiencing the handing down of loftiness that is poetic influence. The poet's vision and revision, turning on a moment of confrontation with higher voice, is like the reader's sight and insight, turning on moments of arrested temporality. In these confrontations the poetry of choice becomes the poetry of the sublime, where grandeur is discovered in facing origins and the moment of creation is re-created now. The process of choice leads to a fork in the road where alternatives are simultaneously present; and since Oedipus' revision of his journey to Thebes, the crossroads have represented the challenge to one's unity of being posed by the recognition that one has been "generated."

Pausing over the intersection till it becomes a pleasance, the poet discovers an interposed ground the vision of which redeems him from both the haste of repudiation and the narrowness of back recoiling on himself. The way is the wait. Milton himself repeatedly demonstrates how the old footsteps point the way to open spaces rather than traumatic intimidation. When Satan seems to tread in Odysseus' shadow, the ghostlier demarcations produce keener sounds, and his voyage takes on the quality of what Poulet calls "free creation"; poised between the overtones of possible literary allusion, we experience an arrested moment of choice. When Satan re-enters paradise, he pauses in a revery that can stand for the romantic brooding over the choice to tread in Milton's shadow. Rapt beyond himself, Satan is caught by this vision of the earth's beauty: "Seat worthier of Gods, as built / With second thoughts, reforming what was old" (PL, IX.100–101). He feels excluded not only from heaven but from the earth as "revision" of heaven; and he feels doubly excluded from this product of second thoughts which has, without him, overcome the problem of loss. His question, "For what God after better worse would build?" may be said to haunt the post-Miltonic poet. But unlike Satan, the romantic comes to see revision as his own work. The more lovely the objects of nature appear to Satan, the more he feels, "I in none of these / Find place or refuge." The romantic, casting out the Satan or selfhood, finds his place or refuge in second thoughts, the labor of reforming his old conception of his literary self.

If a poet is strong enough to get past the solipsistic resignation to the mind as its own place, he assumes the role of chooser, and pausing to confront a poetic father, asserts his right of way. In Stevens' terms he says "yes" to the "no!" of authoritative voice, and in saying "yes" he says farewell. This exchange and the sense of new departure are all myth, to be sure, but the strong poet creates the myth of origin with which he grapples. He takes on a Miltonic blindness, choosing re-vision over the primary vision of the fact that these confrontations are a matter of "false surmise." Rapt in Keatsian "embalmed darkness," the poet transcends the easy daylight demystifications, and finds a choice inaudible to those untuned to voices "heard / In ancient days," invisible to those afraid to reimagine the giant.

Acknowledging his version of those daylight awarenesses ("My house has changed a little in the sun,") Wallace Stevens goes on to his version of the choice:

> It must be visible or invisible,
> Invisible or visible or both:
> A seeing and unseeing in the eye.
>
> ["Notes toward a Supreme Fiction"]

Helen Vendler speaks generally of Stevens' use of "or" as a "device for hovering over the statement rather than making it." [4] What is recreated thus as a habit of speech points to the creative nature of poetic language. Like the hovering over statement in Stevens and Milton is the image of hovering over an abyss. The experience of alternatives points not to weak indecisiveness but to potency; the hovering becomes seminal, the abyss, a womb of time. In a parody of creative movement, Sin and Death "Flew diverse, and with Power (thir Power was great) / Hovering upon the Waters" (PL, X.284–285). One may wish to find here the power that Wordsworth identifies with imagination itself; the difference is that Sin bridges the chaos, while poets like Wordsworth and Stevens make a dwelling of the abyss, not spanning it but brooding on it till it brings forth new imaginative life. The abyss of consciousness opens to reveal, beyond the awareness of loss, the awareness of new worlds. Poetry thus participates in the divine illuminative power, recreating in each new imagining the creative moment when Holy Spirit "Dove-like [sat] brooding on the vast Abyss / And [made] it pregnant" (*PL*, I.21–22).

Imaging an abyss, the conscious will "dissolves, diffuses, dissipates, in order to recreate." Reading Milton, we must see the divine will participating in these recreations, enacting the revisionary power of "secondary imagination." In the begetting of the Second Person, in second thoughts producing this earth, in the revision of history with the Fall, in every expression of the Word become words, creativity is made manifest. For the poet, God's participation is the basis of the complex analogies between aesthetic and religious experience, the reason aesthetic and ethical choice are one; for the critic, the conception of Divinity sharing Milton's poetry of choice extends the possibilities for seeing Milton sharing a poetics with romantic heirs. To attempt to come to terms with Milton on the ground that poetry and theology are separate things and that the reader can accept the one while overlooking the other does this poet, perhaps more than any other, extreme violence. The only option is to see every choice of word as a moral choice, every musical echo as an echo of heavenly music, every proper arrest as an apprehension of the presence of God. One need not, of course, be a believer in Miltonic or any other doctrine, but one must believe in the absolute unity of the doctrine and the poetry, a unity of earthly and heavenly song in which every note is a note toward a supreme fiction. Fiction and faith form a continuum in which false surmise is an imaginative equivalent of transcendence, in which every "perhaps" points to the essential romantic insight that we live beyond ourselves, in possibility.

Leone Vivante cites Milton's Sonnet XXIII to illustrate how much the supreme fiction that is poetry depends on the beauty of the sense of possibility:

> Her face was veiled; yet to my fancied sight
> Love, sweetness, goodness, in her person shined
> So clear as in no face with more delight.

"There is not one single thing with distinct outlines," he notes, and we may think of Wordsworth's description of the Miltonic "indefinite abstraction" as we apprehend the face of Katherine (or an indefinite abstraction of Mary, or of woman more generally). "The 'white,' and the 'clear,' all these terms express here the (in tendency) self- and form-transcending value of deep original freedom; that is, of the active principle in its *potential* intensity, and in its primal character." [5] This is just the relation between "original freedom" and a poetry of choice, one which reaches toward moments of abstraction when alternatives exist as potentialities, when we come upon something forever in the realm of possibility. In "Notes toward a Supreme Fiction," Stevens muses:

> To discover an order as of
> A season, to discover summer and know it,
>
> To discover winter and know it well, to find,
> Not to impose, not to have reasoned at all,
> Out of nothing to have come on major weather,
>
> It is possible, possible, possible. It must
> Be possible.

More prosaically Sartre says that the goal of art must be to restore to the event its freshness and unforeseeability, to "recover this world by giving it to be seen as it is, but as if it had its source in human freedom." [6] If one takes as subject the event of literary composition itself, then one may want ultimately to interpret poetic influence as something neither to be evaded nor imposed, but a process profoundly dependent on a forgetting and a recovery, a new will to come upon a crossroads and "discover an order." What happens in poetic composition is thus analogous to, if not expressed by, what happens in reading Miltonic verse. To confront each choice in its presentness, *as if* order were not already there, to come upon the world of time as a discovery, not an imposition—such is the achievement of Milton's poetry of choice.

Notes

we are lived, the powers
That we create with are not ours.
. . . . .
O sudden Wind that blows unbidden,
Parting the quiet reeds, O Voice
Within the labyrinth of choice
Only the passive listener hears.

W. H. Auden, *New Year Letter*

Abbreviations

BNYPL   *Bulletin of the New York Public Library*
E&S   *Essays and Studies by Members of the English Association*
ELH   *Journal of English Literary History*
MLN   *Modern Language Notes*
N&Q   *Notes and Queries*
PQ   *Philological Quarterly*
RES   *Review of English Studies*
RM   *Review of Metaphysics*
SP   *Studies in Philology*
UTQ   *University of Toronto Quarterly*

Foreword

1. See, for example, James Holly Hanford, "The Temptation Motive in Milton," *SP*, 15 (1918), 176–194; and W. B. C. Watkins, "Temptation," in *An Anatomy of Milton's Verse* (Baton Rouge, La., 1955), pp. 87–146.

2. Christopher Ricks, *Milton's Grand Style* (Oxford, 1963), pp. 81–82.

3. Cf. "those obstinate questionings / Of sense and outward things"

(Wordsworth, Immortality Ode). Perhaps the most seminal comment on the light of sense going out is William Empson's, in "Sense in the Prelude," *The Structure of Complex Words* (New York, 1951), pp. 294–295. The seeming contradiction between the "obscure sense / Of possible sublimity" (*Prelude*, II, 317–318) and the meaning of a beaconing, emanating light when "the light of sense / Goes out" is one way of relating indefinite abstraction to prophetic strain.

4. The borrowing is noted by Ernest de Selincourt, *The Poetical Works of William Wordsworth* (5 vols., 2d ed., rev.; Oxford, 1967), I, 327. Quotations are from this edition. Of another passage that captures lingering lapse "preserv'd while pass away, / The feeble generations of mankind" (A² *Prelude*, VIII.504ff), De Selincourt comments, "The picture of Echo and her sister Silence, added to A, has a touch of suggestive beauty that recalls *Comus*" (*The Prelude*, ed. Ernest de Selincourt; 2d ed. rev. Helen Darbishire [Oxford, 1959], pp. 581–582).

There is no actual synesthesia but surely an evocation of that kind of power in Wordsworth's fragment of a poem on Milton:

> He built an altar, and the fire from heaven
> Came down upon it. Round the growing flames
> That filled the sense with fragrance gently rose
> Sounds . . . [*Poetical Works*, V, 362]

5. "Preface to the Edition of 1815," *Poetical Works*, II, 439.

6. "The phrase 'solution sweet' is Miltonic, both in its inversion of the adjective and in its appositional relation with the rest of the sentence" (Ernest de Selincourt, *The Poems of John Keats* [London, 1905], p. 471).

7. Quotations from Milton's poems are from Merritt Y. Hughes, ed., *John Milton: Complete Poems and Major Prose* (New York, 1957), and are used by permission of The Bobbs-Merrill Company, Inc. *Paradise Lost* is abbreviated *PL*; *Paradise Regained*, *PR*.

8. See Ricks, pp. 94–95. Edward Le Comte, in *Yet Once More: Verbal and Psychological Pattern in Milton* (New York, 1969), p. 97, compares other phrases from Milton: "Fanning their odoriferous wings" (*PL*, IV.156); "flung odors" (*PL*, VIII.515); "odors famed / From their soft wings" (*PR*, II.364–365).

9. *Poetical Works*, II, 437.

10. "Angel Surrounded by Paysans." Quotations from *The Collected Poems of Wallace Stevens* (New York, 1967), copyright 1923–1954 by Wallace Stevens, are by permission of Alfred A. Knopf, Inc., and Faber and Faber Ltd.

Chapter 1. A Better Way

1. Søren Kierkegaard, *Either / Or*, trans. Walter Lowrie, David F. Swenson, and Lillian Marvin Swenson; rev. Howard A. Johnson (Garden City, N.Y., 1959), II, 229. (New York, 1959), II, 229.

2. "Milton: I," *On Poetry and Poets* (New York, 1957), p. 159 (first published in *Essays and Studies*, 1936). One reply to Eliot might be to cite some of his own diction. See the chorus in *Murder in the Cathedral*, where phrases like "the watchman," "the old without fire," "the child without milk," "our laborer," are put in general terms for specific effect.

3. Cleanth Brooks, "The Light Symbolism in 'L'Allegro–Il Penseroso,'" *The Well Wrought Urn* (New York, 1947), p. 50.

4. "Milton's Visual Imagination: An Answer to T. S. Eliot," *UTQ*, 16 (1946), 19.

5. Geoffrey Hartman, "False Themes and Gentle Minds," *PQ*, 47 (1968), 57; reprinted in *Beyond Formalism: Literary Essays, 1958–1970* (New Haven, 1970).

6. The connection between temptation and renunciation is carried to its consequence by Northrop Frye, who points out that the devils cannot die, "because they cannot make the act of surrender involved in death" (*The Return of Eden: Five Essays on Milton's Epics* [Toronto, 1965], p. 81).

7. F. T. Prince, "On the Last Two Books of 'Paradise Lost,'" *E&S*, n.s. 11 (1958), 51.

8. Geoffrey H. Hartman, *Wordsworth's Poetry, 1787–1814* (New Haven, 1964), p. 12.

9. Watkins, p. 58.

10. Cf. Wordsworth:

> With trembling oars I turned,
> And through the silent water stole my way
> Back to the covert of the willow tree. [*Prelude*, I.385–387]

The relation of such turn to lapsed choice is the subject of Chapter 2.

11. J. B. Leishman, *The Art of Marvell's Poetry* (London, 1966), p. 264.

12. See Hartman, *Wordsworth's Poetry*, p. 12.

13. "Milton and Metaphysical Art," *ELH*, 16 (1949), 132–133.

14. Le Comte, p. 15, notes the connection between these passages of waking and loss.

15. Kierkegaard, II, 182.

16. Cf. II.948–950, where Satan

> O'er bog, or steep, through strait, rough, dense, or rare,
> With head, hands, wings, or feet pursues his way,
> And swims or sinks, or wades, or creeps, or flies.

Clearly the verse is itself a muddy tangle, and one could argue that the reason for "or" rather than "and" is that Satan is in the realm of chaos and nonbeing which lacks even the order of hell needed to add rebellious qualities each to each without mutual negation. (His object, after all, is not to multiply "Allegro" experiences or varieties of transportation, but to get past. He is not standing at a moment of choice between "swims" or "sinks," but doing what he can to get by, to deny such moments.)

Cf. Blake's *Book of Los*, where the "or" marks the ability to organize and control chaos:

> Incessant the falling Mind labour'd
> Organizing itself: till the Vacuum
> Became element, pliant to rise,
> Or to fall, or to swim, or to fly:
> With ease searching the dire vacuity. [Plate 4, ll. 49–53]

But one must avoid inventing a system of moral connotation that can be invoked whenever the words "and" or "or" come up; what is needed is simply an awareness that in certain contexts even such small words can take on moral meaning. Blake quotations are from *The Poetry and Prose of William Blake*, ed. David V. Erdman (New York, 1965).

17. *The Early Lives of Milton*, ed. Helen Darbishire (London, 1932), p. 291.

18. "Milton's Corrections to the Minor Poems," *MLN*, 25 (1910), 203.

19. John S. Diekhoff, "Critical Activity of the Poetic Mind: John Milton," *PMLA*, 55 (1940), 751.

20. "A Note in *Comus*," *RES*, 8 (1932), 170–176.

21. See Blake's *Book of Urizen:*

> What Demon
> Hath form'd this abominable void
> This soul-shudd'ring vacuum?—Some said
> "It is Urizen," But unknown, abstracted
> Brooding secret, the dark power hid.   [Plate 3]

In *Blake's Apocalypse* (New York, 1963), Harold Bloom comments, "Blake again parodies Milton's God who created by retraction—'I uncircumscribed myself retire'" (p. 166).

22. The revised "wide" in the Trinity manuscript is "wild" in the Bridgewater manuscript. Milton or someone else must have changed it back to the original Trinity word, seeing how much better "wild" is than "wide." Printed editions retain "wild surrounding waste" (*John Milton's Complete Poetical Works: Reproduced in Photographic Facsimile*, ed. Harris Francis Fletcher [Urbana, Ill., 1943]).

23. E. M. W. Tillyard, *Milton* (rev. ed.; New York, 1967), p. 304.

24. T. S. Eliot, *Selected Essays* (New York, 1950), pp. 255, 246.

25. See especially Paul Goodman, "Milton's 'On His Blindness': Stanzas, Motion of Thought," in *The Structure of Literature* (Chicago, 1954), pp. 192–215.

26. Rosemond Tuve, "Structural Figures of *L'Allegro* and *Il Penseroso*," *Images and Themes in Five Poems by Milton* (Cambridge, Mass., 1957), p. 110. See also Frye: "The kernel of revelation is Paradise, the feeling that man's home is not in this world, but in another world (though occupying the same time and space) that makes more sense" (*Return of Eden*, p. 97).

27. The relationship of Sonnets XX and XXI has been discussed by others. See, for example, Frazer Neiman, "Milton's Sonnet XX," *PMLA*, 64 (1949), 480–483; and John H. Finley, Jr., "Milton and Horace: A Study of Milton's Sonnets," *Harvard Studies in Classical Philology*, 48 (1937), 64–67.

28. Donald Dorian remarks, " 'To Mr. Lawrence,' pleasant as it is, closes with a serious reminder of the need of temperance in the enjoyment of sensuous delights" ("The Question of Autobiographical Significance in *L'Allegro* and *Il Penseroso*," *Modern Philology*, 31 [1933], 180). Compare the "mountain nymph, sweet Liberty" of "L'Allegro." As Brooks points out, "Such pleasures . . . depend upon one's freedom from business appointments and dinner engagements" (p. 51).

In the controversy over the meaning of "spare," both interpretations point to the concept of moderation. W. J. Rolfe says: "He does *not* mean *spare time* for interposing such pleasures oft, but the opposite—refrain from interposing them oft. It is moderation in festive indulgence that he recommends, not the seeking of opportunities for it" (*The Poems of John Milton* [New York, 1887], p. 205). It is clear that "spare" in the sense of "refrain from" calls for temperance in such matters. But even the sense of "spare time" (for something else), surely the more accepted reading, suggests moderate indulgence when placed together with "interpose" and the overtones of more pressing business. See also Le Comte, pp. 146–148.

29. "Milton's Cato," *Times Literary Supplement*, April 5, 1963, p. 233. E. M. W. Tillyard makes a similar point about the "subtle friendliness of tone" in the twin poems (*L'Allegro and Il Penseroso* [London, 1932] p. 9). Milton "tactfully and without undue insistence invites his readers to share his experiences. He adjusts his expression to suit his guests, but never so drastically as to obliterate the sense of his own presence" (p. 11). Such understanding of Milton's tone is even more important in a poem like Sonnet XX, which is openly an invitation.

30. Robert M. Adams, *Ikon: John Milton and the Modern Critics* (Ithaca, N.Y., 1955), p. 28.

31. One might make a similar comparison (and one along the more frequently traveled road of literary history) between Milton's and Spenser's use of the word "or." As has been amply shown by Paul Alpers, "particular attention to sentence structure is almost never helpful in reading *The Faerie Queene*. This is the general rule, whose intensified version is that we do not have to make a choice between alternatives when sentence structure is ambiguous" (*The Poetry of*

the Faerie Queen [Princeton, 1967], p. 88). The whole section on alternatives, pp. 77–95, is of interest in this context.

32. Northrop Frye takes a somewhat analogous short view of Shakespeare and Milton based on Cleopatra and Eve. The later, exclusive poet of choice is contrasted with the earlier, inclusive poet, whose heroine "is vain and frivolous and light-minded and capricious and extravagant and irresponsible and a very bad influence on Antony" (*Return of Eden*, p. 26). Even more descriptive than the specific adjectives—for Frye has chosen but one aspect of Cleopatra —are the cumulated *and*s, for it is just the sense of unnegating fullness that contrasts with the chastity of Milton's muse.

Geoffrey Hartman points to Shakespeare's use of sound and enjambment to express the easy ascent in *Antony and Cleopatra* from mortal to immortal ("The Voice of the Shuttle," *RM*, 23 [1969], 247; reprinted in *Beyond Formalism*).

33. The work of John M. Major, "*Comus* and *The Tempest*," *Shakespeare Quarterly*, 10 (1959), 177–183, and Ethel Seaton, "*Comus* and Shakespeare," *E&S*, 31 (1946), 68–80, supersedes the collections of echoes in Alwin Thaler, "The Shaksperian Element in Milton," *PMLA*, 40 (1925), 645–691, and George Coffin Taylor, "Shakespeare and Milton Again," *SP*, 23 (1926), 189–199.

34. Robert Bechtold Heilman, *This Great Stage: Image and Structure in "King Lear"* (Baton Rouge, La., 1948), p. 155. The punctuation in the *King Lear* passage is my own; the First Quarto is unpunctuated, and this scene is not in the First Folio. See *King Lear: Parallel Texts of the First Quarto and the First Folio*, ed. Wilhelm Vietor (Marburg, Germany, 1886), p. 120. Even if one reads "a better way" as belonging to the phrase before, the point remains the same; regardless of where one places the semicolon, simile is being pointed to as inadequate.

35. *Milton*, Plates 30 (inscription), 40.33.

36. I take the manuscript phrase "another way" (Fletcher, p. 425), because it is closer verbally to "a better way," though the revised wording, "some other means I have" makes the same point.

37. Referring to this use of the term "fancy," Cleanth Brooks contrasts the supernatural lore of "L'Allegro" with the unsphering of the "spirit of Plato" in "Il Penseroso": "In 'L'Allegro' the supersti-

tion is reduced to a charming and poetic fancy; in 'Il Penseroso,' it has been elevated to the level of the philosophic imagination" (p. 53). "Poetic fancy" is precisely the right term for the unpurged multiplicity of "L'Allegro" in contrast to the narrow ladder leading to the elevation of the "Penseroso" Plato.

38. Adams, *Ikon*, p. 34.

39. The voice to be turned from is thus like that of the sirens in *Comus* ("They in pleasing slumber lulled the sense / And in sweet madness robbed it of itself" [ll. 260–261]). Le Comte (p. 12) notes the connection.

40. G. Wilson Knight, "The Frozen Labyrinth: An Essay on Milton," *The Burning Oracle* (London, 1939), p. 69. One might take the renunciation he speaks of as an emblem of the larger renunciation that is the topic of this chapter. Cf. Milton's relationship to allegro music and its chief poet, Shakespeare, who makes his exit in *The Tempest*, where the rod is an emblem of magical powers given up. Frye finds a similar valedictory attitude near the conclusion of *Paradise Lost:* "When Michael comes to earth in Book Eleven, his descent is associated, in the last classical allusion in *Paradise Lost*, with Hermes putting Argus to sleep with his 'opiate rod'" (*Return of Eden*, p. 57).

41. "Milton: I," *On Poetry and Poets*, p. 162.

Chapter 2. A Moment's Space

1. Henri Bergson, *Time and Free Will: An Essay on the Immediate Data of Consciousness*, trans. F. L. Pogson (New York, 1960), pp. 196–197.

2. Bergson, p. 173.

3. Bergson, p. 101.

4. Bergson, pp. 180, 182.

5. *Return of Eden*, p. 36.

6. Roy Daniells, *Milton, Mannerism and Baroque* (Toronto, 1963), p. 38.

7. Tuve, p. 88.

8. Bergson, p. 183.

9. *Return of Eden*, p. 102.

10. Bergson, p. 100.

11. Kierkegaard, II, 168. Why the going back is a going forward is suggested by Hartman (*Wordsworth's Poetry*, p. 255), who calls Milton's verse "forward poetry."

12. *Wordsworth's Poetry*, pp. 10–13.

13. Bergson, p. 12. One possible vocabulary for the difference could be taken from mathematics, of which Milton himself was an avid student. It is the difference between continuous and discontinuous functions. The poet's effort would then be like Newton's, an attempt to find all functions continuous, "every new direction indicated in the preceding one" (Bergson, p. 12).

14. *Milton's Paradise Lost: A New Edition*, ed. Richard Bentley (London, 1732), p. 161.

15. See Hartman, "The Voice of the Shuttle."

16. See Geoffrey Hartman, "Milton's Counterplot," *ELH*, 25 (1958), 2; reprinted in *Beyond Formalism*.

The association of the arrest of time with the noon hour is amplified in the recurrent mention of the noon hour in *PL*, IX.219, 397–403, 739–744. Cf. biblical noon arrests in Deut. 28:28–29, Job 5:14, Isaiah 59:10, Psalms 91:6.

The noon hour and the summer's day recur together as emblems of a suspect stasis when Beelzebub draws attention "still as Night / Or Summer's Noon-tide air" (II.308–309). Milton associates the arrest of time with the arrest that is fiction in *PL*, I.449–453:

> In amorous ditties all a Summer's day,
> While smooth *Adonis* from his native Rock
> Ran purple to the Sea, suppos'd with blood
> Of *Thammuz* yearly wounded: the Love-tale
> Infected Sion's daughters.

Arrest here is an emblem of untruth, a technique Wordsworth inherits when he introduces his dreamy fiction as coming to him when "once in the stillness of a summer's noon, / . . . perusing, so it chanced, / The famous history of the errant knight" (*Prelude*, V.57–59). Wordsworth also uses repetition to capture arrested time, describing how as a child he

Made one long bathing of a summer's day;
Basked in the sun, and plunged and basked again
Alternate, all a summer's day. [*Prelude*, I.290–292]

17. Paul Valéry, "Poetry and Abstract Thought," *The Art of Poetry*, trans. Denise Folliot, *The Collected Works of Paul Valéry*, ed. Jackson Mathews, VII (New York, 1958), 55–56.

"Reading a poem," says Hartman, "is like walking on silence" ("The Voice of the Shuttle," *RM*, 23 [1969], 245). Hartman is interested in looking longer at the depths.

18. Joseph Summers discusses the "me" passages and distinguishes Eve's disordered self-reference—parallel to the arrest of song that is fall—with that of Christ, which reflects history—the arrest of time that is Incarnation ("The Voice of the Redeemer in *Paradise Lost*," *PMLA*, 70 [1955], 1082–89; reprinted in *The Muse's Method: An Introduction to "Paradise Lost"* [London, 1962]).

19. One might wish to make a parallel statement about the stylistic turn in the poem. See J. B. Broadbent (*Some Graver Subject: An Essay on "Paradise Lost"* [New York, 1967], p. 27), who notes that "in the second half of the poem he writes consistently as the poet of thirty years later: 'O more exceeding love . . . '" Le Comte does not admire the repetition: "The formula sticks out [in Elegy VI] even as it does in the unsuccessful, conceited poem "Upon the Circumcision," where again a question is asked and rather too mechanically answered: 'O more exceeding love . . . '" (p. 23).

20. Le Comte (p. 19) says, "Surely only the blind, or rather the deaf, can fail to notice the increase in skill from

Young Hyacinth, born on Eurotas' strand,
Young Hyacinth, the pride of Spartan land; ("Fair Infant," 25–26)

which is no better than its model, Spenser's

Young Astrophel, the pride of shepherds' praise,
Young Astrophel, the rustic lasses' love,

to

or Lycidas is dead, dead ere his prime,
Young Lycidas, and hath not left his peer."

21. Tuve, p. 92.

22. Bergson, p. 11. One can see such "impoverishment" in compar-

ing the passage next quoted, "And wipe the tears for ever from his eyes" with Pope's playfully sweeping "stopping up" of the future: "All tears are wip'd for ever from all Eyes" (*Epilogue to the Satires*, I.103).

23. "Milton's *Lycidas* 29," *Explicator*, 21 (1963), 43.

24. Gretchen Finney, *Musical Backgrounds for English Literature: 1580–1650* (New Brunswick, N.J., 1962), p. 42.

25. Bergson, p. 12. For a discussion of "the periodic returns of the measure," the way Milton variously draws the sense from one line to the next, see especially Donald R. Roberts, "The Music of Milton," *PQ*, 26 (1947), 328–344. On the relation of grammar to verse see also Ricks, *Milton's Grand Style*, and Donald Davie, "Syntax and Music in *Paradise Lost*," in *The Living Milton*, ed. Frank Kermode (London, 1960), pp. 70–84.

26. Jean-Paul Sartre, *Nausea*, trans. Lloyd Alexander (Norfolk, Conn., 1959), pp. 179–180; *Being and Nothingness: An Essay on Phenomenological Ontology*, trans. Hazel E. Barnes (New York, 1956), p. 135.

27. Bergson, p. 13.

28. Finney, p. 200.

29. *Being and Nothingness*, p. 11.

30. See the opening essays in *Language and Silence* (New York, 1967). See more especially, Murray Krieger, "The Ekphrastic Principle and the Still Movement of Poetry," in *The Poet as Critic*, ed. Frederick P. W. McDowell (Evanston, Ill., 1967); reprinted in Krieger's *The Play and Place of Criticism* (Baltimore, 1967).

31. The apprehension of silence between phonemic poles is discussed by Hartman in the "The Voice of the Shuttle." I am indebted to Neil Hertz for emphasizing the effect in this particular line of Milton's; it is related to the Hebrew linguistic pattern of creation in which the biblical past tense is formed by adding to the imperative the single letter "vav" which also means, and is translated in King James, as "and." What differentiates the injunction, "Yihe or" ("Let there be light") from the fulfillment, "Vayihe or" ("and there was light") is the letter "vav," a single scribal stroke. There repetition is the fulfillment; between is the still point.

32. Eve, IV.647, 654, V.39; Adam, VII.106; poet, IV.600, 604.

33. "The Aesthetics of Silence," in *Styles of Radical Will* (New

York, 1969), p. 18. "Words after speech," writes Eliot in *Burnt Norton*, "reach / Into silence." In different ways Eliot and Milton are using the enjambment to express the reach into silence.

34. *Harmonious Vision* (Baltimore, 1954), p. 12.

35. *Prelude*, I.166–169. It is significant that the phrase "power of choice," like many of Wordsworth's profound interactions with Milton (as opposed to the unconscious or trivial verbal echoes) is not in the 1805 version but is a chosen emendation. (See Chapter 5.) Power is energy as yet unspent, and throughout the *Prelude*, Wordsworth identifies it with poetic potential of the unspoken word. De Selincourt (*Prelude*, p. 541) quotes De Quincey: "What you owe to Milton is not any knowledge, what you owe is *power*. . . . The true antithesis to knowledge is not pleasure but *power*"; De Quincey further notes, "For which distinction, as for most of the sound criticism on poetry . . . I must acknowledge my obligations to many years' conversations with Mr. Wordsworth."

36. The quoted phrases are from Anne Davidson Ferry, *Milton's Epic Voice: The Narrator in "Paradise Lost"* (Cambridge, Mass., 1963), p. 133; and Arnold Stein, *Answerable Style* (Minneapolis, 1953), p. 158. On the relation of silence and mantling light to creative imagination compare particularly *PL*, IV.604–609. On clouds or their absence and the mantled vision compare any number of places in Wordsworth. The frequency of clouds, vapors, haze, and mist in Wordsworth is not in itself remarkable, but at moments of revelation the image seems more significantly connected to its literary tradition than to common metaphor or observation of landscape. Passages of unclouding as a mark of higher vision are of course everywhere, especially in *Prelude*, Book XIV. Noteworthy here are the ways clouds stand for the mantled vision once unobscured. Cf. the interposition in *Prelude* A² at VI.425, *Prelude*, I.565, and *Excursion*, IV.83, where the "cloud of infancy" marks a disturbed communion; or *Excursion*, IV.637, where "morning mist" connects man's vision with Adam's. See also Geoffrey Hartman, *The Unmediated Vision* (New Haven, 1954), pp. 10–11.

37. Harold Bloom, *The Visionary Company: A Reading of English Romantic Poetry* (New York, 1963), p. 436.

38. *The Letters of John Keats, 1814–1821*, ed. Hyder Edward Rollins (Cambridge, Mass., 1958), I, 369.

39. *Letters*, I, 193.

40. *The Poems of John Keats*, p. 575.

41. *The Romantics on Milton: Formal Essays and Critical Asides*, ed. Joseph Anthony Wittreich, Jr. (Cleveland, 1970), p. 554. This is a convenient reference for the romantics' comments. Keats's annotations are also in *The Poetical Works and Other Writings of John Keats*, ed. Harry Buxton Forman (London, 1883).

42. *Wordsworth's Poetry*, pp. 11–12. Hartman's comment about Wordsworth's "Solitary Reaper" is worth bringing to a reading of Keats's Nightingale Ode discussed later in the chapter. It is not that both poems have reapers and nightingales, but that both extend the Miltonic "perhaps" in which alternatives are open. Wordsworth, stopping "here" instead of gently passing, arrests time with the reaper, and extends that false surmise by moving back in time with the nightingale; Keats, stopping "here" where there is no light after an instantaneous poetic journey, arrests time with the nightingale, and extends that false surmise by moving in time with the reaper Ruth. If Keats is writing consciously in the tradition of Milton and Wordsworth, then the point about power, the self-assertion amid the embalmed darkness of poetic tradition, is all the stronger. The tune haunts Wordsworth; Keats makes it disappear. The "I" returns at the end of the Wordsworth poem, but the self-assertion is made less certain and more mighty in Keats. See Wordsworth's sonnet "The Resting Place" ("Midnoon is past . . ."), which, though most dubiously connected to the ending of the Keats ode, does perform the movement inward and outward in terms of space.

43. "Keats and the Embarrassments of Poetic Tradition," *From Sensibility to Romanticism: Essays Presented to Frederick A. Pottle*, ed. Frederick W. Hilles and Harold Bloom (New York, 1965), p. 520; reprinted in Bloom's *Ringers in the Tower: Studies in Romantic Tradition* (Chicago, 1971).

44. "Milton's Sonnet on His 'Late Espoused Saint,'" *RES*, 25 (1949), 60.

45. "Tradition and the Individual Talent," *Selected Essays*, p. 5.

Chapter 3. A Space Extended

1. Albert Camus, *The Stranger*, trans. Stuart Gilbert (New York, 1946), p. 74.

2. *Surprised by Sin: The Reader in Paradise Lost* (London, 1967), p. 9.

3. Fish, p. 222. Though the deed itself (when not dreamed but performed) is indicated in the text, more than one reader has drawn an arrow to IX.781 and marked "here." The moment must seem to be subsumed into a larger context; and the moment itself is double—the substantially separated falls of Eve and Adam.

4. Kierkegaard, I, 289.

5. That the response to music is intended to be seen as uncorrupted is confirmed by comparison with the lines in Milton's "Ad Leonoram Romae Canentem":

> Aut Deus, aut vacui certe mens tertia caeli
> Per tua secreto guttura serpit agens.

The connection is made by Sigmund Gottfried Spaeth, *Milton's Knowledge of Music* (Princeton, 1913), p. 50.

6. See the discussion of the "Penseroso" phrase in Chapter 1, above, and Hartman's discussion of the *Comus* phrase "smoothing the Raven doune / Of darkness till it smiled" in "The Voice of the Shuttle," *RM*, 23 (1969), 243–244 (reprinted in *Beyond Formalism*, pp. 340–341).

7. Cf. ll. 800–801 and the manuscript revisions of the speech in and from the Trinity manuscript (Fletcher, p. 424), which show Milton changing Comus from the strength of assured victory to an awareness that he is almost overcome. Laurence Stapleton notes that the momentary rapture beyond self is something Comus shares with Satan, who is "abstracted" from self when he sees Eve ("Milton and the New Music," *UTQ*, 23 [1954] 220; reprinted in *Milton: Modern Essays in Criticism*, ed. Arthur E. Barker [London, 1965]).

8. Daniells, p. 29.

9. *Return of Eden*, p. 22.

10. *Return of Eden*, pp. 22–23.

11. Davie, p. 73. Cf. Ricks, pp. 41–42.

12. Davie comments: "How eventful is 'Day' at the start of line 42! The inversion, 'not to me returns' has forged for the long-awaited subject of 'returns' a link every bit as strong as rhyme, with 'Seasons,' in the corresponding place in the line above, and in the same gram-

matical relation to the identical verb 'return.' Thus, what we expect is a word parallel in meaning, just as it is parallel in metrical placement and grammatical function. We expect 'Spring.' What we get is 'Day.' And this is surprising" (p. 73).

13. John Hollander notes, "It is the doctrine which has suffered in the fall of the rebel angels, rather than the purely musical power to charm and move" (*The Untuning of the Sky: Ideas of Music in English Poetry, 1500–1900* [Princeton, 1961], p. 318; the section entitled "Milton's Renewed Song" is reprinted in Barker). The element Hollander calls doctrine is just that which comes "out of" song; it is fallen doctrine, not fallen song, that must be checked.

14. Masson is cited by Marjorie Nicolson in "Milton and the Telescope," *Science and Imagination* (Ithaca, N.Y., 1956), p. 96.

15. Kierkegaard, I, 288; Jackson I. Cope, *The Metaphoric Structure of Paradise Lost* (Baltimore, 1962), p. 59.

16. Arthur Schopenhauer, *The World as Will and Representation*, trans. E. F. Payne, (2 vols.; New York, 1966), II, 447; I, 257.

17. Johann Wolfgang von Goethe, *Faust: Part One & Part Two*, trans. Charles E. Passage (New York, 1965), ll. 1699–1702; copyright © 1965 by The Bobbs-Merrill Company, Inc.; reprinted by permission of the Liberal Arts Press Division. The translation is unfortunately colloquial, but the line numbers correspond with the original.

18. Le Comte (pp. 98–100, 178) notes how characteristic the phrase is of Milton.

19. Saul Bellow, *Dangling Man* (New York, 1944), p. 148.

20. *The Letters of Percy Bysshe Shelley*, ed. Frederick L. Jones (Oxford, 1964), II, 407.

21. *Letters*, II, 435–436. The relationship of Shelley's sentiments to his imminent death has been argued by James Rieger, in *The Mutiny Within* (New York, 1967), pp. 221–236.

22. *Letters*, II, 308.

23. Preface to *Prometheus Unbound*.

24. Rieger, p. 30.

25. Preface to *Prometheus Unbound*. Cf. the equation of poetry and fighting for freedom in Shelley's "Milton's Spirit":

I dreamed that Milton's spirit rose, and took
From life's green tree his Uranian lute;

And from his touch sweet thunder flowed, and shook
All human things built in contempt of man,—
And sanguine thrones and impious altars quaked,
Prisons and citadels.

26. *The Defence of Poetry*, in *Shelley's Prose, or The Trumpet of a Prophecy*, ed. David Lee Clark (Albuquerque, 1954), pp. 283, 279.

27. *Letters*, I, 251–252.

28. *Shelley's Prose*, p. 238. The lines that precede those quoted from *Prometheus Unbound* are reminiscent of Milton's hell. Those that follow echo Abdiel's advice in *PL*, V.847ff and the passage about interceding words in *PL*, XI.14–20.

29. *PU*, II.iv.107, cf. *PL*, I.48; *PU*, I.37, cf. *PL*, II.595. In the line "Burns frore and cold performs the effect of fire" (*PL*, I.595) the cold-fire would not be enough to establish Shelley's thinking of Milton's line except that, as Richard Pelletier notes, Shelley also borrows the unusual word "frore" in *Prometheus Unbound*, I.120 (Satan and Prometheus in Captivity," *N&Q*, 205 [n.s. 7] [1960], 107).

30. R. Piccoli notes that ll. 200–201, recognizing the experiential world outside song, move outward like *Samson Agonistes*, ll. 102–107 (cited in *Shelley's Prometheus Unbound: A Variorum Edition*, ed. Lawrence John Zillman [Seattle, 1959], p. 565).

31. Peter Blos, *On Adolescence: A Psychoanalytic Interpretation* (New York, 1962), pp. 156–157.

32. Cited by Blos, p. 195.

33. Blos, p. 100. An examination of the relation of repetition to the mourning process would provide a good evaluation of the place of repetition in *Paradise Lost*, if one regards the Fall as a loss like that of the security of the Oedipal parent. See the section "Excursus: Repetition," in Chapter 2, above, and repetition in the larger structure of the epic, as in the dual fall, first of Eve, then of Adam.

34. Rieger, p. 181.

35. *Shelley at Work: A Critical Inquiry* (Oxford, 1967), p. 264.

36. See *The Visionary Company*, p. 295. The Miltonic reference is noted by Lane Cooper, in *Plato* (London, 1938), p. 6. For a discussion of other sources see S. C. Wilcox, "The Sources, Symbolism, and Unity of Shelley's Skylark," *SP*, 46 (1949), 560–576, especially 569n.

37. "Lapis Lazuli" (copyright 1940 by Georgie Yeats; renewed 1968 by Bertha Georgie Yeats, Michael Butler Yeats, and Anne Yeats), *The Collected Poems of W. B. Yeats* (New York: Macmillan, 1956), by permission.

38. Raymond Dexter Havens, *The Influence of Milton on English Poetry* (Cambridge, Mass., 1922), p. 475n.

39. "Note on *Prometheus Unbound,* by Mrs. Shelley."

40. The loss that goes with Miltonic Eden is thus closer to Shelley than the mild absorption of loss into the timelessness of a Spenserian Garden of Adonis. So Frederick L. Jones concludes that "Milton, more than any other English poet, was Shelley's master" ("Shelley and Spenser," *SP*, 39 [1942], 669). On echoes of Milton's paradise see Carlos Baker, *Shelley's Major Poetry: The Fabric of a Vision* (Princeton, 1948), pp. 197–198.

41. *Shelley's Prose,* p. 295.

42. William Butler Yeats, "The Philosophy of Shelley's Poetry," from *Ideas of Good and Evil,* in *Essays and Introductions* (New York, 1961), p. 87.

Chapter 4. A Time to the Space

1. Irene Samuel relates the passage to Adam's superior power of contemplating other times (*Dante and Milton: The "Commedia" and "Paradise Lost"* [Ithaca, N.Y., 1966], pp. 14–15).

2. Kierkegaard, I, 289.

3. Kierkegaard, II, 170–171.

4. Georges Poulet, *Studies in Human Time,* trans. Elliott Coleman (Baltimore, 1956), p. 297. Poulet is talking about replacing grace with memory in Proust, but I use his insight to point to the way grace and memory work together, are part of the same thing, in Milton.

5. Howard Moss, *The Magic Lantern of Marcel Proust* (New York, 1962), p. 93.

6. Kierkegaard, II, 316. Milton, of course, had another point to prove about the hierarchy of the sexes, but introducing Kierkegaard may help explain how psychologically correct the poet makes an otherwise rather banal conception.

7. Sartre, *Being and Nothingness,* p. 7.

8. *Return of Eden,* pp. 79–80.

9. Poulet, p. 24.

10. "Perspectives on Time in *Paradise Lost*," *PQ*, 45 (1966), 740.

11. Kierkegaard, II, 161; Blake, *Milton*, Plate 30, inscription.

12. See D. C. Allen, "Milton and the Sons of God," *MLN*, 61 (1946), 73–79; Robert H. West, "Milton's Sons of God," *MLN*, 65 (1950), 187–191; and John M. Steadman, "Milton's 'Giant Angels': An Additional Parallel," *MLN*, 75 (1960), 551–553. For Raphael and the Sons of God as related to the eighth *sephirah*, see Anthony Edward Waite, *The Holy Kabbalah: A Study of the Secret Tradition in Israel* (London, 1929), pp. 254–256.

13. That the purpose of time designation here is to indicate duration for Adam and Eve rather than for Satan himself is shown by comparing the lack of time designation for Satan's voyage from hell. Stapleton comments: "The building of Pandemonium and the Council in Hell take place without any indication of time, nor is there reason to ponder their duration. More significant is the lack of any evidence of the length of Satan's voyage. This seems to me an example of Milton's judicious choice of an indefinite time when specific detail would detract from rather than add to the power of his narrative over the imagination. Satan voyages through darkness until he reaches the outer limits of creation, and even then, he coasts the wall of heaven 'on this side Night' (III, 71). But to give a part of a day or of night or a number of them to this episode would nullify the effect of the limitless confusion and disorder he has to overcome" ("Perspectives," pp. 738–739).

14. Kierkegaard, I, 290.

15. Roger Shattuck, *Proust's Binoculars: A Study of Memory, Time, and Recognition in "A la Recherche du Temps Perdu"* (New York, 1963), p. 100.

16. Joseph Summers, *The Muse's Method*, p. 190.

17. The first phrase is technically the translator's; Camus wrote, "J'ai pensé à ce moment qu'on pouvait tirer ou ne pas tirer." Gilbert gives, "And just then it crossed my mind that one might fire, or not fire—and it would come to absolutely the same thing." The second phrase, "rester ici ou partir, cela revenait au même," uses the past tense in a way that shows that in grammar as in intent the twentieth-century work confronts a failure of option before the moment of the

fall (*L'Etranger* [Paris, 1942], pp. 83–84; *The Stranger*, pp. 72–73).

18. Wallace Stevens, "Notes toward a Supreme Fiction," sect. iii, "It Must Give Pleasure." The passage follows what is clearly an attempt to imitate Milton stylistically:

> Forth then with huge pathetic force
> Straight to the utmost crown of night he flew.

Stevens is speaking of the imposition of order, like Satan's attempt to build his own order (see Chapter 3, above); Stevens, like Milton, uses images of physical construction to symbolize the violation of the legitimate powers of song. Canon Aspirin, like Satan, undergoes a fall when imposing order; as in Milton, that is the point at which the poet withdraws from his character and declares himself to be of the other party. Interestingly, that separation is also a fall from the time when the canon, as angel of reality, conceived fact and thought together. Compare what happens to Miltonic metaphor.

19. Bergson, p. 10.

20. *Nausea*, pp. 79–80, 58.

21. For a discussion of patience as an active virtue for Adam, poet, and reader, see Paul R. Baumgartner, "Milton and Patience," *SP*, 60 (1963), 203–213.

22. Kierkegaard, I, 290–291.

23. Summers, p. 218.

24. Bergson, p. 197.

25. "Time and Eternity: Paradox and Structure in *Paradise Lost*," *Journal of the Warburg and Courtauld Institutes*, 23 (1960), 132.

26. Summers, p. 192.

27. H. R. MacCallum, "Milton and Sacred History: Books XI and XII of *Paradise Lost*," in *Essays in English Literature from the Renaissance to the Victorian Age; Presented to A. S. P. Woodhouse*, ed. Millar MacLure and F. W. Watt (Toronto, 1964), p. 167.

28. How deliberate is the placing of the Israelites on the shore is noted by John M. Steadman: "According to the Authorized Version of Exodus 14:30, 'Israel saw the Egyptians dead upon the sea shore.' In *Paradise Lost*, on the other hand, the bodies of the Egyptian warriors are described not as scattered along the coast, but as floating on the sea itself. It is the Hebrews, rather than the Egyptians, who are

on the shore." (Steadman quotes *PL*, I.309–311.) Steadman notes that Milton's version "heightens the parallel between the defeated angels and the Egyptians" (" 'From the Safe Shore': Milton and Tremellius," *Neophilologus*, 44 [1960], 218–219).

29. Regarding Mosaic law, see Maurice Kelley, *This Great Argument: A Study of Milton's "De Doctrina Christiana" as a Gloss upon "Paradise Lost"* (Princeton, 1941), pp. 59–65.

30. *Return of Eden*, p. 56.

31. *Heroic Knowledge* (Minneapolis, 1957), pp. 85–86.

32. *Fearful Symmetry: A Study of William Blake* (Princeton, 1947), p. 338.

33. "Per non aspettar lume, cadde acerbo" (*Paradiso*, XIX.48), *The Divine Comedy of Dante Alighieri*, with trans. by John D. Sinclair (New York, 1961), 272–273.

34. *Oedipus the King*, trans. with commentary by Thomas Gould (Englewood Cliffs, N.J., 1970), pp. 103, 149, 156.

35. "Sin apparently is conceived as undergoing a 'two-stage' existence in parallel with that of the Logos: she exists as an idea in Satan's mind and then at a moment in time springs from his head as a real being (II, 755–758)" (William Hunter, "Milton's Arianism Reconsidered," *Harvard Theological Review*, 52 [1959], 34).

36. Milton cites "St. Paul's own interpretation of the second Psalm: 'I will declare the decree; Jehovah hath said unto me, Thou art my Son; This day I have begotten Thee.'" And he points to the begetting "within the limits of time, for the decree itself must have been anterior to the execution of the decree, as is sufficiently clear from the insertion of the word *today*" (*The Christian Doctrine*, in *The Works of John Milton*, ed. Frank Allen Patterson [New York, 1933], XIV, 183, 189). On the double begetting of the Son, see also Walter Clyde Curry, "Milton's Dual Concept of God as Related to Creation," *SP*, 47 (1950), 190–210, and Kelley, pp. 95–106.

37. Harold Fisch, "Blake's Miltonic Moment," in *William Blake: Essays for S. Foster Damon*, ed. Alvin H. Rosenfeld (Providence, R.I., 1969), p. 45.

38. Samuel, p. 75.

39. William Empson, "Milton and Bentley: The Pastoral of the Innocence of Man and Nature," *Some Versions of Pastoral* (London, 1950; rev. ed., New York, 1960), pp. 166–167.

40. Colie, p. 129.
41. *A Vision of the Last Judgment,* in Erdman, *Blake,* pp. 552–553.

Chapter 5. A Second Will

1. *The Visionary Company,* p. 139.
2. Kierkegaard, I, 9.
3. Using "voice" as a critical term was suggested to me by Words-worth—specifically as it occurs in the *Recluse* fragment, line 753, to introduce a higher tone. In a description of effects in Milton's poetry the term is used by Harold E. Toliver, "Complicity of Voice in *Paradise Lost," Modern Language Quarterly,* 25 (1964), 153–170. For a discussion of Milton's own voice in the epic see Neil H. Hertz, "Wordsworth and the Tears of Adam," *Studies in Romanticism,* 7 (1967), 15–33.

The choice is not really open to make vision rather than voice the means of confrontation. ("And the Lord spake unto you out of the midst of the fire: ye heard the voice of the words, but saw no simili-tude; only ye heard a voice"—Deut. 4:12.) One speculates with trepidation about exploiting vision as the mode of generational aware-ness. Eve admits that she has learned "how beauty is excell'd by manly grace" (*PL,* IV.490)—it is not a first reaction—but the point there is the replacement of the visible by nonvisible qualities. Simply in terms of sight, a preference for Adam is at best a taste that has to be cultivated. Generational confrontations across the sexes based on sight rather than sound might go either in the direction of the ludi-crous (e.g., a taste for middle-aged beauties) or the frightening, if not obscene (primal scenes). Milton does not give us Lot and his daughters ("th'obscene dread of Moab's mother" [I.406]) but does repay violation of sight with voice decreeing distance in the case of Ham,

> who for shame
> Done to his Father, heard this heavy curse,
> *Servants of Servants,* on his vitious Race. [XII.101–104]

The son who violates the filial bond is punished with fathering a race whose bondage is the inheritance "of his Father, Ham"

(*Christian Doctrine*, Patterson, XV, 191). Only Chaucer could voice the double entendre of knowing "Goddes pryvetee."

4. Patterson, XIV, 65, 187.

5. "Because he is 'in unity defective,' he requires 'Collateral love, and dearest amity' (VIII.425-26). But if equality is necessary for perfect dialogue, Eve is clearly a danger as well as a solace for Adam, who will be tempted to make her his equal" (Toliver, p. 163).

6. Wittreich, p. 109. Wordsworth's marginalia also appear, with commentary, in Bishop C. Hunt, Jr., "Wordsworth's Marginalia on *Paradise Lost*," BNYPL, 73 (1969), 167-183.

7. *Poetical Works*, III, 116. For Milton the obligation to descend from Parnassus to politics required such a "second will more wise." How personally he conceived of duty as a voice may be illustrated by this passage from the *Second Defence*, which speaks of the warning about the loss of sight: "In no wise dismayed at this warning, methought it was no Physician's voice I heard . . . but of some diviner monitor within; methought, that, by a certain fatality in my birth, two destinies were set before me, on the one hand, blindness, on the other duty—that I must necessarily incur the loss of my eyes, or desert a sovereign duty" (Patterson, VIII, 69).

8. *The Doctrine and Discipline of Divorce*, Patterson, III, ii, 373.

9. *Wordsworth's Poetry*, p. 281.

10. I like to think of the excision of this stanza, not as a second will (that very phrase is sacrificed), but as a failure of the will when the later Wordsworth, prizing restraint farther than second will, moralizes the song and does not allow the creative distinction to stand. On the other hand the *addition* of the Miltonism of stanza I belongs to Wordsworth's more creative years. In general this chapter is not concerned with Wordsworth chronology, for the relation of passing years to passing inspiration has been all too often noted. I wish to focus rather on the fact that the interaction with Milton is inseminating, not stultifying, regardless of the point in the poetic career at which it takes place. Many of the added Miltonisms discussed in the chapter are late indeed, and often stand out as isolated inspirations, instances of second will more wise in the midst of a general failure of imaginative will.

For a judicious view of Milton's influence that accounts for the periods in Wordsworth's development, see Appendix Two, "1798–99 or 1804–5?—A Note on Wordsworth and Milton," in Herbert Lindenberger's *On Wordsworth's "Prelude"* (Princeton, 1963).

11. William B. Hunter, Jr., "Prophetic Dreams and Visions in *Paradise Lost*," *Modern Language Quarterly*, IX (1948), 279. John Smith calls the Bath Kol "the *Lowest degree* of Revelation among the Jews" ("Of Bath Kol, i.e., Filia Vocis," *Select Discourses* [London, 1660], p. 257). In taking issue with Harris Francis Fletcher, George Newton Conklin is certainly right to conclude that "Milton was not a specialist in Hebrew nor a student of the rabbinical literature" (*Biblical Criticism and Heresy in Milton* [New York, 1949], p. 51). But Milton was likely to have known the Cambridge Platonist John Smith's work on prophecy.

12. Rashi, giving the interpretation of the Midrash, says, "NEITHER SHALL YE TOUCH IT—She added to God's command [which did not forbid touching the tree, but only eating of its fruit] therefore she was led to diminish from it" (*The Pentateuch, with Targum Onkelos, Haphtaroth and Rashi's Commentary*, trans. M. Rosenbaum and A. M. Silbermann; I: *Genesis* [New York, 1963?], 13). See J. M. Evans, *Paradise Lost and the Genesis Tradition* (Oxford, 1968), pp. 48–49.

13. A copy of Wordsworth's *Poems in Two Volumes*, 1807, containing corrections made by the poet for the 1815 edition, is in the Tinker Collection of the Yale University Library.

14. Toliver, p. 170.

15. De Selincourt, *Poetical Works*, III, 417.

16. *Edinburgh Review, or Critical Journal*, 11 (October, 1807), 220–221 (quoted by De Selincourt, *Poetical Works*, IV, 419). Harold Bloom is no less strong on this: "Wordsworth's heavens do not renovate themselves by the dictates of law, nor do his stars need preservation by any moral precepts. The Nature of *Tintern Abbey* and *The Prelude* is an unrestrained effluence from a fountain beyond the relevance of traditional morality" (*The Visionary Company*, p. 183). This view may be more judicious, but one must acknowledge, at least, that Wordsworth is attempting a moment of interposed ease in a poem painfully aware of the disparity between poetic myth and plebeian morality. (See also Newton P. Stallknecht, "Wordsworth's

Ode to Duty and the Schöne Seele," *PMLA*, 52 [1937], 230–237.)

17. "The Orpheus Image in *Lycidas*," *PMLA*, 64 (1949), 190. Milton's relation to Orpheus as a figure of the poet is studied by C. F. Stone III in "Milton's Self-Concerns and Manuscript Revision in *Lycidas*," *MLN*, 83 (1968), 867–881. Stone sees beyond the parallel of Milton's own situation to that of Orpheus, and locates "Milton's sense of danger when threatened by a failure of inspiration" (p. 870). (The threat, one needs to specify, does not concern anxiety about whether the poet could "overgo" Orpheus but whether the figure of Orpheus would prove an adequate metaphor to express the poet's own concerns.) I am much indebted to Stone for raising the question of how the failure of inspiration could be felt to be a special threat in just this passage. Milton is not recounting some concern he had in previous pastoral writing; he is encountering the threat right here, in trying to make the experience of temporality and the expression of poetic self-concern metaphors for one another.

18. "Haec quoque, cum iustos matura peregerit annos, / iuris erit vestri" (*Metamorphoses* X.36–37; in Ovid, *Metamorphoses*, with trans. by Frank Justus Miller, Loeb Classical Library [London, 1933], II, 66–67).

19. Finney, p. 218.

20. "Critical Activity of the Poetic Mind," p. 764. See also David Berkeley, "The Revision of the Orpheus Passage in 'Lycidas,'" *N&Q*, 203 (n.s. 5) (1958), 335.

21. Bergson, p. 197.

22. Berkeley says that "by repeating 'the Muse herself' he produces a kind of sobbing colloquial insistence" (p. 335). The phrase may be placed in the context of repetition, discussed in Chapter 2, above, pointing to the incipient turn that is loss.

23. From Marsilio Ficino's *Commentary on Plato's Symposium*, trans. and quoted by Finney, p. 87.

24. P. L. Heyworth, "The Composition of Milton's 'At a Solemn Music,'" *BNYPL*, 70 (1966), 450–458.

25. Richard Hooker, *Of the Laws of Ecclesiastical Polity*, Book V, sect. xxxviii, ed. Ronald Bayne (London, 1925), II, 146, quoted in Finney, p. 53.

26. Hollander, p. 327.

27. Finney, p. 162.

28. Hollander finds another kind of divorce in the lines: " '& in our lives & in our song' clearly differentiates, I think, mundane existence from the special life of religious contemplation and prayer" (p. 328).

29. Hollander, p. 328.

30. To avoid insignificant repetition, "bring" became "throw" when the passage beginning "Bring the rathe" was inserted.

31. "Flowerets and Sounding Seas: A Study in the Affective Structure of 'Lycidas,' " *PMLA*, 66 (1951), 480.

32. See Henry Adams, "The Development of the Flower Passage in 'Lycidas,' " *MLN*, 65 (1950), 471.

33. "A Poem Nearly Anonymous," *The World's Body* (New York, 1938), p. 3.

34. See W. H. Auden's "The Truest Poetry Is the Most Feigning":

> No metaphor, remember, can express
> A real historical unhappiness;
> Your tears have value if they make us gay;
> O Happy Grief! is all sad verse can say.

This quotation from W. H. Auden, *Collected Shorter Poems, 1927–1957* (New York, 1967), copyright 1964 by W. H. Auden, and the epigraph quotation from *Collected Longer Poems* (New York, 1969), copyright 1969 by W. H. Auden, are by permission of Random House, Inc., and Faber and Faber Ltd.

35. *Wordsworth's Poetry*, p. 13.

36. *Poetical Works*, IV, 413.

37. *Wordsworth's Poetry*, p. 149.

38. See 1805 *Prelude*, XII.301–305:

> . . . Poets, even as Prophets, each with each
> Connected in a mighty scheme of truth,
> Have each for his peculiar dower, a sense
> By which he is enabled to perceive
> Something unseen before.

39. Paul de Man, "Symbolic Landscape in Wordsworth and Yeats," in *In Defense of Reading*, ed. Reuben A. Brower and Richard Poirier (New York, 1962), p. 26.

40. De Man, p. 28.

41. Raymond Dexter Havens, *The Mind of a Poet* (Baltimore, 1941), p. 391.

42. An early version went on from the line "What ye have done for me" to the section that became one of the most energetic expressions of willful arrest, "Nutting." See *Poetical Works*, II, 505–506.

43. Compare the description in the opening of Book IX of the progress of the poem as "motions retrograde" (1805 text, IX.8). The 1850 text is more explicit still in likening narrative to journey progress, with turn, return, and halt for interposed ease.

44. The borrowing is noted by Havens, *The Mind of a Poet*, p. 428.

45. I am indebted on this point to Charles F. Stone III.

46. Søren Kierkegaard, *Repetition: An Essay in Experimental Psychology*, trans. Walter Lowrie (New York, 1964), p. 39.

Afterword

1. Poulet, p. 35.

2. Wallace Stevens, "The Sail of Ulysses," in *Opus Posthumous* (New York, 1957), pp. 101–102, copyright 1957 by Wallace Stevens; by permission of Alfred A. Knopf, Inc.

3. Stapleton, "Perspectives," p. 747.

4. Helen Hennessy Vendler, *On Extended Wings: Wallace Stevens' Longer Poems* (Cambridge, Mass., 1969), p. 37.

5. *English Poetry and Its Contribution to the Knowledge of a Creative Principle* (New York, 1950), pp. 73–74.

6. Jean-Paul Sartre, *What Is Literature?* trans. Bernard Frechtman (New York, 1949), p. 57.

Index

Milton's Poetry of Choice
and Its Romantic Heirs

Designed by R. E. Rosenbaum.
Composed by Vail-Ballou Press, Inc.,
in 11 point linotype Janson, 3 points leaded,
with display lines in monotype Janson.
Printed letterpress from type by Vail-Ballou Press
on Warren's 1854 text, 60 pound basis,
with the Cornell University Press watermark.
Bound by Vail-Ballou Press.

Library of Congress Cataloging in Publication Data
(For library cataloging purposes only)

Brisman, Leslie.
    Milton's poetry of choice and its romantic heirs.

    Bibliography: p.
    1. Milton, John, 1608–1674—Influence. 2. English
poetry—18th century—History and criticism. I. Title.
PR3588.B7   821'.7'09   72-13129
ISBN 0-8014-0666-8